The Idea of Welfare

G000041847

Studies in Social Policy and Welfare
Edited by Robert Pinker

In the same series

The Idea of Welfare

Robert Pinker

Professor of Social Work Studies,
London School of Economics and Political Science

HEINEMANN · LONDON

Heinemann Educational Books Ltd
22 Bedford Square, London WC1B 3HH

LONDON EDINBURGH MELBOURNE AUCKLAND
HONG KONG SINGAPORE KUALA LUMPUR NEW DELHI
IBADAN NAIROBI JOHANNESBURG
EXETER (NH) KINGSTON PORT OF SPAIN

British Library Cataloguing in Publication Data
Pinker, Robert
    The idea of welfare. — (Studies in social policy
    and welfare; 9).
    1. Social service   2. Public welfare
    I. Title   II. Series
    361   HV40

    ISBN 0 435 82683 2 Cased
    ISBN 0 435 82684 0 Paperback

© Robert Pinker 1979
First Published 1979
Reprinted 1980

Typeset by The Castlefield Press of High Wycombe
in 10/11 pt Century, and printed in Great Britain by
Richard Clay (The Chaucer Press) Ltd, Bungay Suffolk

To the memory of
Dorothy Wigand

Contents

Preface

This has been a difficult book to write, and its completion has been delayed many times, partly because academic life is rapidly ceasing to be a life of scholarship — a problem shared to some extent by all university teachers — partly because my views about social policy and social welfare changed as I extended my comparative studies, and also because of the nature of the enterprise, which took me across the intellectual boundary of more than one social science discipline. I would certainly disclaim, for example, any special expertise in the history of economic thought and in Russian and American social history. My only justification for having ventured into these subjects is that it was unavoidable in a work which set out to be both a comparative and a synthesizing study.

I would like to have written a more assertively optimistic book, because most students of social policy and administration come to the subject in the hope of making the world a better place to live in, but my expectations of the future are more modest now than they were at the outset. The comparative material in this study is largely retrospective, and in the comparative sections I discuss the social and political conditions under which the enhancement of welfare has been possible. Unfortunately, in my view, these conditions — in Britain at least — are no longer being met.

In his recent novel, *Lancelot*, which is set in third-century Britain, Peter Vansittart describes the state of the Roman Empire at the time as characterized by an '. . . overgrown bureaucracy, debt-ridden peasantry, overworked and insecure professional classes, ever-growing inflation, malaria and occasional plague, a falling birth-rate [and] general initiative sapped by too great a reliance on State subsidies and taxes. . . .' With a little up-dating in the types of disease and social class, the description in other respects fits the state of Britain today.

It is not my wish, however, to add even fractionally to the general climate of introspective criticism, which does little to arrest the decline and fall of a society. There is no evidence that decline is irreversible, unless the citizenry loses respect and affection for its own past and abandons all sense of common worth and common purpose. It is in reading British social history that I have found the most convincing grounds for hope that our national ability to reconcile the claims of self-interest and altruism can still be recovered and adopted as the basis for a better future.

In conclusion I have found that comparative studies tend to make optimism conditional on modest expectation rather than an abundance of supportive evidence. Nevertheless, as Dr Johnson remarked when he was giving his opinion as to whether there had ever been an instance of the ghost of a dead person appearing after death, 'All argument is against it; but all belief is for it.'

Robert Pinker
Blackheath, London
January 1979

Acknowledgements

This book originated in the James Seth memorial lecture which I had the honour to give at the University of Edinburgh in 1972. In that lecture, subsequently published as 'The Welfare State: A Comparative Perspective' and now comprising a large part of Chapter 11, I described in broad outline the main themes of enquiry which I have since explored in teaching and research. While I was writing the book I gave lectures or seminars at nearly twenty colleges on the various subjects on which I was working and I gained enormously from my discussions with teachers and students on those occasions. I am similarly indebted to my own colleagues and students.

I would also like to thank Professor Kathleen Bell, Hilary Land, Sandra Milligan, Professor Roy Parker, Angelo Saporiti, Ivan Sewandono and Mike Winwood for their help and advice on several occasions.

I am greatly indebted to Professor Jay Demarath, Professor Maurice Kogan, Professor Donald MacRae and Professor Della Nevitt for their detailed comments on the final draft, and I owe a special debt to Lord McGregor, whose encouragement, interest and scholarship were extended to me throughout the enterprise.

I was particularly fortunate in having the secretarial assistance of Shirley White, who typed the several drafts of the book with impeccable efficiency and unfailing enthusiasm. Susan Tester prepared the index with great speed and thoroughness. Finally, my thanks to my wife, Jennifer, who checked the various drafts and the references for style and consistency. I alone am responsible for the remaining errors in scholarship and other shortcomings.

My daughters, having reached the age of discretion and relative independence, are now able to put up with the demands imposed on a household by the domestic industry of scholarship, but I thank them too for making sure that such impositions did not trespass too far on the qualities of daily life which have more to do with hedonism than familial altruism.

Part I

The Institutional Frameworks of Social Welfare

1 Egoism and Altruism: A Critique of the Divergence

Any author who takes as his main theme the boundaries of obligation and entitlement in welfare is certain to encounter the spirit of Mrs. Jellyby seeking to push those boundaries into infinity. There is of course nothing intrinsically foolish in trying to broaden the boundaries of our compassion, although there are some dangers in unbridled ambitions of this kind. Just as it is possible for scholars to end up thinking beyond their means, so can philanthropists end up caring beyond their means.

As readers of *Bleak House* will know, Mrs. Jellyby was one of several ladies and gentlemen who found a vocation in the practice of what Dickens describes as 'telescopic philanthropy'. This concept expresses a law of social welfare, the operation of which can still be observed in some circles today. In general terms the law of telescopic philanthropy asserts that the further away the object of our compassion lies the more intense will be the feelings of concern and obligation which it evokes. In the case of Mrs. Jellyby we have a lady who 'devoted herself to an extensive variety of public subjects', in particular the subject of Africa and the establishment of a colony of coffee-growing settlers in the Kingdom of Borrioboola-Gha.[1] In pursuit of these ends Mrs. Jellyby found herself compelled to neglect the welfare of her own children and the management of her domestic life and to reduce her husband to a state of melancholic torpor. Mrs. Jellyby, were she alive today, would undoubtedly receive an accolade for services to humanity in the *Guardian* and a summons from the National Society for the Prevention of Cruelty to Children on the same morning.

Mrs. Jellyby's daughter, Caddy, rebelled against her mother's example and chose to marry a dancing-master in preference to Mr. Quale, another admirer, the roots of whose hair, we are told, 'were almost ready to fly out of his head in unappeasable philanthropy'.[2] In condemning the marriage Mrs. Jellyby remarked, 'If you had any sympathy with the human race, it would raise you high above any such idea. But you have none. I have often told you, Caddy, you have no such sympathy.' To this remark poor Caddy could only reply, sadly but firmly, 'Not if it's Africa, Ma, I have not.'[3]

My own sympathies are with Caddy and certain other characters in *Bleak House* who practise modest forms of altruism. There is, for example, the heroine, Esther Summerson, who purposively made a vocation out of being useful in humdrum, practical ways. Esther was something of a prig as well as a compulsive weeper — for joy as well as sorrow — but like her admirer, Alan Woodcourt, who became a poor-law doctor, she managed to fill her life with a multitude of good deeds, which were no less worthy for being done within a narrow compass.

As Esther herself remarked to her guardian, 'We thought that, perhaps . . . it is right to begin with the obligations of home, Sir; and that, perhaps, while those are overlooked and neglected, no other duties can possible be substituted for them.'[4] Her argument was poignantly driven home when Jo, the crossing-sweeper, was discovered near to death and in a state of destitution. Jo's greatest handicap was that 'he is not one of Mrs. Jellyby's lambs, being wholly unconnected with Borrioboola-Gha; he is not softened by distance and unfamiliarity . . . he is not a genuine foreign-grown savage; he is the ordinary home-made article.'[5]

The present book ranges widely into different times and places because it follows wherever the ideas and directions of welfare take us. By contrast, in altruistic terms its arguments are not ambitious, although I have tried to be purposive and to relate my concepts to actual events and institutions. The first part of this study begins therefore with a review of the moral and institutional frameworks within which social policies and other forms of mutual aid are carried out.

Despite the continuing interest of social scientists in matters such as value freedom, there remains a serious gap between the practical concerns of philosophers and those of the social scientists who are dealing with problems of social welfare and social justice. To a large extent moral theorizing in Western philosophy is indifferent or unrelated to the social contexts within which moral practices occur; equally a high proportion of social welfare theory is formulated with an insufficient examination of the moral beliefs of ordinary citizens and their actual behaviour. In spite of the British tendency to define the subject of social welfare as social policy and administration, we are now experiencing, in company with most other Western industrial societies, a resurgence of interest in community politics and a greater involvement of ordinary citizens in the procurement of welfare resources and the practice of mutual aid. This has been inspired partly by a variety of libertarian and democratic ideologies and partly by more practical considerations, including a greater willingness to recognize that hitherto unutilized resources of goodwill and civic expertise can be mobilized for the common good, that the scale and complexity of our welfare problems make it economically and administratively essential that these human resources should be mobilized and that it is morally right for civic involvement in welfare policy to go beyond the traditional boundaries and forms of self-help. However, any developments which lead to an increase in public participation are just as likely to result in a clear demarcation of sectional interests — including several which have hitherto been neglected — as in the discovery of a new sense of common purpose or agreement on policy objectives. On this matter we can only speculate since we know so little about the welfare beliefs and practices of ordinary people.

Unless we pursue these studies in a comparative context we will fail in our attempt to explain the features of continuity and change in social welfare policy and we will also fail to explore as fully as we might both the possible range of altruism in social welfare and its limits. The assertion of internationalist ideals of social welfare tells us how we ought to help the 'universal stranger', but it is equally important to discover more about how we help our next-door neighbours, and how these two objectives can be reconciled.

The task we face in social welfare studies is not merely to make judgements about the anomalies and paradoxes of our social welfare system but to describe as fairly as possible the scope and limits of social welfare and to account for the phenomena which we are describing. In this we shall be attempting to elicit and clarify 'the ideals and principles of conduct latent in the groping efforts of mankind towards equity and fairness', which in Ginsberg's view was the central task of a rational ethic.[6] We must go beyond the construction of models which set out ideological positions rather than explaining actual situations and events, and models presented in terms which appear to be simply descriptive but which are in fact highly value-laden. The institutional model and the residual model of social welfare are very extensively used in the teaching of social welfare; both of them are charged with value connotations and therefore make a good starting-point for our enquiry.

The institutional model of social welfare treats collectivist intervention in the form of social policy as the most desirable end-product of political action. Priorities are ordered and resources allocated by reference to criteria of need which are based on the welfare ethics of a social market in which the hallmark of good citizenship is the unilateral transfer from one person or group to another. The unilateral transfer is the epitome of social altruism.

By contrast the residual model of social welfare treats as morally commendable actions the individualistic forms of self-help. Priorities are ordered and resources allocated according to the criterion of price, and effective demand is justified by the work ethic of an economic market in which the distinctive feature of good citizenship is the exchange relationship based on reciprocity and bilateral transfers. This kind of exchange relationship occurs between economically motivated citizens who are acting out of self-interest — enlightened though it may be — rather than altruism.

If social science students were not themselves collectivistically disposed, they might pause to wonder why, in the analysis which usually follows this sort of juxtaposition, the residualist always loses, or, rather, why the institutionalist always wins at least the moral victory. What appears to happen is that the argument changes almost imperceptibly from a neutral description to an ethical indictment. Inexorably the residualist is identified — or rather exposed — both as an individualist *and* as an egoist, while the institutionalist is deemed to be inspired by a self-evidently superior form of altruism.

It is possible, however, to argue that much of our moralizing about social welfare is based on an initial terminological confusion. The genesis of this kind of confusion was pinpointed (for other purposes) by Sir Karl Popper in *The Open Society* over thirty years ago.[7] Popper describes the terms in which we are customarily invited to debate the nature of altruism in social analysis. 'Individualism' is defined in two ways by a method of contrast. First it is contrasted with 'collectivism'; then secondly it is contrasted with 'altruism'. The description of two modes of behaviour is thus linked from the start with value judgements about each of them. Collectivism is assumed to be altruistic, while individualism, in associational default, is left with equivalents like egoism and selfishness. So long as the terms themselves are left unexamined, this crude comparison carries a measure of analytical conviction. It is set out by Popper as follows:

(a) *Individualism*   is opposed to (a') *collectivism;*
(b) *Egoism*   is opposed to (b') *altruism;*

and for our purposes I will add two further comparisons:

(c) *Residualism*   is opposed to (c') *institutionalism;*
(d) *Selectivity*   is opposed to (d') *universalism.*

Popper reminds us, however, that any of these terms can 'be combined with either of the two terms which stand on the other line'.[8] In practice collectivism, for example, can represent highly sectional interests, for example those of trade unions, professional associations, consumer groups and whole social classes. In such contexts, it is suggested, the term 'group egoism' would not be an inappropriate one to use, and similarly it is possible that an individualist may act in altruistic ways, making considerable sacrifices on behalf of others. Popper's criticism of this confusion of patterns of behaviour as well as the terms used to describe them is part of a much more general debate about the nature of justice and the relationship between the individual and the state. Nonetheless what he says has great relevance to our present examination of certain specific issues of social policy. Outside the confines of academic and political debate one rarely encounters a confrontation between either individualism and collectivism or egoism and altruism, in their uncompromising forms. In any case we shall discover more by looking at the various forms of qualified egoism or altruism which set the tenor of everyday welfare practices.

In a discussion of Adam Smith's views on the morality of economic practice Thomas Wilson advances an argument similar to Popper's. Wilson points out how seriously the moral basis of the competitive market economy continues to be misunderstood by many social scientists.[9] First, he reminds us that individualists may be motivated as much by sympathy as by egoism, and that even 'the pursuit of personal advantage' is not 'in itself inherently immoral', since it may result in socially beneficial outcomes. Secondly, he develops Philip Wicksteed's definition of an economic relationship, namely, one which 'does not exclude from my mind everyone but me, it potentially includes everyone but you'.[10] Wicksteed's conclusion is that 'The specific characteristic of an economic relationship is not its "egoism" but its "non-tuism" '.[11] Even within the totally planned economy, Wilson reminds us, individual government departments press their claims for extra resources against those of other departments. The same point is made by Milton Friedman with regard to the traditional distinction drawn between the *public* interest and the *private* interest. In practice government bureaucrats serve departmental and private interests as well as government interests and through the political process they have to be sensitive to what are often highly sectional interests amongst the electorate.[12] Once again a consideration of real life draws us away from a universe of moral absolutes characterized by sharp differences in belief and practice. The moralities of the competitive economic market reveal certain definitely altruistic qualities, albeit of a conditional and limited type, while those of the planned economy are less altruistic than collectivists are disposed to believe.

The traditional methods of classifying the moral components of social welfare are deficient in a number of other respects. In the first place both 'institutional' and 'residual' are insufficiently comprehensive terms because they represent only the statutory or formal policy aspects of welfare. They are *par excellence* the terms of administrators within whose chosen ambience whatever is institutional carries connotations of fullness and maturity and whatever is residual suggests that which is run down, undeveloped or withered on the branch.

Secondly, the sociological and philosophical antecedents of the related notions of 'altruism' and 'egoism' give an additional historical assurance to the commendation which the one evokes and the censure which the other calls down upon itself. Durkheim, for example, defines as 'egotistical' the forms of conduct which are 'determined by sentiments and representations which are exclusively personal'.[13] In his *The Division of Labour in Society* Durkheim challenges Spencer's view of competitive individualism by comparing with it 'the essential element of moral life, that is, the moderating influence that society exercises over its members, which tempers and neutralises the brutal action of the struggle for existence and selection. Wherever there are societies, there is altruism because there is solidarity'.[14]

Durkheim's response to Spencer's sociology was part of a wide-ranging debate about the nature of human solidarities in industrial societies. Another neglected facet of this debate is Kropotkin's critical response to Huxley's essay, 'The Struggle for Existence'.[15] In his study of mutual aid Kropotkin criticized what he rightly believed to be Huxley's gross distortion of Darwinian theory. One significant feature of this debate was that both Spencer and Huxley dramatized the issue, seeing it as a conflict between individual citizens and the state, and attributed a potentially major role to collectivist social policies, which they considered to be destructive of true social progress. They both anticipated the institutional/residual cleavage, and their analyses both fit into its terms of reference.

By contrast neither Durkheim nor Kropotkin gave much attention to collectivist social policies, but in differing degrees both of them expressed grave reservations about the virtues of state intervention. Kropotkin held that state intervention of any kind was intrinsically destructive of social welfare, whether it was aimed at protecting the free play of market forces or mitigating its worst effects. Both writers placed their trust in the informal and spontaneous practices of mutual aid and saw in them the necessary and convincing evidence of the human propensity to be altruistic. In this respect the writings of Durkheim and Kropotkin have greater relevance to contemporary debates about civic participation and community development than those of Spencer and Huxley, or those which come within the Webbian tradition of social administration.

The development of explanatory concepts and theories in social welfare is inhibited by the fact that concepts defining the modes of service organization are often used as value judgements and that these value judgements have not been properly examined. Approaches which restrict the term 'altruism' to any one set of policies or practices prejudge the relevant moral issues. For example if we enquire as to who would define himself as an egoist, and if the answer happens to be 'no one who is in any way admirable', we will probably conclude that the term is intrinsically a derogatory one. Rawls, for example, describes an egoist as someone who would never act 'as justice requires except as self-interest and expediency prompt'.[16] Egoism, in Rawls's view, cannot provide a basis for any moral theory or action and is incompatible with the notion of social justice as fairness.

I would argue that both of the terms, 'egoism' and 'altruism', used in an unqualified way, are largely irrelevant to the study of

social welfare because they are inapplicable to the most characteristic forms of social behaviour. While it would seem that an
egoist is a person who is incapable of friendship, an altruist is
someone who is exploitable by every 'friend' and stranger,
unless they also happen to be altruists; for the egoist a social
life is meaningless, and for the altruist it is impossible. The
egoist could be likened to a black hole in the social universe,
devouring everything which comes within its range, while the
altruist may be compared to a brightly burning star, ineffec-
tually striving to illuminate and warm a dark and limitless
universe.

In the more homely contexts of kinship and the local community it is equally difficult to draw sensible distinctions between egoism and altruism. There is no self-evidently governing
principle by which the claims of one social group may be
measured against the claims of others, once we have abandoned
the crude utilitarian principle of seeking the greatest good
for the greatest number, and there are several good reasons
why it might be better to define the objective of social policy
as 'minimizing suffering' rather than 'maximizing pleasure'
(or 'happiness').[17]

Until recently collectivists have tended to argue from the
latter sort of utilitarian assumption, so that the welfare claims
of kinship and community groups have been treated as un-
questionably subordinate to those of the wider society. Yet
within their relatively narrow confines families practise forms
of mutual aid which can be described as altruistic, if only
conditionally so. All too often in discussions of self-interest
and egoism one gets the impression that the subject of concern
is a single individual, acting exclusively on his own behalf. In
everyday life, however, the majority of working citizens are
trying to act in the best interests of their dependent and even
their less favoured kin as well as themselves. Any model which
makes it possible for familial altruism to be subsumed under the
category of egoism is seriously defective. And it is equally
misleading to class familial welfare practices under the category
of altruism. In short, any analysis which treats egoism and
altruism as alternatives fails to take adequate account of the
subtle interplay of loyalties which characterize people's notions
of welfare obligation and entitlement.

It would be worth our while to note the distinction drawn
by Urmson between moral conduct which occurs within the
requirements of duty and that which exceeds the normal

expectations of ordinary citizens.[18] Bernard Williams also reminds us that 'Some of our decent actions come not from that motive which Christians misrepresent as our loving everybody, but just from our loving somebody.'[19] A great deal of what can be described as familial altruism falls within this second category of actions.

There are secular as well as religious moralities which present a hierarchical model of altruism. Marxists see these issues in terms of class interest and class conflict and they emphasize the connection between economic inequalities and the family as a social institution. This kind of analysis, however, is only a partial one. The conflicts which arise between familial and extra-familial forms of altruism are fundamental to the concerns of social policy and social justice because it can be shown that they regularly transcend and survive changes in class structure. The family nurtures a very distinctive sense of privacy and exclusive loyalty which few citizens appear to be willing to give up as the price of belonging to a wider community. This distinction between familial and extra-familial altruism is important because it reminds us of the dilemmas of moral choice and of the fact that we can seldom be certain that we have taken the right decisions.

Many social administrators stress the importance of the family and of parental responsibility in the pursuit of social welfare, arguing at the same time that stringent limits should be put upon the scope of parental choice and the parental ordering of priorities. Social administration tries to resolve this basic ethical problem by prescribing methods of political or administrative action. Yet the resistance to certain of these directives persists, and its social and ethical foundations seldom receive the attention which they merit. On what ethical grounds and at what stage, we may ask, ought these forms of familial self-interest and altruism to be written off as intrinsically inferior types of welfare practice? On what ethical grounds should we seek to modify them? Even within the context of the social market it is difficult to draw a line between the point at which the concept of relative poverty ceases to be a device for remedying minority injustices and the point at which it becomes instead a doctrine through which each disgruntled citizen lights up his darkness with the green and fitful light of envy.

What matters for all practical purposes is how and to what extent the claims of familial altruism can be reconciled with those of extra-familial forms of altruism relating to communal, national and international interests. Before exploring these issues we shall have to construct a relevant institutional framework for the study of social welfare which accepts as constant features of social life the interplay of these familial and extra-familial loyalties and the ways in which these networks of obligation and entitlement are expressed in a variety of exchange relationships.

References

[1] Charles Dickens, *Bleak House*, Penguin, Harmondsworth, 1978, p. 82.

[2] ibid., p. 225.

[3] ibid., p. 386.

[4] ibid., p. 113.

[5] ibid., p. 696.

[6] Morris Ginsberg, *On the Diversity of Morals*, Mercury Books, Heinemann, London, 1962, p. xi.

[7] K. R. Popper, *The Open Society and Its Enemies*, Vol. I, Routledge & Kegan Paul, London, 1957, pp. 99 et seq.

[8] ibid., p. 101.

[9] Thomas Wilson, 'Sympathy and Self-Interest', unpublished paper, given at the Adam Smith Bicentenary Conference, April 1976.

[10] See L. Robbins (ed.), *The Common Sense of Political Economy*, George Routledge, London, 1933, p. 174.

[11] See P. Wicksteed, ibid., p. 179.

[12] Milton Friedman, 'The Line We Dare Not Cross', *Encounter*, November 1976, pp. 11-12.

[13] Emile Durkheim, *The Division of Labour in Society*, Free Press of Glencoe, Collier-Macmillan, London, 1964, p. 197. See also Gianfranco Poggi, *Images of Society*, Stanford University Press, Stanford, California, Oxford University Press, London, 1972, pp. 194 et seq.

[14] Durkheim, op. cit., p. 109.

[15] Peter Kropotkin, *Mutual Aid: A Factor of Evolution*, edited and with an introduction by Paul Avrich, Allen Lane, London, 1972; and T. H. Huxley, 'The Struggle for Existence: A Programme', *Nineteenth Century*, February 1888.

[16] John Rawls, *A Theory of Justice*, Oxford University Press, London, 1972, p. 488.

[17] Popper, op. cit., pp. 235 and 285.

[18] J. O. Urmson, 'Saints and Heroes', in Joel Feinberg (ed.), *Moral Concepts*, Oxford University Press, London, 1969, p. 68.

[19] Bernard Williams, *Morality*, Penguin, Harmondsworth, 1973, p. 85.

2 Family and Community

As we have seen, mutual aid is practised in a variety of institutional contexts. In seeking to understand the nature of these welfare practices we shall need to give special attention both to the distinction, insofar as it can be drawn, between familial and extra-familial social institutions, and to the quality of the relationships within each separate institutional context. The potential scope for co-operation and conflict between familial and non-familial forms of altruism is illustrated in Litwak's essay, 'Extended Kin Relations in an Industrial Society'.[1] Litwak sets out a theory of shared functions and institutional balance. He distinguishes four types of family structure — the traditional extended type, the modified extended type, the isolated nuclear type and the dissolving nuclear type — and he relates their welfare functions to those of other forms of welfare organization. Litwak argues that families are more suited than other groups to meeting needs of an idiosyncratic nature, since 'because of its small size' the family can 'define much more uniquely what is to be valued' and respond with speed and flexibility, whereas welfare bureaucracies are better equipped to deal with routine needs requiring special skills and knowledge.[2] The most generally preferred forms of exchange are those in which the person in need can avoid total dependence on both familial and non-familial forms of aid, and this situation is most likely to occur with regard to members of modified extended families. As Litwak suggests, 'Where the giver is never in a position to provide the entire service, then he is not in a position to ask for complete subservience.'[3]

Like any other social institution the family has great propensities for conflict as well as for co-operation. Since it is bound up with so many of our dearest expectations it is inevitably also the cause of many of our deepest disappointments. The incidence of divorce is only one of many indicators of familial disharmony. Within the family there are complex networks of interdependence and dependency involving the exercise of power between and within the generations and the sexes which affect many of the elements of everyday life. These networks provide the framework within which the most important forms of mutual aid occur. The studies carried out by Rosser and Harris, Willmott and Young, and Townsend, for example, illustrate the delicate nature of these relationships and the importance of maintaining a norm of reciprocity whenever it is possible.[4] In addition to providing personal services the family continues to be the key institution by which wealth and differential advantages are transmitted from generation to generation.

Social welfare studies have given careful and sustained attention to the relationship between the forms of family life and the effect of social policies, but priority has naturally been given to the problem of controlling the influence of the family which is exercised in the transmission of its differential advantages and wealth to its own members, as well as to members of other families which are under stress or at risk in one way or another. In recent years much attention has been given to the social disadvantages experienced by 'dissolving' nuclear families, which have incomplete membership or are on the brink of complete breakdown.[5]

In practice, however, the development of collectivist social policies designed to make a positive contribution to the general enhancement of familial welfare has often encountered strong political resistance. The distinction between familial and extra-familial forms of altruism is never more vigorously asserted than at times when social reforms are thought to be eroding the 'responsibility' of parents for their dependent kin. Hilary Land has described the long-drawn-out campaign for family allowances as a sustained attempt to establish the 'legitimacy' of the sort of policy which it 'was believed would interfere with the prevailing patterns of family responsibility, thus reducing the dependency of wives on husbands and children on parents'.[6] Fears on the part of trade unions that family allowances would undermine the processes of collective wage bargaining were complemented by Conservative anxieties concerning their effect on work incentives.[7] The victory was eventually won because these risks were deemed to be less important than the dangers of inflation and a falling birth rate. Another important factor was the influence of John Maynard Keynes, who, as an economic adviser to the government, supported family allowances for both economic and social reasons.

The ambivalence of government policy and of public opinion

regarding the need to protect the family and at the same time to respect its autonomy is displayed even more dramatically in the treatment of one-parent families, especially those which are created by illegitimacy or marital breakdown. At the end of their definitive review of the history of the obligation to maintain, Finer and McGregor observe that 'The upshot was that the principles on which the State made provision for one-parent families remained after the Beveridge Report precisely what they had been before. Widows received pensions with the possibility of supplementation, from the poor law or public assistance or, after 1948, from national assistance. But divorced, deserted or separated wives and unmarried mothers remained throughout dependent on the poor law or its substitutes, in the event of their receiving no support from their husbands. On the other hand, their children benefited from the introduction in 1945 of the family allowances for which Eleanor Rathbone had pleaded in 1924.'[8]

Finer and McGregor conclude that the commitment to a traditional view of the obligation of liable relatives to maintain their familial dependants — dating from the seventeenth century — has survived the transfer of powers from the National Assistance Board to the Supplementary Benefits Commission which took place in 1966. They note 'one major departure', namely, that 'It was the express intention of the poor law to impose a stigma upon those whom it relieved, and it was the express intention of the National Assistance Act, as of the Ministry of Social Security Act, that the Board and the Commission should not impose stigma upon recipients of benefit.' The situation remains one in which the unsupported wife or mother both retains her legal right of maintenance, which she may seek to enforce through an order of the court, and also enjoys, in her capacity as citizen, a right to support from the social security authorities which carries no stigma. Finer and McGregor suggest, however, that 'In the minds of many citizens the old stigma still carries over to the social benefits of the welfare state.'[9]

The financial hardships of many one-parent families cannot be effectively relieved until this anomalous situation is changed. In aggregate the problem grows steadily as the incidence of divorce in Britain continues to rise, as does the number of divorced persons who do not subsequently remarry. Approximately one in ten families in Britain is a one-parent family. It would, however, be misleading to infer from these trends that the family is ceasing to be the primary locus of our sense of welfare obligation and entitlement. It is still exceptional for one or both spouses to reject the obligation to maintain one another in adversity and even more exceptional for both spouses to abandon their children. The bitterness which attends such failures to maintain does not indicate any general change in moral beliefs about familial altruism. It serves rather to demonstrate the enduring strength of these beliefs and the fear and resentment evoked by their violation. Furthermore these beliefs still find a sufficiently powerful expression in public opinion to inhibit changes in law and social policy, so that the growing minority of one-parent families remains at serious financial risk.

It is possible that these processes of social and cultural change will compel us to review some of the traditional assumptions on which current policies are based with regard to family life and also to revise our typologies of family structure and sexual relationships. With regard to tax law and income maintenance services new feminist ideologies are already forcing governments to undertake a radical reappraisal of their family policies, and of the assumptions about the status of women upon which these policies have customarily rested. While these trends may be observed with regard to income maintenance services, contrary patterns of development appear with regard to services of a personal caring nature. The underlying assumption appears to be that it is a desirable end of social policy that stable family structures should be sustained when in peril and restored whenever possible if they should suffer dissolution, and furthermore that the great majority of citizens share this objective. Despite some radical views to the contrary this assumption is still probably correct. For example the principles and practice of community care policies rest on such assumptions, but they seem to go further in taking for granted not only the permanence of existing family structures but also the immutability of sex and occupational roles within the family.

Major policy documents such as the Seebohm Report, which gave so much impetus to the campaign for community care, offer us little or no help in defining either the family or the community and hence the nature of their interdependence. In some respects the policy of community care is taking on the appearance of a leap into institutional uncertainty and theoretical oblivion. Not only does the working definition of what counts as a family vary greatly between societies, it also varies within societies over time. The only regularity which we can discern in the literature on the family regarding the boundaries of what Morgan calls 'the kinship universe' is that 'However vague and fluctuating this outer cloud of relationships might be, the inner nuclear core of parents and children would appear to be much more definite.'[10] Morgan describes how individual families all construct their own 'subjectively understood realit[ies]' which are influenced by a variety of external forces, including social and fiscal policies.

Despite the rapid development of personal social services and social work the goal of achieving a sensitive adaptation of social policies to all these idiosyncratic variations in family life remains a seemingly impossible one. One difficulty is that we still know so little about what is most 'uniquely' valued, in Litwak's sense, by family members regarding their capacity for self-help and their disposition to accept outside help or to provide it for others. In a recent study of fifty-four families caring for mentally handicapped relatives Bayley draws attention to the subtly interactive forms of mutual aid which occurred between the kinsfolk involved. He characterizes these relationships as 'structures' for 'coping' and for 'living' which provide for both the functional and the expressive needs of their members. Bayley draws attention to two recurring features of these patterns of support which he considers to have had a considerable influence on the extent to which outside forms of support from social welfare agencies were utilized. First, there was a general reluctance to admit the need for outside help from strangers, and beneath this reluctance he notes the fear of being stigmatized as a consequence of becoming dependent. Secondly, there was a reluctance on the part of ordinary citizens to intrude upon the concerns of other families or to be made the subject of outside interest. Most of the families in his sample placed great emphasis upon the value and rights of privacy. These attitudes were probably reinforced by the apparent failure of local authority social workers to make any useful contribution when their services were accepted.[11]

In her study of community life in Banbury Stacey was similarly impressed by the complexity of the helping networks which she observed, the importance which the members attached to informality as a quality in social relationships, their close sense of localism and their caution with regard to accepting offers of help from outsiders.[12] The relative marginality of help from formal welfare agencies outside the family is further emphasized by Eda Topliss in her study, *Provision for the Disabled*.[13] She concludes that 'The expansion of personal social services . . . while

desired by some handicapped individuals living in private households, would not meet the idiosyncratic needs of the majority
of disabled people and their families.'[14] Disabled citizens wish
in the main to 'salvage as much as possible of their lives' in a
context of familial and local friendships and social activities,
and the major obstacle they face in seeking to do so is lack of
money. When personal social services are needed they seem
most likely to be accepted without reluctance if they are provided on a regular basis, if there are opportunities to reciprocate
or make restitution and if they are locally based.

Empirical studies of this kind illustrate not only the problems
of defining the family for analytical and policy purposes but
also those of separating it conceptually from the even vaguer
notion of the community. Indeed in societies where the range
of operative extended family ties is sufficiently extensive, any
such distinction becomes almost meaningless, since the one concept is encompassed by the other.

Whatever problems we encounter in seeking to define the
family for social policy purposes, they are of minor significance
compared with those we meet in attempting to define the community. Robert Nisbet defines community as 'all forms of relationship which are characterized by a high degree of personal
intimacy, emotional depth, moral commitment, social cohesion
and continuity in time. Community is founded on man conceived in his wholeness rather than in one or another of the
roles, taken separately, that he may hold in a social order.'[15]
The problem with such definitions is that they are so vague
and general as to serve little analytical purpose. Plant refers
to one authority, writing in 1955, who assembled some ninety-four definitions of community, all of which share a common
element insofar as they 'deal with people. Beyond this there is
no agreement.'[16] In reviewing the literature of community
studies, Margaret Stacey doubts whether the concept 'refers to a
useful abstraction'[17] and adopts in preference the term 'local
social system' to describe 'a set of interrelated social institutions
covering all aspects of social life, familial, religious, juridical, etc.,
and the associated belief systems of each' occurring in 'a geographically defined locality'.[18]

Stacey goes on to emphasize that the concept of a local social
system 'involves *structure* and *process*'. She suggests that the
development of such systems is contingent on a 'majority of the
local population' having 'been present together in the locality
for some period of time'. Such development is 'highly likely' to

occur when 'the majority of the population have been born and bred in the locality', but apart from such cases it 'does not necessarily follow that common residence over a period of time will lead to the emergence of local social systems'.[19] Migration into a locality will eventually change the nature of the system, when a certain critical stage is reached — one 'determined by the number and/or type of migrants in relation to the host population' — and, if the inflow continues, another critical stage will be reached at which the system will be destroyed altogether. Stacey emphasizes our lack of precise knowledge regarding the empirical conditions under which these processes will occur.

Stacey then proceeds to outline the characteristic role relationships of local social systems. We are told that 'Some or all of the actors in the population to which the system relates play multiplex roles to each other', and that the chances that this will happen increase in relation to the number of institutions present in the system. The type as well as the number of these existent institutions — for example the presence or absence of workplaces or sub-systems of local power — greatly affects the nature of the system.[20]

Reference is also made to the belief systems of localities. Where such systems exist they will be shared 'through the multiplex role-playing and the overlapping group memberships of the local population'. Stacey appears to treat the presence of local belief systems as a matter of fundamental importance. She contends that in cases where 'a majority of the population do not share to any considerable extent common groups, institutions, beliefs and expectations, there can be no *one* local social system for that locality'. Stacey stresses once again that 'The empirical meaning of "majority" and "considerable extent" are at present not at all clearly known.'[21]

In the final sections of her paper Stacey reminds us that in Britain local social systems are never socially self-contained. Residents have affiliations outside their localities; local political, economic and religious systems are related to national systems. Furthermore physical proximity over time does not of itself ensure that local social relationships will develop. The fact that some residents are not actively involved in these relationships, allied to the presence of 'elements of other systems' within the locality, ensures that 'the local social system will be sensitive to changes which take place in these social systems outside itself.' Stacey also stresses the point that within localities social relationships 'include those of conflict as well as co-operation'.[22] We are also reminded that although 'a totality of social relations are not to be found within a locality', this does not place 'the future of locality studies in doubt'. The lesson to be drawn from such a conclusion is that local social systems must be studied in relation to the wider society of which they are a part, and that such study must be both empirically and theoretically grounded. Although Stacey's paper was published ten years ago, it remains, in my view, the best conceptual review available. Apart from its manifest virtues of clarity and caution it sets out a number of crucially important propositions in a testable form.

The concept of community has subsequently become inextricably interwoven with various ideologies of community participation and policies of community care. Consequently it serves as an instrument of both political debate and social enquiry. It has of course always carried certain ideological connotations of a general nature. The study group on community work teaching (of which I was a member), in noting how these connotations have recently changed, observed that

> It is a paradox of our time that the idea of community — which historically has been one of the more conservative expressions of social welfare — has become so attractive to social innovators and agents of change. We can only guess at this stage why this is taking place. It is possible that the idea of community and the practice of community work now offer the most propitious context within advanced industrial societies for regenerating the principles of democracy and re-affirming the links between these principles and vigorous policies of social reform. In affluent industrial societies the claims of the severely deprived can too easily be treated as the marginal claims of a residual minority. By narrowing the initial focus of action to local contexts, the community worker hopes to give a new quality of conviction and authority to the claims of social justice through recourse to local democratic processes and by appeal to general democratic principles.[23]

This new commitment to localized social action and the nurturing of informal modes of welfare practice is often associated with a hostility towards the administrative ethos of both central and local government. It represents the revival of a collectivist tradition which is not only highly localized in its concerns but populist in its inspiration and outlook. By contrast the history of social reform in twentieth-century Britain has been inspired by collectivist values but committed to policy and administrative processes directed by elected representatives and paid experts. The arch-apostles of this administrative tradition, on which the foundations of the welfare state were based, were the Webbs, who held a generally poor opinion of 'the average sensual man' and believed that enlightened administrators were the most reliable interpreters of what constituted the best interests of the general public. A similar view was held by Beveridge, who as Harris suggests, 'envisaged that a more "socialistic" organization of society would be achieved, not through working-class pressure, but through an enlightened, bureaucratic, public-spirited élite'.[24] A deeply held belief in the importance of voluntary effort was, however, an equally important element in Beveridge's philosophy of welfare. His notion of a welfare society was one in which the major enterprises of the state, funded through social insurance and taxation, were complemented by a rich variety of voluntary endeavours directed especially towards 'the special needs of untypical distressed minorities'.[25]

Beveridge believed that voluntary effort was an expression of civic responsibility which was vital not only to the enhancement of welfare but to the survival of democracy itself. These views, which were set out at length in *Voluntary Action*,[26] provide an intellectual and normative bridge between the earlier tradition of voluntarism in Victorian and Edwardian Britain and the emphasis on community development of our own time. The conceptual importance of Beveridge's idea of community derives, however, from the fact that voluntary action was but one element in his total idea of welfare. In the last analysis Beveridge's ideal of the good society was based on a model of consensus in which all sectional concerns and loyalties would be reconciled within the terms of a comprehensive plan directed towards the national interest. Furthermore Beveridge conceptualized the nation in terms of a common ethnic identity and the perpetuation of a distinctive Anglo-Saxon race and culture. In defending his proposals regarding the treatment of women in his social insurance scheme Beveridge suggested that 'In the next thirty years housewives as mothers have vital work to do in ensuring the adequate continuance of the British race and of British ideals in the world.'[27]

Patriotism is the sentiment in Beveridge's grand design which provides the political rationale for his report and binds together within one framework his concern for the welfare of families, for local communities, for the nation as an entity and for international reconstruction. Time and change have rendered obsolescent his prescriptions for social policy, but the sense of national destiny and the certainty of principle which inspired his vision of the future have not lost their relevance to the present, though they may seem alien to a generation riven with cynicism and self-doubt.

References

[1] Eugene Litwak, 'Extended Kin Relations in an Industrial Society', in Ethel Shanas and Gordon F. Streib, *Social Structure and the Family: Generational Relations*, Prentice-Hall, Englewood Cliffs, New Jersey, 1965.

[2] ibid., p. 299.

[3] ibid., p. 310.

[4] See for example C. R. Bell, *Middle Class Families: Social and Geographical Mobility*, Routledge & Kegan Paul, London, 1968; R. Firth (ed.), *Two Studies in Kinship in London*, Athlone Press, London, 1957; C. Rosser and J. Harris, *The Family and Social Change: A Study of Family and Kinship in a South Wales Town*, Routledge & Kegan Paul, London, 1966; P. Willmott, *The Evolution of a Community*, Routledge & Kegan Paul, London, 1963; M. Young and P. Willmott, *Family and Class in a London Suburb*, Routledge & Kegan Paul, London, 1960; M. Young and P. Willmott, *Family and Kinship in East London*, Routledge & Kegan Paul, London, 1957; J. Platt, *Social Research in Bethnal Green: An Evaluation of the Work of the Institute of Community Studies*, Macmillan, London, 1971; and P. Townsend, *The Family Life of Old People*, Routledge & Kegan Paul, London, 1957.

[5] See for example P. Marris, *Widows and their Families*, Routledge & Kegan Paul, London, 1958; E. Mills, *Living with Mental Illness*, Routledge & Kegan Paul, London, 1962, J. Eekelar, *Family Security and Family Breakdown*, Penguin, Harmondsworth, 1971; O. R. McGregor, L. Blom-Cooper and C. Gibson, *Separated Spouses*, Duckworth, London, 1971; P. Morris, *Prisoners and their Families*, Allen & Unwin, London, 1965; and *Report on the Committee on One-Parent Families* (Finer Report), Vol. I, Cmnd 5629; and Vol. II, Cmnd 5629-1, HMSO, London, 1974.

[6] Phoebe Hall, Hilary Land, Roy Parker and Adrian Webb, *Change, Choice and Conflict in Social Policy*, Heinemann Educational Books, London, 1975, p. 227.

[7] ibid., p. 228.

[8] Finer Report, Vol. II, para. 111, p. 148.

[9] ibid., p. 149 and fn.

[10] D. H. J. Morgan, *Social Theory and the Family*, Routledge & Kegan Paul, London, 1975, pp. 206-7.

[11] Michael Bayley, *Mental Handicap and Community Care*, Routledge & Kegan Paul, London, 1973.

[12] Margaret Stacey, *Tradition and Change: A Study of Banbury*, Oxford University Press, London, 1960.

[13] Eda Topliss, *Provision for the Disabled*, Basil Blackwell, Oxford, Martin Robertson, London, 1975.

[14] ibid., p. 135.

[15] Robert Nisbet, *The Sociological Tradition*, Heinemann Educational Books, London, 1971.

[16] Richard Hillery, 'Definitions of Community: Areas of Agreement',

Rural Sociology, XX, 1955, quoted in Raymond Plant, *Community and Ideology: An Essay in Applied Social Philosophy*, Routledge & Kegan Paul, London, 1974, pp. 37-8.

[17] Margaret Stacey, 'The Myth of Community Studies', *British Journal of Sociology*, XX, 2, 1969, p. 134.

[18] ibid., p. 140.

[19] ibid., p. 141.

[20] ibid., p. 142.

[21] ibid., p. 143.

[22] ibid., pp. 143-5.

[23] Central Council for Education and Training in Social Work, *Social Work Curriculum Study: The Teaching of Community Work*, CCETSW Paper 8, London, 1974.

[24] José Harris, *William Beveridge: A Portrait*, Clarendon Press, Oxford, 1977, p. 441.

[25] ibid., p. 458.

[26] William Beveridge, *Voluntary Action: A Report on Methods of Advance*, Allen & Unwin, London, 1948.

[27] *Social Insurance and Allied Services* (Beveridge Report), Cmd 6404, HMSO, London, 1942 (1958 edition), para. 117, p. 53, also quoted in Robert Pinker, 'Social Policy and Social Justice', *Journal of Social Policy*, 3, 1, 1974, p. 11.

3 Nationalism and Internationalism

Beveridge's patriotism was qualified by a keen awareness of both the various sectional loyalties which created conflict within nations and those which created conflict between nations. In his report Beveridge argued that 'In seeking security not merely against physical want, but against all these evils (Want, Disease, Ignorance, Squalor, and Idleness), and in showing that security can be combined with freedom and enterprise and responsibility of the individual for his own life, the British community and those who in other lands have inherited the British tradition have a vital service to render to human progress.'[1] Beveridge believed that the claims of collective and individual welfare could be reconciled since they were mutually interdependent. Although he took 'the British community' as his context for redistribution, he was equally convinced that the claims of national and international welfare were also reconcilable. He saw the creation of a welfare state in Britain as a partial fulfilment of the wider aims of the Atlantic Charter. The proposals in his report represented 'not an attempt by one nation to gain for its citizens advantages at the cost of their fellow fighters in a common cause, but a contribution to that common cause'.[2] Beveridge was appealing to sentiments of communal and patriotic loyalty which were inclusive rather than exclusive, reaching out to an ideal of international welfare embodied in a future world-wide community of united nations.

The problems which arise in the attempt to make a reality of this philosophy of social welfare stem from the fact that every institutional claim on our loyalties and interests is potentially exclusive as well as inclusive. A love of one's country, like a love of one's local community, can be inward- as well as outward-looking, and this applies equally to their popular and intellectual manifestations. Patriotism, for example, is a folk sentiment, but in providing the basis for nationalist ideologies it becomes associated with theories of national self-determination and social improvement. More recently the loyalties which ordinary people feel towards their local community have been incorporated into theories of community participation and action. Once upon a time the term 'nationalism' must have seemed as artificial and alien to the untutored ear as the concept of 'a local social system'. Plamenatz defined nationalism as 'the desire to preserve or enhance a people's national or cultural identity when that identity is threatened, or the desire to transform or even create it where it is felt to be inadequate or lacking'.[3] Ginsberg offers us one of the best considered definitions of a nation: 'a body of people, associated with, if not actually inhabiting a certain territory, who have in common a stock of sentiments, thoughts and conative tendencies, acquired and transmitted during the course of a common history, and who have the will to be, or to become, politically independent . . . or have at least some measure of autonomy in cultural affairs'.[4]

These attachments to family, community, nation and beyond define the boundaries of our felt objectives and entitlements. They are a part of the 'three conditions' of 'attachment to self, and to things and to persons' which Eliot singles out as giving meaning to our daily lives.[5] They are all mutable under the impact of change.

In the tradition of European and American social thought there has always been a concern about the degree to which industrialization, bureaucratization and increasing social and geographical mobility have led to massive concentrations of power and a widening of the distance between individuals and their families and the wider society of which they are a part. One of Durkheim's preoccupations was the extent to which modern citizens lacked commitment to clearly defined collective ideals. He argued that men and women need to discover some attachment to altruistic purposes which might counterbalance the self-interestedness of their economic activities. Without that balance, life in industrial societies becomes characterized by a restless, egoistic search for new experiences and gratifications which is accompanied by an intolerable degree of moral uncertainty and distress. This social, or asocial, state Durkheim described as 'anomie'.

Durkheim feared that 'the radical disappearance of intermediate groups' would weaken public morality, 'unless the spirit of association comes alive, not only in a few educated circles, but in the deep mass of the people'.[6] Tönnies showed a similar concern about this sort of eventuality over fifty years ago, when he observed how 'The State serves progress, the development of independent personalities, but always at the expense of the folk, and their rich . . . co-operative life'.[7] It was his view that when social welfare 'ceases to rest in the community . . . it demoralizes poverty and reassures the wealthy in their complacency'.[8] The same concerns preoccupy and inspire the present revival of community studies and activities. I have stressed the commitment to change and reform expressed in this revival as distinct from the concern of writers like Nisbet with the links between social order and the nurturing of 'meaningful groups and associations lying intermediate to the individual and the larger values and processes of . . . society'.[9]

In recent times Dahrendorf has argued that the ideology of community is essentially antipathetic to any notion of citizenship which is based upon equal rights and opportunities within a truly pluralistic society. He describes Tönnies's distinction between *Gemeinschaft* and *Gesellschaft* as 'one of those unfortunate dichotomies in which German thought is rich', and as being 'historically misleading, sociologically uninformed and politically illiberal'.[10] Dahrendorf's critique of community is part of his attack on certain features of German nationalism. He argues that the fundamental illiberality of Tönnies's model stems from the fact that, while the model seems to imply a basic harmony and identity between community and nation, this consensus is essentially suppressive of innovation, conflict and personal liberty. Dahrendorf concludes that 'The ideology of an inner unity of society generally appeared in the other ideology of a state of national emergency. Because the nation is surrounded by enemies, it must close its ranks inside and form a "forsworn community". . . . Thus society and its classes disappear behind the nation and a fictitious community of its people.'[11] There is no doubt that it was this type of interpretation of Tönnies which provided ideological support for the tyrannies of Nazism. In fairness to Tönnies, however, one must add that he objected with equal passion to Bolshevik and Nazi programmes of community organization, arguing that they created a '"*Volksgemeinschaft*" by compulsion'.[12] He believed that 'A people which is in the process of becoming spiritually more mature and stronger will again want to be its own master. It wants to recognise its own identity in the State and to form itself into the State. It wants to again be self-ruling in the smaller groups.'[13]

Durkheim's view of the relationship between community and nation was more positive and explicitly developmental. It was grounded in the belief that the boundaries both of egoism and of altruism had to be governed by compromise and realism.[14] He describes family, nation and humanity as reflecting a hierarchy of moral goals in which the family, being 'closer to the individual . . . provides less lofty goals' than the others.[15] He suggests that the nation derives its moral value from its close approximation to 'the society of mankind, at present unrealised in fact, and perhaps unrealisable, yet representing the limiting case, or the ideal limit toward which we always strive'.[16]

It is at this point that Durkheim tries to define a realistic limit to practical altruistic concerns. He contends that 'There is nothing to justify the supposition that there will never emerge a State embracing the whole of humanity . . . [but] there is no reason for considering it at this time. . . . It would seem impossible to subordinate and sacrifice a group that does in fact exist, that is at the present a living reality, to one not yet born and that very probably never will be anything but an intellectual construct. According to what we have said, conduct is moral only when it has for its object a society having its own structure and character. How can humanity have such a character and fill such a role since it is not a constituted group?'[17]

The claims of internationalism are therefore demoted, if not debunked, in Durkheim's analysis. One's own country has prior claims to moral allegiance. In his review of Durkheim's ethical theory Ginsberg points out that he saw no problem in reconciling the rivalry between 'cosmopolitanism and patriotism', provided that 'each state gives up the pursuit of selfish ends', and that all states abandon the 'policy of expansion at the expense of their neighbours and [take] for their ends the realisation of justice within their own domains'.[18]

Durkheim's theory of moral education attributes a key role to patriotic sentiment: it serves as a natural bridge between local and international forms of welfare. The discharge of social obligations requires collective efforts, for which the child must be suitably educated. From his immediate involvement in the mutual aid practices of his family, school and local community the child can be prepared to take part in 'the pursuit of great collective ends', and 'The spirit of devotion to patriotic objectives can furnish this necessary end.'[19] Durkheim does not, however, recommend a patriotism which is either uncritical or unreflective: 'We need not fear', he concludes, 'on occasion to show what is necessarily incomplete in our way of life.' Neither is a love of one's country incompatible with a concern for other nations, since 'If one loves his country, or humanity in general, he cannot see the suffering of his compatriots — or more generally, of any human being — without suffering himself and without demonstrating, consequently, the impulse to relieve it.'[20]

Durkheim's theory suggests that there is a natural and desirable progression from a person's attachment to his family and local community associations to an informed and inclusive love of his country. There are understandable reasons why liberal intellectuals should feel uneasy when the word 'patriotism' is used, since it is so often taken to imply ethnocentrism, prejudice and other undesirable sentiments although it need not imply anything of the sort. Tocqueville distinguishes between an instinctive and a rational patriotism. He describes the former as an 'undefinable and unpondered feeling that ties a man's heart to the place where he was born'. He contrasts this with a rational patriotism, which is 'less generous, perhaps, less ardent, but more creative and lasting . . . engendered by enlightenment, grows by the aid of laws and the exercise of rights, and in the end becomes, in a sense, mingled with personal interest'.[21] With characteristic finesse Tocqueville goes on to describe the mental state of those who under conditions of change and moral uncertainty are able to 'find their country nowhere' so that 'they retreat into a narrow and unenlightened egoism. Such men escape from prejudices without recognising the rule of reason: they have neither the instinctive patriotism of a monarchy nor the reflective patriotism of a republic, but have come to a halt between the two amidst confusion and misery.'[22]

There may be equally unfortunate outcomes if the lack of patriotic attachment encourages a flight into a boundless altruism rather than 'a narrow egoism' — an internationalism which is a substitute for rather than a complement to patriotism. In these circumstances the confusions and miseries to which Tocqueville alludes would be attended by that 'pessimism [which] always accompanies unlimited aspirations'.[23] It may be argued for example that much racial prejudice occurs among people who *lack* an informed and authentic attachment to their country and their local community, or in whom there has grown no balance of moral sentiments. They come to resent the apparent incorporation and acceptance of minorities into a society of which they do not feel themselves to be a part. Those who feel a sense of belonging to their society may be more disposed to share it with others and to accept cultural diversity without feeling themselves to be threatened by it. Nor is there any convincing reason why, in treating the subject of patriotism, we should equate it with jingoistic intolerance. Yet the literature of social administration scarcely touches upon it at all except with reference to the evident connections between war and social policy. War often provides a context in which the heightening of patriotic feelings can be used to inspire a collective spirit of self-sacrifice and an augmented desire among people to work together for a better society. A nation in political and economic crisis cannot act otherwise if it hopes to survive. Nonetheless, despite the succession of crises which we have suffered since 1945, we have to go back as far as the Beveridge Report to find an unequivocal assertion of the positive links between social policy and the recovery of a sense of national purpose.

The world wars discredited the concepts of patriotism and nationalism among large sections of the liberal and socialist intelligentsia of the West. Nationalism became a noble cause only when it was practised abroad by foreigners — notably those engaged in wars of liberation against imperialist powers. This association between nationalism and imperialism in the West and political and economic exploitation in the Third World has inhibited a positive appraisal of the links between nationalism and social policy in industrial societies. Theories of class conflict rather than of national consensus have tended to dominate the debate about social welfare. It has become a part of the conventional wisdom of collectivist thought to assert that the inequalities within Western capitalist societies are functionally associated with the inequalities that exist between those societies and the Third World.

In discussing the connection between nationalism and imperialism Lichtheim suggests that imperialism as a political movement 'latched onto nationalism because no other popular base was available. But this statement can also be turned round: nationalism transformed itself into imperialism whenever the opportunity offered. It can be argued that popular patriotism was systematically corrupted when it passed into the service of the imperialist movement, but the speed with which the transformation was accomplished suggests that no deep resistance had to be overcome.'[24] This pattern of historical association goes some way towards explaining why, among radicals, both nationalism and patriotism are disparagingly equated with chauvinistic ideologies, and why they evoke little positive response save for embarrassment among moderate reformers.

At the root of this diffidence about patriotism lies a fundamental hostility towards capitalism. In the collectivist ideologies
of the Left it is possible to delineate a hierarchy of moral obligations in which the needs of local social systems rank above
those of family and kinship and the needs of the international
community rank above those of individual nations. The patriotic card is seldom played, except when it can be argued that
one's own country is more collectivist and less capitalist than
some others. This was the case in the great debate about the
United Kingdom's entry into the Common Market. Left and
right wing on this occasion played patriotic cards of different
suits. The Right opposed entry on the grounds that national
sovereignty would be imperilled. The Left opposed entry on the
grounds that the European Economic Community was marked
with the stigma of capitalism and thus derived its rationale not
from the altruistic motives of the social market and a benevolent
internationalism but from the profit-seeking motives of a
capitalist economy which was entering into a new period of
imperialist exploitation.

This opposition goes back to the early 1960s. Anthony
Wedgewood Benn (as he then was) briefly summed up the
socialist case when he opposed entry into the Common Market,
on the grounds that the Common Market 'entrenches *laissez-
faire* as its philosophy and chooses Bureaucracy as its administrative method'. Such a political system would be antipathetic
to the growth of 'social justice under democratic control, both
within its member nations and in the underdeveloped countries'.
Benn argued that the exports of these countries would be
damaged, and that 'Relevant internationalism today means
accepting disarmament controls, following liberal tariff and
trading policies' and working towards a policy of co-operation.[25]
Titmuss was hostile to entry on the grounds that the levels of
social service provision in Western Germany and France were
inadequate, and that official attitudes to dependency and
deviance in those countries were so lacking in humanity that
they gave us little reason to hope that the Common Market
would develop into a 'compassionate and civilised' country 'in
world terms'.[26]

Two idealistic traditions are often found together in the
literature of the social sciences. One of them is retrospective
and looks back to forms of social organization which are
deemed to be simpler and more wholesome than the com-

plexities of industrial societies. The other looks forward to an integrated world healed of the divisions and antagonisms of nation states. This second tradition expresses a passionate internationalism which seeks to encompass a whole world of strangers in its beneficence. In the West both of these two traditions are antipathetic to the values and practices of capitalism. Indeed the rhetoric of internationalism is so much a part of contemporary socialist thought that we sometimes forget that another great internationalist ideal was once a fundamental element in classical economic theory and the doctrines of *laissez-faire*. This theory purported to show how the exchange mechanisms of the free economic market could not only reconcile the interests of individual egoism and collective welfare within single nations but could also create, on the basis of free trade, an international framework of concord between nations. The doctrine of *laissez-faire* challenged the established mercantilist doctrines of the seventeenth and eighteenth centuries which had emphasized the overriding claims of national interests and sovereignty.

This brings us to a second set of contradictory theories which define the boundaries of obligation and entitlement, and which have served historically as the criteria for inclusion and exclusion in social and economic exchanges. In order to explore this territory it will be necessary for us to review trends in social and economic thought which are not customarily treated as central to the study of social policy. The practical outcomes of the great historical debates about mercantilism as against *laissez-faire* and protection as against free trade, for example, had a profound influence upon social welfare and the making of social policy. Within this broader framework we cannot but be reminded that in nineteenth-century Britain economic policies had a far greater and more positive influence than social policies upon social welfare. Social policies, as we understand them today, scarcely existed outside the fields of environmental health and charitable endeavour. The purpose of the new poor law was not to contribute directly to the improvement of living standards but to serve as an instrument by which an old order of economic life, already demoralized, could be finally destroyed.

It may be that the generally anti-capitalist bias of social administration students stems in part from the preoccupation of their tutors with the English poor law. A student whose study of nineteenth-century capitalism is mainly confined to the workings of the poor law would indeed be an unfeeling scoundrel were he not to conclude that the rise of capitalism had been an unmitigated disaster for the poor of Britain. This emphasis on deterrence and injustice can easily extend into the study of contemporary social policies, so that the subject becomes primarily a study of the persistence of poverty rather than the creation of opportunity and wealth, and of the failures rather than the successes of the economic market. In this way the subject becomes steadily more overcast with a subsistence mode of thought, in which the past is a cause for lament, the present an object of regret and only the future a source of hope.

Marxists and supporters of the free market economy alike tend to dismiss as Utopian any optimistic outlook on the future which does not link social reform with radical social change. Marxists criticize what they deem to be the excessive concern of social administrators with the symptoms of poverty, and they also criticize their neglect of the fundamental causes of poverty, which are inherent in the structure and function of economic markets under capitalism. Coercion, they argue, will always be a feature of social policies under capitalism, although its form and intensity will vary in response to the needs of the exploiting class. Liberal economists argue that only a return to a greater reliance on the operations of a free market will lead to increased national prosperity and the realization of the aim of alleviating poverty, both of which collective intervention has so far failed to achieve. They suggest that if the humiliations of the poor law were functionally necessary for the production of wealth under capitalism, then the same point ought to be made regarding the relationship between forced labour and economic growth under communism.

Social administrators who occupy the ideological ground between these two traditions of thought face the most intractable dichotomy of all when they are considering the means and ends of social welfare. Among their number are those who wish to continue to reform capitalism without abolishing it as well as those who wish to transform it by peaceful means into a democratic socialist society. The latter are probably in a majority, and a part of their difficulty lies in a problem of morale, since they have to face at least in the short run the prospect of living in a type of society for which they have very little enthusiasm. It is this tradition in social administration, defending itself against cynicism and despair, which is the least able to do without intimations of Utopia, universal altruism and brotherhood.

I have suggested elsewhere[27] that the Utopian tradition and injunctions to unconditional altruism remain powerful elements in the work of many non-Marxist social administrators. These elements are of course exemplified in the work of Titmuss, who wrote so disparagingly of those who are disposed to treat social services as a residual institution, imposing burdens on the productive forces of capitalism. Titmuss was equally disparaging of capitalism. Nonetheless his hostility towards many features of British economic life was always complemented by a commitment to Britain, its democratic institutions and values. At the same time he was a committed internationalist. *The Gift Relationship* stands as his most developed apologia of an internationalist welfare ethic. In this work Titmuss's defence of unilateral altruism and gift relationships rests on what he describes as three interrelated theses: 'First, that gift exchange of a non-quantifiable nature has more important functions in complex, large-scale societies than the writings of Lévi-Strauss and others would suggest. Second, the application of scientific and technological developments in such societies, in further accelerating the spread of complexity, has increased rather than diminished the scientific as well as the social need for gift relationships. Third, for these and many other reasons, modern societies now require more rather than less freedom of choice for the expression of altruism in the daily life of all social groups.'[28] The altruistic sentiments of men and women can, however, only find their full expression in societies in which the basic institutions — particularly those of health and welfare — positively encourage and sustain such choices. Titmuss concludes that 'It is indeed little understood how modern society, technical, professional, large-scale organized society, allows few opportunities for ordinary people to articulate giving in morally practical terms outside their own network of family and personal relationships.'[29]

The morality underlying the practices of small groups such as the family, peers, workmates and friends is seen to be in large part contingent on and derived from the dominant values of the wider society. Titmuss's master stroke was to develop his thesis from the example of blood donorship, which is immediate and familiar to ordinary people and yet has international implications.

Given its collectivist bias, the subject of social policy and administration has been more deeply influenced by socialist than by classical economic theory. Its major writers on internationalist themes, Titmuss, Myrdal and Galbraith, for example, have been inspired by the collectivist values of the social market rather than those of competitive individualism. In a subsequent chapter I shall look more closely at the connections between collectivism and socialism, since they are not always compatible doctrines. The collectivist tradition in social policy and administration owed much to both Marxist and non-Marxist theories of social-ism, and socialists until now have remained remarkably confident about the practicability of their internationalist ideals. With the recent increase in the number of socialist and quasi-socialist governments in the Third World, these ideals are currently being put to the test. Despite the present evidence of a vigorous and seemingly pervasive nationalism in those countries — as well as in the Soviet Union and China — socialists continue in the hope that their philosophy will prove sufficiently altruistic to transcend national frontiers. Capitalist economic theory, in contrast, is no longer sustained by a spirit of committed and confident interna-tionalism, although one of the main elements, not only of the moral appeal but of the very rationale of classical economic theory, was its advocacy of international free trade. Furthermore the radical appeal of *laissez-faire* was not restricted to economic issues. It was a powerful element in the traditions of earlier nineteenth-century liberalism, closely associated with the enlarge-ment of political freedoms and hostile to the acquisition and ex-ploitation of overseas colonies.

The subject of this chapter has been the nature of the insti-tutional forces and boundaries which determine the intensity and range of the welfare obligations which citizens accept and of the welfare rights to which they feel entitled. I have tried to explore some of the familial, communal and national aspects of this subject, despite the general lack of empirical evidence about their relative importance in the lives of ordinary people. A much clearer impression remains regarding the views of social ad-ministrators about the ethics of social welfare. Above all else there seems to be a general assumption that universalist and inclusive forms of social policy are morally superior to selectivist and exclusive forms. Charity may begin at home but it ceases to be charity if it stays there. Few people would quarrel with this view of welfare ethics. Disagreements arise about the extent to which the range of obligations and entitlements ought to be en-larged. The logical end result of the universalist argument is the internationalization of welfare as a system of exchange.

In any model of welfare which treats internationalism as its ethical ideal we will find that capitalism and the philosophy of the free economic market are likely to be judged and found wanting. Their defenders are handicapped by the evidence of the past, which suggests that the internationalist theories of *laissez-faire* have failed whenever they have been put to the test. Britain's great essay at free trade throughout the greater part of the nineteenth century is, however, the only major example we have. In its contemporary forms capitalism tends to be viewed by collectivist social administrators as being essentially predatory. It is internationalist only insofar as it is imperialist. By contrast, socialists seem able to preserve against the gathering tide of evidence a belief that their internationalist ideals may yet be realized. Time may eventually prove them right, although it is too early to say.

The consequence of this imbalance of ideological commitment within the discipline is that it becomes extremely difficult to bring together within one analytical model the general institutional and specific policy dimensions of social welfare. In seeking to understand the ordering of priorities in welfare obligation and entitlement it is necessary for us to refer to some hierarchy of moral sentiments and the cultural processes by which the various levels of the hierarchy are interrelated. The institutional components of that hierarchy will include family, community, nation and an international dimension — although their actual positions in the hierarchy may vary from one society to another. Such a model, however, cannot be an entirely intellectual construction in a normative sense. It must take account of the sentiments of ordinary people and of the stages by which they extend and order their knowledge of the world. They are unlikely to bridge any serious institutional gaps in this progression by acts of imagination or faith.

Within both socialist and non-socialist hierarchies of moral sentiment the most serious hiatus concerns the sentiment of patriotism and the nation state itself. Marxist theory copes with this problem by seeking to demonstrate that under capitalism there can be no genuine consensus at a national level regarding welfare means and ends. Class conflict is at present the expression of irreconcilable interests among the citizenry and will in future serve as the means for ending the exploitation of one class by another. Under capitalism patriotic loyalties only serve to perpetuate the alienation of the citizenry and the existence of the institutions which oppress them. At least, in a negative and highly pejorative sense, Marxist theory does accord a place to nationalism and patriotic sentiment, although, as John Rex once observed, after 'the revolution' Marxists might do well to reconsider what Durkheim had to say about the making and remaking of social consensus.

There is no comparable theoretical treatment of the phenomena of patriotism and the nation state in the non-Marxist tradition of social policy and administration. This is a strange omission, since the tradition is still strongly collectivist, and, given its non-revolutionary socialist overtones, it is also redistributive in outlook. Any such philosophy of welfare implies sacrifices on behalf of one section of society by another and by one generation for the next, and hence the subordination of familial and local interests to some higher ideal. That ideal is more likely to be realized if it can draw upon the patriotic sentiments of ordinary people rather than the internationalist beliefs of intellectuals. As Orwell remarks, 'Within the intelligentsia, a derisive and mildly hostile attitude towards Britain is more or less compulsory.' Orwell defines patriotism as 'devotion to a particular place and a particular way of life, which one believes to be the best in the world but has no wish to force upon other people'.[30] The difficulty for collectivistically-minded intellectuals is that it is very hard to feel patriotic about Britain in this sense without also feeling some commitment to capitalism. Perhaps this inhibition explains in part the recent revival of interest in local communities as foci of moral obligation.

We no longer live in times when social scientists can unashamedly love their country and think it right to put their country's interests first — as was the case with Tocqueville, Weber and Durkheim. We need no longer trouble to ask of our radicals, as in *Felix Holt* the vicar asked of Harold Transome:

'You may pepper the bishops a little. But you'll respect the constitution handed down, eh — and you'll rally round the throne — and the King, God bless him, and the usual toasts, eh?'

or, if we do so, to expect the same kind of reply:

'Of course, of course. I am a Radical only in rooting out abuses . . . I remove the rotten timbers . . . and substitute fresh oak, that's all.'[31]

Today they are more likely to tell us that the vocation of being a woodworm in the framework of capitalism is an honourable calling in itself.

References

[1] Beveridge Report, p. 170.

[2] ibid., p. 171.

[3] John Plamenatz, 'Two Types of Nationalism', in Eugene Kamenka, *Nationalism: The Nature and Evolution of an Idea*, Edward Arnold, London, 1976, pp. 23-4.

[4] See Ginsberg, op. cit., p. 244.

[5] T. S. Eliot, *Little Gidding*, Faber & Faber, MCMXLII, p. 12.

[6] Emile Durkheim, *Moral Education*, Free Press of Glencoe, 1961, p. 238.

[7] Ferdinand Tönnies, *Custom: An Essay on Social Codes*, Free Press of Glencoe, 1961, p. 137.

[8] ibid., p. 102.

[9] Robert A. Nisbet, *The Quest for Community*, Oxford University Press, 1970, p. 70.

[10] Ralf Dahrendorf, *Society and Democracy in Germany*, Weidenfeld & Nicolson, 1968, pp. 127-8.

[11] ibid., p. 131.

[12] Tönnies, op. cit., p. 27.

[13] ibid., pp. 141-2.

[14] Durkheim, *Moral Education*, p. 49.

[15] ibid., pp. 74-5.

[16] ibid., p. 81.

[17] ibid., p. 76.

[18] Ginsberg, op. cit., pp. 47-8.

[19] Durkheim, *Moral Education*, pp. 102-3.

[20] ibid., p. 83.

[21] Alexis de Tocqueville, *Democracy in America*, Harper & Row, New York, 1966, p. 217.

[22] ibid., p. 83.

[23] Durkheim, *Moral Education*, p. 40.

[24] George Lichtheim, *Imperialism*, Allen Lane, 1971, pp. 81-2.

[25] Contribution to 'Going into Europe' Symposium (II), *Encounter*, January 1963, p. 64.

[26] Contribution to 'Going into Europe' Symposium (IV), *Encounter*, March 1963, p. 77.

[27] See R. A. Pinker, Preface to David Reisman, *Richard Titmuss: Welfare and Society*, Heinemann Educational Books, London, 1977, pp. vii-xvi.

[28] Richard M. Titmuss, *The Gift Relationship: From Human Blood to Social Policy*, Allen & Unwin, London, 1970, p. 224.

[29] ibid., pp. 225-6.

[30] See 'Notes on Nationalism', in George Orwell, *Decline of the English Murder and Other Essays*, Penguin, 1975, pp. 173 and 156.

[31] George Eliot, *Felix Holt the Radical*, Panther Books, p. 50.

4 Social Change and Social Welfare

The family has always been an object of suspicion amongst social reformers. In recent times psychoanalytic theory has sought to explain the pathologies of family life, while the main thrust of Marxist sociology has indicted the family as a repressive social institution, inextricably associated with the source of all repression — private property. The family is of course the most subversive of all social institutions since it accommodates both its apologists and its antagonists with equanimity. There is an implicit conflict in collectivist social welfare, given that one of the primary aims of social policy is to preserve and restore families and hence the emotional foundations of the institution of private property, while it seeks at the same time to achieve a more equitable distribution of property in general terms.

The concept of community and the ideals of community consciousness and participation have become the most recent institutional repository for this conflict. In one sense they may be seen as an attempt to widen the frontiers of human obligation and fellowship. In another sense they could equally develop into a new institutional network of loyalties, each of which is stronger than individual, nuclear family or extended family loyalties and hence capable of expressing both a slightly more generous definition of conditional altruism and a stronger resistance to more widely based claims of national or international welfarism. A disenchanted outside observer might be tempted to conclude that, at a time when most developing countries of the Third World are seeking to eradicate or control the sectional interests of tribal loyalties, the countries of the West are busily trying to create a *Gemeinschaft* spirit of tribalism in their own cities and towns.

In addition to the family and the local community we have considered the national boundaries of welfare practice. That men and women are able to think at all about the collective well-being of such an extensive and complex phenomenon as the nation state in which they live might seem to signify a triumph of the human imagination and might give grounds for optimism regarding the capacity of our moral sentiments. None-theless this association between social policy and national interests still leaves us falling short of the internationalist ideals of unilateral service to the universal stranger. Indeed the intel-lectual climate of our time — and that of the social sciences generally — encourages us to take a negative view of the moral sentiments which we once called 'patriotism'.

It may be argued that all the institutional supports of these conditional forms of altruism — family, community and nation, and we could add race and religion — are products of false con-sciousness and the exploitative nature of the class system under capitalism. Class generates its own group interests and loyalty, but, the argument goes, class conflict might yet serve as a means of breaking down these conditional forms of altruism, which are both protective of their members and hostile towards those who are strangers.

Much depends on whether we take the view that social insti-tions are largely the product of our moral sentiments, or the converse view that these sentiments are largely shaped by insti-tutional forces. I suspect that social scientists a century from now will look back with amused incredulity on our present ob-session with social class, much as a present-day natural scientist would view his medieval counterpart's preoccupation with phlogiston — a mythical substance, which was said to inhere in all combustible elements and to be the cause of conflagrations. We treat social class in a similar manner today — as a universal component of political heat, whether it be the warmth of partial consensus or the flames of revolutionary conflict.

Class consciousness is undoubtedly an important contributory factor in the growth of conditional altruism, and social research tells us much about the processes of change which intensify or weaken class loyalties as well as those which generate conflict between classes. My concern, however, is as much with the commonplace as with the exceptional situations which affect the balance between loyalties and antipathies, between giving and receiving, and between including and excluding which determines how welfare resources are allocated.

Social and cultural change can radically affect these felt boundaries of entitlement and obligation. Social and geogra-phical mobility, urban growth and industrialization create new forms of attachment and experiences of loss, but the meanings which intellectuals place upon these events are not necessarily the same as their meanings for the ordinary citizens who also experience them and who may prefer not to think in theoretical or abstracted terms. As Peter Berger argues, 'Policies that ignore the indigenous definitions of a situation are prone to fail',[1] and 'All material advances are pointless unless they preserve the meanings by which men live or provide satisfactory substitutes for the old meanings.'[2] I have throughout this section emphasized the kinds of institutional attachment which give meaning to the social life of citizens and argued that the integrity of these cognitive and normative universes depends on the preservation of the boundaries of moral obligation. Furthermore these conditional forms of altruism are deserving of respect in their own right and ought not to be too readily judged by reference to the broadest possible definitions of moral obligation.

My proposed model of social welfare emphasizes the social institutions which make their several claims on our loyalties and thereby compel us to define the scope and limits of our conditional forms of altruism. These loyalties so often conflict that the practice of welfare in industrial societies seems to be governed by a sequence of antinomies. In some cases we are left to our own devices to reconcile these conflicts especially with regard to familial and neighbourly claims and duties. Through the agency of social policies we are also compelled to order our priorities by reference to criteria more or less generous than we might otherwise adopt. Insofar as social policy is concerned with redistribution it also functions as an agent of discrimination which always seems to favour some at the expense of others.

I set out these institutional aspects in order to emphasize the conditional nature of so much of our welfare altruism. It is within this variety of institutional loyalties that we can also locate the many forms of discrimination, both positive and negative, which characterize welfare practices in complex societies. The key differences between societies lie in the extent to which such diversities of interest are tolerated and the degree to which one set of discriminatory criteria is imposed to the exclusion of others. The question for all practical purposes is not whether discrimination occurs, but who practises discrimination and upon whom, on whose behalf and at whose expense?

Governments differ not only in their use of discriminatory criteria but in the kinds of sanctions with which they enforce conformity. Every government, given the variety of social interests over which it presides, must seem to favour some groups to the detriment of others and hence must encounter differing degrees of resistance. The family is one of the most potent sources of what might be called the 'counter-policies' of social welfare. The characteristic type of counter-policy is what I have described as families practising positive discrimination on their own behalf either to protect their privileges or to redress their deprivations.[3] In pursuit of these ends families may, if they possess sufficient power, confidence and skill, act in isolation to further their own interests, but more frequently they combine with other families. Families which are intrinsically weak because of their incompleteness or poverty or ill health must combine with each other if they are to have any hope of success. Trade unions, professional associations and other special interest groups represent typical forms of the conditionally altruistic group practising positive discrimination on its own behalf.

Conditional forms of altruism may find their expression in the sacrifices which one generation is disposed to make for another over time or in the sacrifices which one group may voluntarily or involuntarily make for another at a given time. The more these sacrifices are required to transcend kinship affiliations, the more likely it is that compulsion and sanctions will be employed by the government.

It is the quality of this interaction between formal government social policies and the informal practices of mutual aid which is of crucial importance in the study of altruism. The boundaries between these two sets of activity are never clearly drawn, but when shifts of emphasis occur they have profound significance. The history of the application of the family means test under the poor law is an example of what can happen when the sanctions of formal social policies intrude too forcefully upon the privacy of familial patterns of voluntary mutual aid. There is also much research to be carried out on the changing forms of voluntary aid and charitable enterprise, since the success or failure of community care is now heavily contingent upon the creation of a new set of understandings and working relationships between formal welfare agencies and informal welfare practices.

A theory of moral sentiments which seeks to make sense of the determinants of the giving and receiving of welfare resources must therefore take account of the institutional context in which giving and receiving occur; of the chief forms of positive and negative discrimination practised by the government; of the interplay between these formal policies and the beliefs and informal practices of ordinary citizens, their families and other sectional groups; and of the extent to which such moral diversity is tolerated by governments. Furthermore we need to understand more fully the ways in which and the extent to which changes occur among ordinary people with regard to their definitions of felt obligation and entitlement, because such shifts in opinion and belief provide the groundswell of support for official policies as well as the counter-policies which are the neglected dimension of social welfare studies.

In trying to make sense and create order out of an increasingly complex process of social change men and women learn to systematize and extend their conceptual universes. Social policies are attempts to give, through the force of statutes and administrative practice, a relative continuity and permanence to what might otherwise be only transient extensions of human imagination and empathy. However, the counter-policies and counter-claims of family and local social systems continue to influence the formal rules of social policy. Every exercise of discretion, every so-called anomaly and inconsistency in social policies can be explained partly as a response to these external pressures and partly by the internal propensities for growth and replication which form part of the dynamics of bureaucracy. Here we come up against what Kathleen Bell describes as the 'more serious difficulty' of *'conceptual lag'*.[4] The 'labyrinthine complexities' of the administrative welfare state become so far removed from 'the levels of everyday conception of the social world' that ordinary people are baffled by the experience of 'language and logic'[5] which are quite alien to them. The philosophy of community participation is inspired by the belief that a closer involvement of ordinary citizen in the administration of social services will resolve many of these anomalies and conflicts. It is difficult to follow the reasoning behind this view. Social policies were evolved to meet needs which would not have been effectively met by informal welfare practices, and they are able to meet those needs only insofar as they continue to be governed by formal rules which can be consistently applied in highly generalized systems of exchange.

Titmuss delineated his social division of welfare by reference to the formal administrative boundaries between three major areas of welfare provision and by making explicit the extent to which they shared a common aim but in practice served to reinforce inequalities of welfare provision. In this respect he contrasted the public social services with those of the fiscal and occupational welfare systems. The typology of social welfare which I have tried to set out has a less precise framework. It is concerned more with the conflicts which occur between the various institutional contexts of welfare practice and the notions of obligation and entitlement which they embody. These two approaches are complementary, and both are necessary, if we are to increase our understanding of the relationships between informal and formal modes of welfare practice and between the loyalties evoked by familial, communal, patriotic and internationalist sentiments.

We must also give more attention to the ways in which changes of a more general nature occur in moral sentiments and welfare practices. Such changes cannot be explained simply by a historical progression from small societies based on familial and status networks of mutual aid to complex societies relying mainly on formal welfare bureaucracies. Whole sets of beliefs and practices are not conveniently and totally discarded in favour of better ones in response to economic and technological imperatives. Historical study shows us, rather, how the residues of older welfare practices persist and adapt and reassert themselves in new contexts, so that the practices of social welfare in complex industrial societies become a network of antinomies which is far too complex to be explained simply by class conflict.

Despite conflicts of interest and loyalty societies hold together so long as some continuity is maintained between popular and expert opinion about welfare means and ends. Eighty years ago Dicey explored the effects of change on the relationship between public opinion and law. In defence of the individualist tradition he argued that 'To the ordinary man who knows something of human nature . . . it must seem that the love of self, whether justifiable or unjustifiable, is due to causes deeper than any political or social reform will even touch.'[6] The record of collectivist reform since then suggests that Dicey exaggerated the innate conservatism of public opinion. Nonetheless it can be argued that change in the direction of a more generous definition of welfare obligation will carry the support of public opinion only if it can be shown to have relevance to changes in the institutional order of society. The acceptability of social policies derives not only from their instrumental effectiveness but from the sense of meaning and significance they have for the citizenry.[7]

Public opinion has come to accept a very high degree of

collectivist intervention in the form of the redistributive social policies of central and local governments. It may be argued that, given time, the majority of citizens will also come to accept more generously redistributive policies in favour of poorer nations. There are as yet, however, few convincing signs that this is likely to happen. With regard to immigration policies, for example, the evidence points in the other direction, namely, that the recent tightening up of immigration laws was a popular measure, and also that public opinion favours retrenchment rather than greater generosity in international aid.

Internationalism would seem to be a largely intellectual construct, which draws its support from expert rather than public opinion. Compared with the idea of community, it holds an insignificant place in the popular folklores of welfare and mutual aid with which men and women create a sense of stability and meaning in their lives. In his book, *Chance and Necessity*, Jacques Monod suggests that 'The ideas having the highest invading potential are those that *explain* man by assigning him his place in an imminent destiny, a safe harbour where his anxieties dissolve.'[8] The need to belong to some form of group or community, suggests Monod, is one such idea which is so all-pervasive and reassertive that it might be 'inscribed somewhere in the genetic code'.[9] This is an argument which comes very close to Dicey's views about human nature.

If we cannot yet hope to make one society out of our world we equally cannot return to archaic or primitive forms of community and exchange without also returning to the economic realities and moral traditions which gave them meaning. Our systems of mutual aid must be grounded in the realities of an industrial civilization of which the wealth and expertise derive from science and technology. Our capacity to help poorer nations comes from that wealth and knowledge. Older traditions of mutual aid persist in the present welfare practices of families and local communities. The values which they embody and the ranges of entitlement and obligation which they encompass could not dominate our moral universe once again without severely reducing even the conditional ranges of altruism which we have so gradually come to accept. The revival of interest in local communities as informal agencies of welfare can never be more than a necessary counterpoint to the gradual extension of the boundaries of our welfare responsibility. Those who believe that the idea of welfare rests upon an inclusive rather than an exclusive ethic of mutual aid must reject the sociological tradition which is characterized by its retrospective longing for the simpler life of noble savages, patrician Romans and medieval guildsmen. Nothing can bring back those gardens of Eden — if that is what they were — short of the demise of industrial civilization. The gates of paradise are closed for ever, but we may yet, like Dante's unbaptized and virtuous pagans, make a decent habitation out of Limbo.

References

[1] Peter Berger, *Pyramids of Sacrifice: Political Ethics and Social Change*, Basic Books, New York, 1974, p. 182.

[2] ibid., p. 167.

[3] Robert Pinker, *Social Theory and Social Policy*, Heinemann Educational Books, London, 1971, pp. 189-92.

[4] Kathleen Bell, *Disequilibrium in Welfare*, University of Newcastle upon Tyne, 1973, p. 19.

[5] ibid., p. 20.

[6] A. V. Dicey, *Law and Public Opinion in England During the Nineteenth Century*, Macmillan, London, 1962, p. lxxx.

[7] See Berger, op. cit., Ch. V, pp. 166-89.

[8] Jacques Monod, *Chance and Necessity*, Fontana Books, Glasgow, 1974, p. 155.

[9] ibid., p. 156.

5 Patterns of Exchange in Social Welfare

Economic and social exchange

The notion of exchange is fundamentally important in the study of social welfare. Exchange relationships are intrinsic to all types of welfare practice occurring in both formal and informal contexts. 'Formal' practices of social welfare are the institutional activities which are entirely or largely governed by statute and constitute the accepted subject-matter of social policy and administration. 'Informal' practices are the aspects of social welfare which are entirely or largely the spontaneous activities of ordinary citizens, either in groups or as individuals. This distinction is a useful one, provided that it is loosely drawn and treated as provisional, because the scope of voluntary effort and mutual aid is sometimes influenced by statute, and the conditions of regulation vary over time and among different societies.

From the extensive and growing literature on the subject[1] two basic characteristics of exchange relationships can be identified. First, exchanges can be classified by the number of their participants. We begin with unilateral transfers, in which a gift or grant is given by one person or group to another person or group. In the strictest sense unilateral transfers are not exchanges at all, although the beneficiary may make a response — in the form of gratitude or resentment. Next, there are bilateral exchanges, which occur between two individuals or between two groups, and, last, there are multilateral exchanges, which involve more than two individuals or groups. Simmel's notion of a dyadic relationship refers to a direct form of reciprocal exchange between equals. In triadic relationships the reciprocities become indirect and are both the cause and the consequence of hierarchy in relationships. The inclusion of a third party, making a triad, brings about a fundamental change, in that both direct and indirect relationships then become possible. Mediating roles may emerge, and whenever this happens, hierarchies of power become more common and more complex.

Secondly, we should distinguish between economic exchanges and social exchanges. Economic exchanges are forms of bilateral or multilateral transfer in which each of the parties is both a giver and a receiver and in which the end result is parity between the parties to the exchange. Social exchanges imply a measure of redistribution, and, although all the interested parties may act as both givers and receivers to some degree, the end result is one in which some have given more than others and some have received more than others. Each of these types of exchange embodies a different notion of distributive justice and also different rules regarding the criteria of entitlement and obligation. Titmuss argued that the unilateral transfer is the 'hall-mark of a social policy'[2] in order to emphasize what he believed to be a significant moral difference between economic and social exchanges. In its extreme form the social exchange becomes an outright gift.

We can make a useful distinction between economic and social exchanges by separating transactions in which equivalence is the dominant norm and desired outcome from those in which it is not. Members of private insurance schemes, for example, have reciprocal rights and duties. Due to the nature of risk-pooling some members pay in more than they take out and vice versa, but this occurs within a formal context of reciprocity, and there are contractual limits to such eventualities as well as limitation of membership. Similarly, in the case of schemes of social security based on modified forms of the insurance principle, all members make some contribution; indeed such systems can only function because unilateral transfers are exceptional and residual events.

Unequal exchanges can therefore result from associations which begin on terms of reciprocity and end with one party as an outright beneficiary. However, there are also unilateral transfers in which one person or group gives unconditionally to another person or group. The process may be a simple bilateral one or it may involve a large number of individuals, groups or formal welfare agencies. Clearly it is often very difficult to make a clear moral distinction between reciprocal and unilateral forms of exchange. Participants may or may not be volunteers. Intentions and consequences must both be taken into account. Given the vagaries of human nature and social life, it is often difficult if not impossible to separate prudential self-regard from altruism, as they are conventionally understood, and we have to remember this when we seek to distinguish these categories. A further problem is posed in the definition of altruism and its association with unilateral transfers. Writers like Titmuss restrict the term 'altruism' to the belief that it is morally right to extend collective aid to any person who is in proven need, even to strangers.

In complex industrial societies the distribution of knowledge about social reality is ordered not only by factors such as differential degrees of access to knowledge but also by natural differences in people's ability to comprehend highly complex phenomena. In the modern world the potential scope of generalized exchanges is universal. The continuum of obligation can be extended from kinship to international aid, and this has a bearing on three of Lévi-Strauss's assertions — first, that there are general properties of mind which have their origins in an unconscious which is a natural rather than a cultural phenomenon.[3] Secondly, the most fundamental of these properties, or universal mental structures, is concerned with exchange and reciprocity. Lastly, the rules governing social behaviour are not immutable, and there is ample anthropological and historical evidence of our capacity to change them, although the range of options open to us is finite. The crucial factors therefore appear to be the rate and intensity of the changes to which individuals are subjected, and the extent to which individuals have the freedom and ability to initiate and direct changes by reference to the cultural imperatives and exigencies of their 'own customs, and not those of societies foreign to their own'. These conditions, however, no longer prevail in a world where primitive and modern societies alike are exposed to the influence of radical agents of change both within and outside their boundaries. Furthermore, in default of empirical evidence, we can only speculate upon the different capacity of individuals to preserve a sense of meaning and identity under the stress of change and whether their reaction to change will be hostile or welcoming.

The same problem of the relationship between mind and culture was explored by Simmel in his analysis of exchange relationships. He portrays man having to assimilate a culture, the complexities of which eventually overwhelm and alienate him. Society strives after a wholeness, while each individual has the 'capacity to decompose himself into parts and to feel any one of these as his proper self. . . . In other words, the conflict between society and individual is continued in the individual himself as the conflict among his component parts. . . . It does not derive from any single "anti-social", individual interest.'[4]

Knowledge and power are hierarchically distributed, and so are the capacity and willingness to use them in the furtherance of change. Account must also be taken of the conflicts which often arise between popular or public opinion and expert opinion. In the sphere of expert opinion change is promoted or opposed by those who propagate ideas and by those who directly exercise power in policy-making and administration. Membership of these groupings is frequently overlapping and never constant, but, as the rate of change becomes intensified, there is a tendency for the boundaries to harden which is both a cause and a consequence of conflict. It is possible to infer from Lévi-Strauss's analysis the probability that even in complex industrial societies, whose citizens are relatively accustomed to change, the folklore of popular welfare beliefs is generally resistant to new ideas about obligation and entitlement. The natural disposition of ordinary men and women is to practise highly conditional forms of altruism which are grounded in the institutional realities of their everyday lives. These institutions may collapse under the impact of radical or sudden change but, if they are left alone to recover, they will nearly always return to a similitude of their prior state. It is tempting to attribute the guiding power of these tendencies to the psychological phantoms of Levi-Strauss's universal mental structures, enduring through all the vicissitudes of change. The problem is that we will never know whether or not such phantoms exist, because the theories from which they originate are not set out in a testable form.

In discussing the differences between industrial and pre-industrial societies Titmuss refers to Dalton's thesis that Western economic theories cannot be applied to the study of exchange in primitive communities. At the same time Titmuss insists that there is much of moral worth which Western societies can learn from the exchange practices of simpler societies, and that the residue of such practices in our societies is still sufficiently extensive and important to provide the basis for a new moral order. Following Polanyi, Dalton explains how formal economic theory was developed in response to the analytical problems posed by industrialization and the growth of economic markets which were motivated by profit and which used money as the nexus of exchange.[5] The development of the modern economic market created a new system of exchange relationships based on buying and selling in markets and governed by norms of reciprocity. The whole thrust and tenor of nineteenth-century economic theory was directed towards answering the question, 'What are the forces which determine prices in a market organised economy?'[6] Dalton elaborates this point in his later work, *Economic Systems and Society*, when he remarks that 'Before

Ricardo . . . there was political economy but not economics. From Aristotle to Adam Smith economic issues were analysed only to argue social policy: why prices should be "just"; why usury is a sin; the need for mercantilist market controls; the need to remove mercantilist market. controls. It was Ricardo who outlined the descriptive models of the purely economic market forces that made possible the asking of purely economic questions.'[7]

Thereafter economic theory became divorced from social life and, endowed with the positive moral and psychological sanction of Benthamist utilitarianism, came to be accorded an authority over and above other societal considerations. In this sense the laws of the economic market acquired the status of natural law, reconciling the fact of universal scarcity with the insatiability of human needs and desires.[8] The rules of the economic market were designed to be multi-purposive, like its means of exchange. Dalton concludes that 'When all-purpose money is absent in primitive economy, it is because market exchange as the economy-wide principle of integration is absent.' Primitive exchange economies are based on transactional principles which are essentially different from ours, and, while a 'primitive community often has a market place', it does not have a 'market system'.[9]

Given the nature of these differences, ought we to conclude not only that the economic theories developed to analyse complex industrial societies are 'not relevant to primitive economies' but also that the study of exchange in primitive economies has little or no relevance to 'the structures, processes and problems of market-organized industrialism'.[10] This inversion of Dalton's thesis would not have satisfied Titmuss for the following reason. Titmuss did not accept that the values and processes of economic market exchange provided a sufficient or satisfactory basis for social integration. He rejected any principle of integration based on competition and self-interest. He was therefore compelled to look for evidence in support of his own principle of social integration which he found in the example of blood donorship and other gift relationships in industrial societies.

These examples, however, are all taken from an entity which Titmuss called the social market, and it was a necessary part of his thesis to insist that the social market was governed by a morality different and superior to that of the economic market. In the social market needs were characteristically met through gifts, or unilateral transfers. In the economic market (regulated by effective demand) needs were met through exchanges, or bilateral transfers. By making this distinction Titmuss was able to demonstrate the relevance of his philosophy to the distribution of social welfare. He tells us far less about its relevance to the production of goods and services in the economic market upon which distribution is contingent.

The enhancement of social welfare depends equally upon the production and distribution of goods and services, and the problems of allocation in social policy arise not because one set of principles is morally superior to the other but simply because they are different. The fact remains that most primitive societies are materially poverty-stricken. The extent to which their poverty is caused by lack of natural resources or lack of entrepreneurial skills and values is a debatable question. It is a sufficiently open question, however, to remind us of the considerable 'disservices' and 'diswelfares' we might suffer if we gave too much scope to the free play of social market values. The first condition for a gift relationship is the existence of a gift worth giving.

Finally, there is the problem of extending the scope of exchange systems. Industrialization provides the economic means by which the boundaries of generalized exchange can be made international, but the economic markets of industrial societies are governed by norms of reciprocity. Their dynamic principle is the profit motive. Socialism purports to offer an ethic of altruism as an alternative principle on which an international welfare system might be based. If this goal is to be achieved, there will have to be a radical change in the present ordering of loyalties which ordinary people feel towards family, local community, occupational group, class and nation. I do not, however, believe that much will be gained by searching the past and present for archaic or primitive forms of exchange on which to found our theories of social welfare. The mutual aid systems of these primitive communities often achieve a high degree of universal inclusiveness which is particularly attractive to collectivists. Nonetheless the universal inclusiveness of these primitive communities may well be explained, paradoxically, by the smallness of their cognitive and normative worlds. Mutual aid systems are characterized both by the intensity of the loyalties which they engender and by the size and range of their membership. Unfortunately we live in complex industrial societies where the factors of intensity and scale are both operative. We have therefore become only too well acquainted with the difficulties of reconciling them, but at least industrialism provides us with the resources and skills which allow us to try.

For several centuries the inhabitants of primitive societies were afflicted with the attentions of Western missionaries insisting upon the superiority of their own moral beliefs and practices and enforcing their adoption in cultures which they neither understood nor respected. In recent times the tide of evangelism has turned back on us. The citizens of Western societies are now subject to the exhortations of social scientists insisting that there is much of value to be learned from the moral beliefs and practices of so-called primitive societies. These social scientists are undoubtedly more sensitive to the distinctive properties of industrial and pre-industrial cultures and to the limited degree to which these properties may be transferred from one to the other. They also understand even if they do not greatly admire the industrial societies which they are seeking to improve. At least it could be said of the missionaries that, having diagnosed the moral ills of a society, they neither entertained nor expressed doubts about the cure.

Nationhood and citizenship

In *Social Theory and Social Policy*[11] I explored some of the factors likely to influence patterns of welfare giving and receiving between individuals and groups within the context of single societies. I argued that we know relatively little about the 'conditions of provision and usage under which [stigma] is most likely to be encountered',[12] and that on the subject of dependency we know far more about the opinions and attitudes of experts than about those of laymen. In this chapter I wish to extend the analysis from exchanges between individuals and groups within nations to exchanges between nations.

At the level of international exchange the distinction between economic and social policies becomes exceedingly vague as to means and ends, but it continues to be a vital distinction when we examine exchange transactions and study the criteria which determine whether the transaction is an exchange based upon the norms of reciprocity and an obligation to repay or whether it is a unilateral transfer or gift. One nation may assist the welfare of another either by economic aid in the form of industrial or agricultural investment grants or by social aid in cash, in kind or in the form of specialized types of labour. Either form of aid can be provided with or without an obligation to repay.

It is an obvious but inescapable fact that, however much more highly we may rate the values of the social market as against those of the economic market, nevertheless the capacity of the social market is contingent on the wealth-producing capacity of the economic market. International aid may, however, enable a nation to live for some time beyond its economic means. In *Social Theory and Social Policy* I argued that in all known industrial societies the processes of formal and informal socialization are directed towards encouraging the virtues of work and self-help and that social services are used not only to succour the needy but to penalize those whose needs are not considered to be entirely legitimate. One of the most effective and universal sanctions employed is the imposition of stigma.[13] The extent to which our use of social services causes us to experience stigma is partly determined by whether other people as well as we ourselves consider our declared state of dependency to be a legitimate or an illegitimate one. This consciousness of being esteemed or despised greatly influences in turn the degree to which 'we believe in the authenticity of our citizenship'. Those with the poorest record of success in the economic market will be the most exposed to stigmatizing experiences in the social market.[14] I recommended a greater reliance upon the impersonal forms of public services, rather than the personal social services, as a means by which susceptibility to stigma could be reduced. Impersonal services put greater reliance on measures such as tax reliefs, tax credits and subsidized transport.

In the model of welfare outlined in *Social Theory and Social Policy*, I put great emphasis on the norm of reciprocity and the avoidance of total dependency upon any one donor. The quality of exchange and transfer relationships is influenced by the often conflicting nature of the sentiments which are evoked by giving and receiving. The factors of proximity and distance illustrate these contradictions. The majority of citizens (*pace* the Jellyby principle of 'telescopic philanthropy') are more likely to be aware of the needs of those who are nearest to them both socially and spatially. Closer proximity, however, may increase not only the propensity to give but also the capacity to impose sanction. Even in families intense shame and resentment may be experienced by receivers who are totally and permanently dependent. Similar feelings may be evoked by the intervention of local and national welfare agencies because strangers enter into such cases, and the gaps of distance and knowledge must be narrowed by an investigation of personal circumstances.

In setting out this model of social welfare I put forward the hypothesis that 'A sharp distinction exists in the consciousness of ordinary people between "givers" and "receivers" of social services, whose respective statuses are elevated or debased by virtue of their exchange relationships.' In complex industrial societies the relatively narrow sense of familial obligation, the greater awareness of social inequalities and the dominance of economic market values ensure that social services will 'combine both therapeutic and sanctioning functions'.[15] It cannot be assumed that the altruistic values of social reformers and those of many members of the caring professions are shared by ordinary citizens in their roles either as givers or receivers. Formal social services exist because it is necessary to compel taxpayers to give before the needful can experience either the satisfaction or the stigma of receiving.

While it is always inherently 'less prestigious to receive than to give', the variables of *depth*, *time* and *distance* greatly influence the quality of the relationships of giving and receiving. 'The variable of *depth* refers to the extent to which the recipient is made aware of his dependence and sense of inferiority and accepts the definition of his status as legitimate.'[16] Among the factors influencing his status I included the consciousness of receiving something either in return for past services or of a kind which is likely to increase the recipient's own future giftgiving potentialities.

The variable of *distance* 'may be social or spatial', and 'The more distant the recipient is from the giver, the less is he likely to receive.'[17] Social distance can be measured by criteria such as class or ethnic differences or the extent of isolation imposed by institutional residence. The variable of *time* refers to the length of the period during which dependency is experienced. Over long periods the individual will tend to become adapted to his dependent status.

A number of important differences become apparent when we apply this model to exchanges and gift giving between nations. The ordinary processes of international trade are regulated by the norms of reciprocity which characterize the economic market. The economic market also contains a complex system whereby both nations and firms may lend and borrow on terms of reciprocity, with rates of interest and so on agreed to on strictly competitive terms. It is difficult to draw a dividing line between exchanges of this sort and ex-

changes based on social market values, because many transactions take the form of 'soft loans' which last over very long or
indeterminate periods and at very low rates of interest. In situations of disaster nations also make unconditional gifts to a
stricken country. International charities play an important part
in this respect in maintaining a flow of voluntary aid not only
in crises but on a permanent long-term basis.

Given the variables of scale, complexity and distance, international transactions are the business of experts to a far greater
degree than is the case within nations. Even within the voluntary sector, which relies heavily upon countless individual decisions to give, the decisions about allocation are taken by small
groups of experts. At the international level the distances between givers and receivers are such that there is little scope for
spontaneous personal activity beyond the acts of giving.

In the sphere of international welfare we must also note that
even in the charitable sector the fund-raising agencies emphasize
whenever possible that the primary aim of welfare aid is to help
recipient groups and nations to achieve self-sufficiency. This
aim is emphasized partly in order to alleviate the real or imagined
sense of collective stigma felt by the recipients and partly to
persuade prospective donors that charitable giving makes good
economic sense. The use of euphemisms such as 'developing
nations' in place of 'undeveloped nations' has become a customary device employed to avoid injuring collective sensibilities
and to convey an impression of gradual advance towards self-
sufficiency.

Another consideration is the extent to which international
aid is used, like social services within nations, to impose sanctions as well as to provide welfare. The sanctions imposed on
persistent borrowers or supplicants for gifts usually take the
form of more stringent conditions, higher rates of interest,
shorter repayment periods and requirements or requests for the
recipient nation to adopt social policies which are more economically acceptable to the donor. Conditions of this sort may be
applied not only to underdeveloped countries but to the relatively affluent nations like the United Kingdom and Italy. Again,
on the basis of my model, it is the nations with the poorest
record of success in the economic market which will be the
most likely to experience the stigma of dependency in the social
market of international aid.

Nations, like individuals, may seek to avoid undue dependence
on any one other nation, but the reasons for this are often better

explained in terms of politics than of group psychology. It is questionable, however, whether we can sustain an analogy between the means-testing of nations and that applied to individuals as a condition of aid. The susceptibilities of ordinary individuals as donors or recipients are obviously of less importance than those of nations with regard to official as distinct from voluntary forms of international aid. Foreign aid is frequently given on very generous terms to nations whose political systems violate many of the values which are most esteemed by the donor nations. As Bauer points out, the persecution of minorities is a common feature of political life in many of the poorest countries of the Third World.

The fact that earlier loans or gifts have been spent uneconomically by the recipient nation or have failed to reach its most needy citizens rarely prevents the giving of further aid. Recipient nations sometimes respond with resentment rather than gratitude and adopt hostile rather than co-operative economic policies in their dealings with donor nations. Furthermore it is not uncommon for nations which are receiving foreign aid to continue functioning also as providers of foreign aid. Clearly the norms which appear to hold in transactions between individuals do not have much relevance to transactions between nations. The reasons for this frequently noted difference in standards are well known. In the first place individual citizens have very little choice as to whether they give or whether they receive. It is Bauer again who reminds us that 'Foreign aid is taxpayers' money — the donors have to pay whether they like it or not. . . . Aid lobbyists do not give away their own money.'[18] Secondly, transactions in international aid are governed by political considerations and criteria as well as those of the economic and social markets.

The three variables, depth, time and distance, however, have some supplementary bearing on the extent to which stigma and dependency influence the propensity of nations to give and receive amongst themselves. The variable of depth is clearly important in this connection, if we substitute for the individual awareness of authentic citizenship the collective sense of national esteem or patriotism. There is some evidence that recipient governments emphasize whenever possible the connection between aid for their present needs and their entitlement to some return for services which they have rendered in the past. This has been the case with the United Kingdom since the end of the Second World War, although our references to the war effort have steadily lost credibility, now that other victors and vanquished nations alike have long since recovered their economic self-sufficiency. Nonetheless the price which the United Kingdom paid to the USA in return for Lend-Lease was high by any standards, since it involved among other things the disclosure of scientific knowledge of great potential economic value to the United States government.

A government may put equally strong emphasis on its nation's entitlement to aid, when it has suffered past disservices from a prospective donor. This is an argument frequently advanced by former colonies. They, among others, claim that the affluence of the former imperial powers is based to a greater or lesser extent on the past exploitation of their former colonies. Such lobbyists often find support among influential constituencies within the donor nations. The case for aid may also be based on the claim that it will increase not only the self-sufficiency of the recipient nation but also its eventual ability to assist other nations or to enter into more mutually beneficial economic trade relationships. This argument has been a significant element in the rationale of Marshall Aid, the Colombo Plan and the activities of UNESCO. All arguments of this kind contribute to a more authentic sense of collective entitlement. Their frequent advancement suggests that there may be some connection between the intensity and extent of patriotic sentiments in a nation and its disposition to accept aid on social market terms.

The most recently independent nations — and therefore the ones which will probably be the most sensitive regarding their national independence — are also the poorest ones. In the case of China the heightened consciousness of recovered political independence coincided with the adoption of a political system and an ideology which are intensely hostile to imperialism and capitalism. China was consequently very selective in its choice of aid donors. Since its split with Russia it has become still more selective. The Chinese government recently declined all offers of official and voluntary aid after a devastating earthquake which killed or maimed many hundreds of thousands of people.

The same commitment to economic self-sufficiency cannot be observed in the case of the United Kingdom. This may be explained in the first place partly by the fact that its citizens have a far higher standard of living than the Chinese, and it is a political truism that the privileged never give up their advantages except under extreme duress. Secondly, the past economic record of the United Kingdom — as well as its capacity for recovery — is still better than those of any of the non-industrial nations. Thirdly, foreign aid between industrial nations does not carry the historical connotation of past or present inequality and dependency carried by transactions between developed and undeveloped nations. Fourthly, the United Kingdom has been an independent nation for so long that its rulers and citizens are unlikely to consider aid as an encroachment upon their sovereignty. In any event they are able to go on deluding themselves about their true economic status by continuing to give foreign aid to nations of the Third World. Writing in 1974, Bauer observed that the British aid contribution of about £275 million per annum was exceeding 'by more than one third the total British contribution to the European Economic Community plus all other expenditure on external relations; it is equal to the yield of surtax and twice that of betting and gaming taxes; and it is about one quarter of the expected balance of payments deficit for 1973.'[19] When we substitute the concept of patriotism for that of citizenship the variable of depth can still be said to have some relevance to an understanding of the propensities of nations to give and receive, but it seems that there are many other devices and rationalizations whereby collectivities — as compared with individuals — are able to avoid loss of status in situations of dependency.

It is difficult to assess the effect of the variable of distance on the propensity for international giving. It appears to be self-evident that the greater the distance is, the greater will be the compassion gap — if citizens were better acquainted at first hand with the sheer volume and intensity of unrelieved misery in the Third World they might be more generous in its relief. On the other hand there are rich but apparently indifferent citizens living in the countries of the Third World who show little practical compassion for their own countrymen. It is quite possible that if our citizens knew more about the failure of international aid to reach those in greatest need, they would be less willing to continue giving, either as taxpayers or as charitable donors. It seems reasonable to infer, however, that the less we know of other people's need, the less incentive we will have to find out more and the less likely we are to feel either responsibility or guilt.

With regard to the variable of time few of the nations that establish a pattern of receiving soft loans or free gifts ever achieve self-sufficiency. It is hard to say whether this is more an

indication of their extreme and intractable poverty than of the
fact that they 'adapt to their poverty' and become 'apathetic
regarding their condition'[20] in the manner of Matza's 'disreputable poor'. The comparison with individual types of behaviour
is, however, not sustainable in all respects. Nations do not experience birth and death like individuals. Modern medicine preserves the lives of many marginally viable infants, who would
formerly have had no chance of survival, but the arts of political
expediency can perform far greater miracles than that in the
birth of new nations and the preservation of old ones. The right
to national independence has now become such a commonplace
that it extends to societies which can never hope to become truly
self-sufficient. They are in fact moribund nations which survive
in a state of permanent economic dependency without actually
ceasing to exist. In 1934 the Dominion of Newfoundland went
bankrupt and voluntarily gave up its dominion status; this was
the last occasion on which a nation voluntarily gave up its right
to self-government. In the post-war world we no longer consider
economic self-sufficiency to be a precondition of sovereignty
and an independent state of the size of Newfoundland would
today constitute a whale amongst a shoal of minnows.

The status of citizenship would seem to be far less effective
than the status of nationhood as a protection against having to
experience the stigma which is associated with dependency.
Indeed political independence is often a compensation for
economic dependency, even when it is the main cause of such
penury. In *Social Theory and Social Policy* I suggested that
'Concepts like the "Caring Society" and the "Welfare State"
are subjectively meaningless to those who have not achieved
citizenship in an authentic form. It may be that effecting
changes in the social consciousness of ordinary people is now
becoming more important than further changes in the statute
book.'[21] In comparison with individual changes of this kind, it
appears to be much easier to effect changes in the national
consciousness of whole societies. Whatever personal humiliation
is experienced by the British Chancellor of the Exchequer as
our representative debtor, he appears to accept it in the line of
duty. His electorate shows little sign of suffering from shame or
stigma. Indeed its appetite for public holidays appears to grow
greater as its foreign debts mount up. The problem for the
borrowing nations of the Third World is one of raising sufficient
aid rather than managing on less of what they already have.

A comparison between the chronic recipients of the industrial

West and those of the Third World does, however, suggest one important difference with regard to the significance of patriotic sentiments. In the new nations of the Third World a heightened sense of national consciousness is often associated with a sense of entitlement which is based on a particular interpretation of colonial history. Their patriotism is of a kind to protect both rulers and citizens from the experience of collective stigma. Paradoxically a nation may last for so long and sink so far into the status of collective pauperism that it loses all sense of national pride. The gradual weakening of patriotic sentiment sometimes prepares the way for economic decline and a subsequent cheerful adoption of pauper status which is immune to the imposition of stigma. We do not have to look far for examples of this.

Britain and America: a special exchange relationship

No chapter on nationhood, citizenship and social exchange would be complete without some reference to the sequence of exchanges which determined the development of British social policy in its entirety after the Second World War. The contribution of American capitalism to the making of the British welfare state is an event which has been oddly neglected by historians of social policy. Our post-war system of welfare was built by a Labour government, but, although the general design was collectivist when it was not overtly socialist, we tend to forget that the foundation stones of British welfare were quarried and shipped from Fort Knox.

Even with the benefit of American aid the margin of success was an extremely narrow one for several reasons. First, despite the duration and scale of the British war effort the US Senate was by no means enthusiastically committed to aiding our economic recovery. It required the decisive intervention of President Truman to restore the cuts in Lend-Lease which had been implemented even before the end of the European war.[22] Secondly, the Labour government, on taking office in 1945, faced a daunting list of economic problems, including a seriously adverse balance of trade, a depleted mercantile marine and reduced overseas markets, diminished foreign investments and a domestic economy still directed at war production. Thirdly, the government was committed not only to the implementation of the Beveridge proposals for social reform but to a sizeable programme of nationalization. Fourthly, there were extensive overseas commitments in which, as Hugh Dalton observes, 'We were undertaking liabilities all over the world and slopping out money to the importunate' with serious consequences for our own balance of payments. Dalton described the situation as a 'financial Dunkirk'.[23]

The initial British request to the USA for a unilateral gift of $6,000 million was rejected, as was a second request for an interest-free loan. Keynes, as a principal negotiator, had confidently expected a more generous response. He returned to advise Dalton that 'The Americans were now interested in the future, not the past, and that the old soldier showing off his medals would not be a persuasive advocate.'[24] Eventually a loan of $3,700 million at 2 per cent interest was secured from the American government, and to this was later added a Canadian loan of $1,250 million.[25] The repayment of the American loan was to take place over fifty years and to start in 1951, but the loan provided the necessary financial basis from which post-war reconstruction could begin, with regard to export recovery, nationalization and social policy planning. In addition to starting repayment of the American loan in 1951, Britain was also required under the Bretton Woods agreement to prepare for the restoration of full convertibility of sterling in 1947, without any guarantee that the USA would lower its own tariffs against British exports.

By contrast the American government made a very generous final agreement on Lend-Lease amounting to a further credit of $650 million. Dalton, paraphrasing Churchill, described it in the House as 'a fine clean end' to 'that most unsordid act in history'.[26] It is interesting that ten years later Titmuss used the same phrase when he described the National Health Service as 'the most unsordid act of British social policy in the twentieth century',[27] without referring to the particular gift relationship that had made it possible.

Despite these relatively stringent terms the Labour government implemented the greater part of the Beveridge proposals and carried through a modest nationalization programme. Partly as a result of the severe winter of 1946-7 and the incidence of strikes, industrial output remained low. By the start of 1947, as Medlicott observes, 'the honeymoon of Labour and Welfare on Uncle Sam's money was nearing its end',[28] and the first major monetary crisis came a few months later, when sterling was made convertible.

Even on the terms described the debt which Britain owes to the highly conditional altruism of American capitalism is considerable although *The Economist* ruefully observed at the time that 'In moral terms we are creditors; and for that we shall pay $140 million a year for the rest of the century. It may be unavoidable but it is not right.'[29] Indeed only two of Britain's sterling creditors were willing to write off the balances owed to them, and these were New Zealand and Australia. Nonetheless within the year Britain became a major beneficiary under the terms of Marshall Aid.[30] Without this sudden injection of funds into the failing British economy, there is little doubt that there would have been a drastic fall in imports and an equally sharp rise in unemployment, with appalling consequences for the entire social policy programme.

By March 1947 Britain's dollar credits were being drawn upon at such a rate that they would have been exhausted, at the latest, by the middle of 1948. This situation had come about partly because of the depreciation in the value of the dollar and partly because of the high cost of feeding the Germans in the British occupation zone. In his third budget Dalton imposed further austerities, including drastic cuts in the import of food and tobacco and an increase in taxation designed to raise an additional £200 million. The British government had only recently announced its intention to withdraw from financial and defence involvements in Greece and Turkey as a means of reducing our economic commitments. This decision was swiftly followed by the announcement of the Truman Doctrine.

The doctrine entailed asking Congress to grant special aid to Greece and Turkey but was also extended to include an offer of aid to any nation resisting internal or external communist subversion.[31] Marshall Aid became the major instrument by which the economic and social reconstruction of Europe was to be financed under the Truman Doctrine. Britain eventually became the second biggest beneficiary of Marshall Aid, receiving $1,263 million in September 1948 — over a third of the total sum made available. A part of this sum was set against other British grants. Marshall Aid was the third major American intervention in support of post-war British economic and social recovery. This programme, following the continuance of Lend-Lease and the 1947 loan, was the most important single determinant of the subsequent course of British social policy. Without this support we would have been forced in 1951 to resort to policies far more drastic than the imposition of health service charges.

On balance American aid to post-war Europe must count as one of the most creditable instances of conditional altruism in human history. Under the terms of the Marshall Plan alone, the American government offered to provide credits to the value of more than $18 billion over a period of four years. The Russians rejected the plan and went on to form their own military and trading bloc. The sixteen participating nations of Western Europe joined the plan and became partners in the European Recovery Programme and the Economic Co-operation Administration set up to implement its schemes.

In retrospect it might be argued that Britain deserved more than was given and on terms more generous than those which were granted. It can also be claimed that the Truman Doctrine gave birth not only to the Marshall Plan but to the politics of the Cold War. A more realistic interpretation would be that the doctrine was a response to a cold war which had already started and which swiftly became intensified, with the Stalinist take-over of Czechoslovakia.

What can be said about the imputation that America lacked generosity of spirit in not having made at the start an unconditional and unilateral gift to her closest wartime ally? It is embarrassingly difficult to answer this question by reference to the literature of social administration, since the subject of American aid is scarcely touched on. It is as if the post-war British welfare state leaped fully financed out of the pockets of the altruistic British taxpayer. Indeed the innocent reader of our major collectivist authorities on social policy will find that almost every reference to America is disparaging in tone. In Titmuss's eschatology of welfare the USA seems to be cast exclusively in the role of Antichrist. Looking back on these momentous post-war events, Dalton concludes that, had the American loan not been forthcoming, 'more severe austerity would [have been] necessary than at any time during the war, and an indefinite postponement of the best hopes, and the social programmes of the new government. After a few years of this poor life, some slight improvement might have been possible.'[32]

What does it say of the traditions of parochial insularity in our subject, that its only major study of exchange relationships deals with one aspect of the British National Health Service and unquestioningly presents British practice as the paradigm of altruism in social welfare? How is the student of social welfare ever to set this achievement in perspective unless he is made equally aware of the momentous acts of giving and exchange which made a national health service possible? The terms of the loan were indeed stringent, but it is again too easily forgotten that it was made by a government having little if any sympathy for socialism or the collectivist social policies which the loan would make possible. When, we may ask, did a socialist government last make such a loan to a capitalist society tottering on the edge of dissolution?

In this example of American aid we are certainly considering a case in which assistance was given in order to further social policies which were anathema to the donor government. The terms of the loans were stringent but by no means exclusively governed by economic market criteria. They were agreed entirely between experts, with little reference to or regard for public opinion in either country. Our subsequently poor record of economic performance has not prevented us from securing further assistance from the USA and other sources, although the terms of aid have become increasingly more stringent. As for the effects of this continuous dependency on others, it may be relevant to draw a distinction between our collective self-esteem as a nation and the self-esteem of collectivists. I have already suggested that there is little evidence that our sense of patriotic propriety has been deeply wounded by continuous borrowing. There is some evidence — admittedly of a negative kind — with regard to the events of 1945-8, that the obligation which British collectivism owes to American capitalism offends the sensibilities of certain social policy analysts. They have written so little about these events, while finding time to write about so much else. In social history what we choose to forget is often as important as what we prefer to remember.

The notion of exchange is not only of fundamental importance in the general study of social welfare — it is crucial to our understanding of the particular origins of post-war British social policy. All the frequently rehearsed explanations as to why the greater part of the Beveridge Report was implemented — the experience of the war, the heightened sense of social expectation, the electoral victory of a reforming Labour Party — sink to a level of secondary importance when they are set against the contribution of American aid. Certainly the political will was present in Britain, but America provided the means, and without the means our welfare ends would not have been realized. It is possible that, by facing the dilemma of choice between cutting welfare or cutting defence expenditure, the social reform programme might still have been carried through. There were those who thought so at the time, even in the early frosts of the Cold War.

Clearly the decision to aid Britain was influenced more by political than by economic or social considerations. The American government was sensible enough to recognize that British parliamentary socialism was not to be equated with communism and that a British economic recovery was essential for the defence of post-war Europe. Had there been clear evidence to the contrary — that Britain was not intending to play an active role in the strategic defence of Western Europe — it is unlikely that aid would have been forthcoming.

Much of the literature on the dilemmas of choice in social policy deals with choices between different philosophies and systems of welfare. There is, by contrast, little informed comment on the choices which have to be made in every society between welfare and defence. Instant assumptions of shared piety render such debate unnecessary. Parliamentary democracies are deemed to be 'welfare-warfare' states of a uniquely hypocritical type in budgeting for their armed services and their social services at the same time. Yet the massive defence expenditures of the communist bloc — in company with those of the poorest nations of the Third World — receive relatively little adverse comment. Again, parliamentary democracies are either indicted for spending insufficient sums on welfare, or for spending as much as they do for reprehensible reasons — namely, the abatement of social unrest and the maintainance of the *status quo.*

Of course the fundamental issues of choice regarding defence and welfare expenditures are not debated in social policy circles because they can only be resolved in terms of a value choice — a clearly expressed preference in favour of one type of social order as against another. Such a choice would have to be based on a considered appraisal of the positive and negative features of capitalism and communism and this analysis would also have to include the non-material as well as the material dimensions of welfare, political as well as social and economic.

All these criteria influence the decision of one country as to whether or not it will aid another in adversity. The donor nation may well be prepared to offset a possible economic loss against a political gain, and even to support another nation which does not entirely match up to its criteria of political excellence. Such reservations may indeed be mutual. This is only to point out an obvious fact of political life — that it is a futile exercise to go looking for unconditionally good deeds in a largely naughty world. In this respect American aid to Britain in the immediate post-war years ought to count at least as the next best thing to a good deed, and such deeds have done more for social welfare than acts of unconditional altruism are ever likely to do.

Several key features can be identified in the institutional framework of social welfare which I have outlined in the foregoing chapters. First, I attempted to characterize moral sentiments which citizens hold about welfare in terms of their notions of felt obligation and entitlement. I argued that welfare practices and the search for both personal and collective welfare are features of economic behaviour as well as social policy. In the real world both spheres of human activity involve egoistic and altruistic practices which are bounded and modified by the restraints of common sense and human fallibility.

Secondly, I described how the complex interplay of self-interest and familial, communal and national loyalties places institutional limits on people's notions of felt obligation and entitlement. These loyalties will be seen to have a limiting effect if the ideal of welfare is defined in internationalist terms, but from an alternative and more conditional point of view they can be seen as providing the moral justifications and the welfare resources by which our boundaries of obligation and entitlement can be extended from the narrowest of familial loyalties to include at least an awareness of national interests.

Thirdly, I discussed the main forms of economic and social exchange in order to describe the ways in which citizens put into practice their normative beliefs about welfare. I concluded with a critique of internationalist ideals of welfare and a defence of patriotic sentiments which identify welfare primarily with national interests. I used the example of American aid to Britain after the Second World War to illustrate the complexity of the reasons why gifts are given and why exchanges occur between nations.

My fourth theme was an enquiry into the relationship between changes in popular welfare beliefs and practices and the impact of various theories and ideologies which either uphold or challenge existing structures of obligation and entitlement.

In order to explore these major themes of enquiry in greater depth I have chosen three particular societies as the subject matter of the following part of the book, because each of them has had its own specific traditions of mutual aid and welfare practice and because the ways in which these societies have changed over time have been significantly different in each case.

I begin with Britain, because it was the first great nation to experience industrialization. The terms on which this economic transformation occurred were greatly influenced by the outcome of the conflict between the older mercantilist doctrines and the new theories of classical political economy. These new theories set out the possibilities for internationalizing economic markets and hence for improving the quality of individual and collective welfare. In this respect, these new theories dramatically extended the scope for competition and self-help, which were deemed to be the most appropriate and effective basis for the enhancement of welfare. Traditional notions of obligation and entitlement were greatly modified, and they became more generally grounded in systems of exchange based on the norm of reciprocity. The new poor law served as an instrument of social discipline designed to compel citizens to seek their welfare in the economic market.

I then explore the reasons why Britain, under the impact of successive economic crises and wars, gradually abandoned its internationalist policies of free trade in favour of modified forms of protection and belatedly assumed an imperial role, drawing upon its still considerable military and naval capacities. I argue that these changes were a precondition of the growth of the new forms of social protection which we now call the welfare state. Thereafter, I suggest, our retreat from empire and economic pre-eminence has been complemented by the gradual extension of these forms of social protection. Despite the survival of internationalist ideals in the practice of giving aid, the scope of our external welfare obligations has narrowed to match our diminished means. Only in our notions of entitlement have our expectations continued to grow.

Next I look at nineteenth-century Russia, beginning with a description of its deeply traditional system of mutual aid based on narrowly defined but intensely felt sentiments of familial and communal obligation and entitlement. I examine how these long established networks of obligation and entitlement were radically transformed and eventually destroyed by a sequence of dramatic social changes — the emancipation of the serfs, the belated but determined attempt by a minority of reformers to increase the rate of industrial growth and modernize the economy within an autocratic political framework, and the experience of a disastrous war. These changes left a still numerous and backward peasantry with little more than the illusion that they were about to inherit their long cherished land. This simple welfare aspiration was extinguished by the forceful intervention of a handful of revolutionaries and intellectuals who were committed to the political transformation of a stricken nation and the eventual triumph of a new ideology, the implications of which were truly international. Apart from these internationalist aims I also explore the central role which Marxist and other types of socialist theory accord to conflict as an agent of change and to radical institutional change as a precondition of the strengthening of altruistic sentiments and the enhancement of welfare.

In the case of Russia it is possible to study the effects of a striking sequence of conflicts between popular forms of welfare belief and practice on the one hand and the political, economic and social objectives of a succession of ruling minorities on the other, and to examine the consequent undermining of traditional notions of obligation and entitlement, and the way in which the eventual failure of these innovatory policies led to widespread political disaffection.

Finally, I have chosen to study the impact of social change on welfare beliefs and practices in nineteenth-century America, because it held out a new promise of welfare based on economic opportunity and free land. The promise was exaggerated, but the fulfilment was sufficient to ensure political continuity within an established democratic tradition. As a new society the United States was paradoxically internationalist in a nationally inclusive sense. It created a sense of nationhood by incorporating into one culture the hopes and values of countless immigrants. Out of these origins the relationships between citizens and the government assumed a distinctive form characterized by confident expectations of a prosperous future.

I describe how the contingencies of frontier life helped to forge new bonds of solidarity based on the family and the local community, while those of city life gradually transformed the traditional beliefs about mutual aid which were brought by successive generations of newcomers. In the countryside and cities alike industrialization and the predominance of the popular belief in the virtues of competition and self-help contributed to the development of new modes of welfare practice whose boundaries were set by economic norms of reciprocity as well as the social bonds of kinship and community.

I suggest that the time of disillusionment came later in America than it did in Britain — after the 'closing of the frontier' in the 1890s, the economic crises of the inter-war years and the long delayed challenge of black Americans for their share of the national well-being. Initially this mood of chastened hope found expression in isolationist doctrines and protectionism, but the period of optimism after the Second World War lasted long enough for the United States to assume the role of a universal provider and sponsor and more particularly to play a vital part in the financing of Britain's post-war social reconstruction.

I then take up the general theme of population movement to illustrate the way in which nations seek to limit the scope of their own welfare obligations by regulating immigration. I use evidence of the extent to which different nations take measures either to restrict the number of new entrants or to forbid emigration as an indication of their relative success in enhancing welfare as it is perceived by sections of their own citizenry.

In the last chapter I try to identify the ways in which the dominant criteria of welfare allocation changed over time in Britain, Russia and America, and I close with a defence of the welfare values and practices which embody a compromise between claims to welfare resources based on economic merit and those based on social need. I criticize policies of welfare allocation which are based on any criterion of political desert which differentiates positively or negatively between the citizens of a nation, whether these criteria be expressed in ideological, religious or racial terms. I accept the validity of any political criterion which respects a status of citizenship shared equally by all members of a nation — not because I believe that it is most likely to maximize welfare but because I am persuaded by the historical evidence that it is likely to minimize diswelfare.

Consequently I settle for a highly conditional model of altruism which would give priority to national interests, even though it might push the boundaries of felt obligation and entitlement to the limits of popular tolerance. In contrast I suggest that internationalist doctrines of welfare require processes of such radical change and entail such violation of traditional and popular notions of obligation and entitlement that they can be realized in practice only by small minorities of people who are willing and able to impose their own objectives on a recalcitrant majority. There is undoubtedly a role for internationalist sentiments and practices in a civilized model of welfare, but that role should properly be subordinate and supplementary to national interests.

I close by arguing that the principles of political liberty and political toleration are essential elements in any conceptualization of welfare, and that a balance must be preserved between the material and the non-material qualities which go to make up a good society. With regard to the internationalization of welfare, therefore, it is an overriding commitment to parliamentary democracy which compels me in the last analysis, in decisions affecting the boundaries and priorities of obligation and entitlement, to accept the mandates of popular opinion rather than the prescriptions of reforming intellectuals.

The historical material which I have used seems to me to offer ample evidence that there is much to be said in favour of confining the prophet, without honour, to his own country.

References

[1] Reference may be made in particular to George Dalton, 'Economic Theory and Primitive Society', in Edward E. LeClair Jr. and Harold K. Schneider, *Economic Anthropology: Readings in Theory and Analysis*, Holt, Rinehart & Winston, New York, 1968; Robert Pruger, 'Social Policy: Unilateral Transfer or Reciprocal Exchange', *Journal of Social Policy*, 2, 4, 1973, pp. 289-302; Alvin W. Gouldner, 'The Norm of Reciprocity', *American Sociological Review*, 25, 1960, p. 169; George C. Homans, *Social Behaviour: Its Elementary Forms*, Routledge & Kegan Paul, London, 1973; Peter M. Blau, *Exchange and Power in Social Life*, John Wiley & Sons, New York, 1964; P. Ekeh, *Social Exchange Theory*, Heinemann Educational Books, London, 1975; and A. Heath, *Rational Choice and Social Exchange*, Cambridge University Press, 1976. There is a useful summary chapter on exchange and field theory in Calvin J. Larson, *Major Themes in Sociological Theory*, David McKay, New York, 1973, Ch. 6.

[2] Richard M. Titmuss, *Commitment to Welfare*, Allen & Unwin, London, 1968, p. 22.

[3] This chapter originally included a lengthy section on the relationship between Lévi-Strauss's theories of exchange and systems of mutual aid in advanced industrial societies which has been held over for future publication. The sources which I consulted include the following: Claude Lévi-Strauss, *The Elementary Structures of Kinship*, Eyre & Spottiswoode, 1969; *World on the Wane*, Hutchinson, 1961; *Race and History*, UNESCO, 1952; *The Savage Mind*, Weidenfeld & Nicolson, 1966; and *Structural Anthropology*, Allen Lane, Penguin Press, 1968; Edmund Leach, *Lévi-Strauss*, Fontana, London, 1970; Edmund Leach, 'Claude Lévi-Strauss — Anthropologist and Philosopher', *New Left Review*, 34, 1965; and Clifford Geertz, *The Interpretation of Cultures*, Basic Books, New York, 1973.

[4] Kurt H. Wolff, *The Sociology of Georg Simmel*, Free Press of Glencoe, Collier-Macmillan, London, 1964, pp. 58-9.

[5] George Dalton, 'Economic Theory and Primitive Society', p. 143.

[6] ibid., p. 145.

[7] George Dalton, *Economic Systems and Society*, Penguin, Harmondsworth, 1974, p. 57.

[8] George Dalton, 'Economic Theory and Primitive Society', pp. 146-7.

[9] ibid., pp. 157-9.

[10] Titmuss, *The Gift Relationship*, pp. 210-11.

[11] Pinker, *Social Theory and Social Policy*, Ch. 4.

[12] ibid., p. 156.

[13] ibid., pp. 138-41.

[14] ibid., pp. 141 and 144.

[15] ibid., p. 167.

[16] ibid., p. 170.

[17] ibid., p. 173.

[18] Peter Bauer, 'A Myth of Our Time', *Encounter*, March 1974, p. 25.

[19] ibid., p. 16.

[20] David Matza, 'The Disreputable Poor', in Reinhard Bendix and Seymour Martin Lipset (eds), *Class, Status and Power: Social Stratification in Comparative Perspective*, second edition, Routledge & Kegan Paul, 1967, p. 292.

[21] Pinker, *Social Theory and Social Policy*, p. 174.

[22] See Hugh Dalton, *High Tide and After: Memoirs 1945-1960*, Frederick Muller, London, 1962, pp. 68-9.

[23] ibid., pp. 71 and 73.

[24] ibid., pp. 74.

[25] W. N. Medlicott, *Contemporary England, 1914-1964*, Longmans, 1967, pp. 474-6.

[26] Hugh Dalton, op. cit., p. 81.

[27] Titmuss, *The Gift Relationship*, p. 225.

[28] Medlicott, op. cit., p. 481.

[29] Quoted ibid., p. 476.

[30] See Medlicott, op. cit.; and James Joll, *Europe Since 1870: An International History*, Penguin, Harmondsworth, 1976, p. 452.

[31] Medlicott, op. cit., p. 494.

[32] Hugh Dalton, op. cit., p. 73.

Part II

Capitalism, Socialism and Collectivism

6 Welfare and the Free Market

Mercantilism and laissez-faire

In Book IV of *The Wealth of Nations*[1] Adam Smith outlined a sustained critique of mercantilism, which was then the dominant economic doctrine in Britain and the other major nations of Europe. In one respect mercantilism was a political rather than an economic doctrine, since it placed the goal of national power above that of national prosperity. Lichtheim observes that the chief aim of mercantilist policies was 'not to maximize welfare but to promote the economic and political independence of the nation state'.[2] The primary sources of a nation's power were held to be precious metals and a large population. Protective tariffs, the prohibition of emigration and extensive governmental regulation of the activities of the economic market were considered to be the best policies for achieving national security and greatness.

Mercantilist ideas became steadily more influential throughout Europe during the seventeenth and eighteenth centuries and they were closely associated with the rise of nationalist sentiments. Hicks suggests that mercantilism 'marks the discovery that economic growth can be used in the *national interest*'.[3] Viner, however, points out that within the terms of mercantilist teaching it was possible to achieve a 'long-run harmony' between the ends of power and prosperity, 'although in particular circumstances it may be necessary for a time to make economic sacrifices in the interest of military security and therefore also of long-run prosperity'.[4]

It was a fundamental tenet of mercantilist teaching that '*Under prevailing conditions*, increases in heads would increase real income per head', and this proposition 'during the greater part of the eighteenth century' was, according to Schumpeter, 'manifestly correct'.[5] As for the distribution of these increases in real income, the earlier mercantilist writers argued in favour of repressive poor laws and low wages. Given the choice, they argued, the poor would always prefer idleness to work, and habits of industry could best be enforced by keeping wages low.

The larger the population, the easier it would be to control the level of wages without hindering the growth of industry. Consequently every effort was made in Britain, France, the German states and Russia to discourage emigration. (In Britain, for example, the emigration of skilled workers was prohibited between 1782 and 1824.)

During the seventeenth century, however, a more socially conscious version of the doctrine was developed by writers like Hartlib, Chamberlen and Goffe in response to the growing problems of poverty and social unrest.[6] Wilson notes the growing concern of the Commonwealth and post-Restoration mercantilist writers with the 'chronic problem of poverty which affected severely somewhere between a quarter and a half of the whole population'.[7] The declining demand for labour encouraged mercantilists to seek ways of diversifying the national economy and to propose new schemes for the employment of paupers and the training of pauper children. Hartlib believed that, if the poor could be rendered industrious, the nation would be preserved from dependence on foreigners.[8] Hartlib, in company with Goffe, was among the most eminent of a number of Commonwealth authorities who wrote about social policy and provided, in Wilson's view, 'the basis of almost all later economic thought for more than a century. The recognition that the problems of poverty, employment and national welfare are all linked together was never subsequently lost sight of.'[9]

In describing the major social and economic changes which had helped to bring about these modifications of mercantilist theory, Schumpeter emphasizes the gradual breakdown of the medieval village community, which 'provided a berth for everyone whom it recognized as a member', and whose 'structural design excluded unemployment and destitution'.[10] James draws attention to the social distress and economic upheaval which followed the Civil War in England from the collapse of local industries to the decline and corruption of charitable enterprises and the general increase in vagrancy.[11] At the time, Hartlib recommended not an increase in poor relief 'so much as instruction in the doctrine and practice of self-help'.[12] He therefore advocated both the suppression of vagrancy and a more systematic attempt to train the children of the poor. In his view it was not right for the vagabond to 'go whither his lust as the manner now is' but to 'return to the workhouse from whence he came'.[13] The Act of Settlement of 1662 came at the end of a period during which the increase in the number of vagrants had become a political as well as an economic danger.[14]

During and after the Restoration the debate about national poverty continued in largely mercantilist terms. The traditional tendency of mercantilist thinkers to associate national welfare with 'the net amount of bullion gained or lost via the balance of trade' was broadened to include an active and genuine concern for the social needs of the community.[15] Wilson recognizes that in practical terms few of the poor derived much benefit from these changes in outlook. At the same time he insists that 'The collective charge that a whole class was through several generations guilty of social irresponsibility must . . . be rejected as non-proven.'[16] Effective and humane social policies failed to develop, 'because the supply of those capable of organizing and administering [charities and poor relief] with reasonable efficiency, honesty and compassionate understanding was totally inadequate'.[17] The same point is made by Hicks: the early mercantilists simply lacked the necessary economic and administrative expertise.[18] The clearest indication of progress and the most explicit commitment to change were embodied in the provision of more education and schemes of apprenticeship for the children of the poor. The progress of social reform was, however, still held to be contingent on the maintenance of protectionist economic policies and the control of migration.

Charles Wilson summarizes the main tenets of mercantilist theory by reference to Thomas Mun's major work, *England's Treasure by fforraign Trade*, which was published in 1664.[19] He points out that, like the other mercantilist writers, Mun was concerned less with setting out a body of theory than with finding an answer to 'a pressing economic problem; not to amass bullion but to explain its loss. And, as Keynes pointed out in the 1930s, while economists might later have come to regard the favourable balance of trade as a "puerile obsession", those more immediately concerned with policy in the centuries that followed have continued to regard it as a prime object of practical statecraft.'[20]

From this preoccupation with the trade balance developed the various strands of mercantilist policy — the imposition of restrictions and prohibition of certain exports; the encouragement of the immigration of skilled workers; the stimulation of the import of raw materials from colonies; the imposition of tariffs to check the import of foreign luxuries; and the passing of the Navigation Acts in 1651 and 1660 designed to give British shipping a monopoly of British trade. Behind these economic defences it was hoped that the national economy would steadily diversify and grow, to the benefit of all citizens.

In contrast to mercantilism *laissez-faire* was an internationalist doctrine. The classical economic theories on which the popular notions of *laissez-faire* were based sought to demonstrate that human welfare could best be enhanced if goods and services were allowed to move without hindrance between nations, if labour was allowed to move with similar freedom and 'find its own price in the market' and if the 'creation of money' was made subject to 'an automatic mechanism' of gold.[21] Once these interdependent mechanisms were allowed to operate in a largely self-regulatory way, a natural coincidence would occur between self-interest and the welfare of all.

During the first quarter of the nineteenth century the conflict between mercantilist and *laissez-faire* doctrines centred upon a number of major issues, which included the Corn Laws, the Navigation Acts, the Settlement Acts and the future of the colonies. All of these issues had some bearing on the great debate about free trade and protection. The implications of this debate for social welfare are the subject of this and the following chapter.

It is true that this promised Utopia could not emerge unless the poor remained content with only a modest level of expectation; indeed Ricardo's iron law of wages promised little more than subsistence for the labouring classes. Nonetheless, as Polanyi reminds us, Adam Smith was confident that some of the increases in wealth which would follow industrialization would filter down to the poor.[22] Ricardo was also mindful of the ameliorating influence of custom on the definition of subsistence. There is a passage in *Principles of Political Economy* in which Ricardo suggests that 'the natural price of labour . . . always depends on the price of food, clothing and other necessaries', but that this price is never 'absolutely fixed and constant' since it depends upon 'the habits and customs of the people. . . . Many of the conveniences now enjoyed in an English cottage would have been thought luxuries at an earlier period in history.'[23]

The passing of the Corn Law in 1815 provided an issue over which the exponents of *laissez-faire* were able to begin cultivating popular support and to appeal directly to the rising class of manufacturers. Coats reminds us of the disagreement which occurred between Ricardo and Malthus concerning the effect of the Corn Laws. Ricardo argued that enforcing an artificially high price for corn would not only raise food prices but would push up the level of money wages to the detriment of profits. A fall in the rate of profit would discourage capital accumulation, and in the resulting economic slump the living standards of the labourer would be catastrophically affected. Malthus, however, took the view that free trade in corn would destroy the landed classes and thereby undermine the political stability of the nation. Furthermore a nation overly dependent upon imported foodstuffs would be strategically at a disadvantage in time of war.[24]

It is also important to recognize that very few of the classical political economists were committed in an unqualified way to what became the popularized doctrines of *laissez-faire*. They favoured free trade but were not indifferent to the need to afford some protection to the living standards of ordinary citizens in times of adversity. It was from the group of thinkers and political activists loosely termed the Manchester school that the most dogmatic and unqualified doctrines of free trade and individualism began to circulate and gain public support. An anti-Corn Law association was formed in Manchester during 1838, and under the leadership and inspiration of Richard Cobden this group formed the nucleus of the Anti-Corn Law League. Opposition to the Corn Law was only one part of the campaign of the Manchester school to make *laissez-faire* an internationalist doctrine in practice as well as in theory. It also adopted a strongly anti-colonialist policy, at a time when Britain was beginning to acquire a second empire.

Within the terms of mercantilist theory 'The colonies and the mother country were to supplement one another as producers of raw materials and of manufactured articles respectively', which meant that Britain would retain 'a monopoly of the colonial markets and the inter-imperial shipping trade', while the colonies would be granted 'substantial tariff preferences' in their trade with Britain.[25] That policy would have been anathema to Cobden and the Manchester school, looking forward, as they did, to an ideal economic world in which every nation would eventually adopt free trade and live at peace with its neighbours. In contrast with mercantilism free trade was, as Fuchs describes it, an essentially cosmopolitan theory, 'the object of which is not so much the highest development of the nation and the national character, as the greatest possible levelling down of national barriers'.[26] Its fundamental economic principle was 'buying in the cheapest and selling in the dearest market' within the context of an international division of labour. An essential part of the theory is the doctrine of the 'harmony of interests according to which it is impossible that one country can develop at the expense of another, or that the progress or advantage of one is not at the same time in the interests of all'.[27] The case for free trade follows naturally from the very notion of reciprocal exchange: in every condition of free exchange both parties derive some benefit.

Free trade offered the possibility of an unlimited system of exchange, while protectionism accepted the necessity of limits which were determined by the conflicts of economic interest both within and between nations. For the free trader the Titmussian problem of altruism did not exist, since a natural coincidence would occur under free conditions between self-interest and the welfare of all at both individual and collective levels. Nonetheless protectionism can be said to express a definite, if highly conditional, notion of altruism. This notion derives from the mercantilist argument that welfare is not definable in purely economic terms, in other words the maximization of exchange values. The prosperity of a nation depends on the achievement of a balance between the several productive processes of that nation, and only extensive governmental intervention can assure the achievement of such an equilibrium between the interests of agriculture, commerce and manufacturing. The free market could not be relied upon to bring about a natural reconciliation of individual and national interests. Only governmental regulation could ensure that the long-term needs of the nation were not jeopardized by the short-term interests of individuals and sectional groups. These were the central tenets of Friedrich List's defence of mercantilism and critique of Adam Smith. As Sir Eric Roll puts it, in List's view 'The atomism of Smith took no account of the national bond: in considering man, the producer and consumer, Smith had forgotten the citizen.'[28] Such an indictment, however, appears to have more relevance to the popularized versions of *laissez-faire* than to Smith's own work.

Adam Smith and Karl Marx

It was not only Marx who criticized Adam Smith's notion of civil society and human self-interest. There were other authorities who were greatly influenced by mercantilist doctrines, such as Daniel Defoe, John Cary and Jonas Hanway who argued that the claims of national security and social welfare must take precedence over the pursuit of profit.[29]

A key point about classical economic theory is that in positing a natural coincidence between self-interest and collective welfare it seems to render altruism an irrelevant concept. The free market *was* the welfare society. In this sense it is pointless to judge the humanity of capitalism simply by reference to the new poor laws, because less eligibility and deterrence were only the negative instruments designed to force men and women to seek their welfare in the economic market. And it was only in this economic market that positive welfare could be found.

A part of the perennial attraction of Marx's social theory is that it does provide an analytical framework within which the student can seek to relate theory to practice. It is a system of thought in which the political theory derives from and acts back upon the social theory. It purports to tell us not only how societies change but something about the role of political theory as an agent in those processes of change.

Marx conceptualized social reality as a man-made reality which was the product of human choice and action. Man was the product of his social relationships and at the same time he could experience his selfhood as an 'inalienable property' in its own right. In *Grundrisse* Marx elaborated this view of the self by comparing it with that of the classical political economists. 'The economists', he suggested, 'express this as follows: Each pursues his private interest and only his private interest; and thereby serves the private interests of all, the general interest without willing or knowing it. . . . The point is rather that private interest is already a socially determined interest, which can be achieved only within the conditions laid down by society and with the means provided by society.'[30]

We might remind ourselves at this stage that the perfectly competitive economic market was not and never could be some natural state of affairs which appears when all the unnatural restraints upon competition are removed. Both the creation and preservation of competitive markets depends upon extensive legislation and government controls. This point has been made clearly by Polanyi in *The Great Transformation*, by Schumpeter in *Capitalism, Socialism and Democracy* and of course by Adam Smith himself.[31]

For Marx the key agents in this creation and re-creation of social realities were social groups — especially social classes — rather than individuals. I find it very difficult to understand Marx's notion of praxis, that is, the union of theory and practice by which men make sense of their world, act upon it through the exercise of choice and experience in turn the counter effects of their own action. I find it easier to comprehend the relationship between individuals and their culture in Simmel's more fatalistic or tragic sense, namely, that culture will always deny freedom to those who seek it in any unconditional sense.[32] Or one may take the functionalist view that men treat their culture as an entity over and above themselves because it is useful and necessary to do so.

Marx, as we know, took a contrary view. He saw the disposition of men to reify their culture — to treat, for example, the complete marketization of social life under capitalism as a necessary fact of life regulating the conditions of life — as evidence of the way in which private property, the division of labour and the pursuit of profit alienated them from each other and the products of their own labour. Through such a process individuals lose control of their own lives and labour and thus become involved in 'a contradiction between the interest of the separate individual (or the individual family) and the communal interest of all individuals who have intercourse with one another.'[33]

But both Marx and Smith recognized the absolute centrality of the *productive process* in structuring the meaning and the sense of reality of the individual members of industrial societies. For Smith it was *through* the productive process that individuals sought their own interests. For Marx the key agents were social classes rather than individuals. Although both writers drew different conclusions regarding the outcomes of this competition, in terms of the consequences for human welfare and its enhancement, these differences should not be allowed to obscure the common emphasis which Smith and Marx placed on production.

Marx was, however, highly critical of political economists like John Stuart Mill who, in his opinion, drew a sharp distinction between production and distribution and then treated this model as if it were 'encased in eternal natural laws independent of history', when in fact it only typified 'bourgeois relations'. Marx's 'very short answer' to this approach was that all production involved the 'appropriation of nature', and that 'every form of production' created its own distinctive set of social and political relationships.[34] But Marx was not content to let the matter rest there. He went on to ridicule the 'syllogism' by which political economists treated production as 'the generality, distribution and exchange the particularity, and consumption the singularity by which the whole is joined together'. He was equally dismissive of the critics of political economy who argued that distribution was as important as production, only to fall into the same error of treating production and distribution as 'independent, autonomous neighbours'.[35]

Marx contended that, although production, distribution, exchange and consumption are not identical, they 'all form the members of a totality, distinctions within a unity. Production predominates not only over itself, in the antithetical definition of production, but over the other moments as well.'[36] The fact that changes in demand influence the character of production only underlined the 'organic' nature of the whole process. As for exchange, Marx described it as merely 'an act comprised within production itself', contingent on the division of labour, the forms of which are in turn determined by production. Similarly the forms of distribution were shaped by 'the existence of capital and landed property as independent agents of production'.[37]

Smith begins *The Wealth of Nations* with an analysis of the division of labour. He argues that it is 'the great multiplication of the production of all the different arts, in consequence of the division of labour which occasions, in a well-governed society, that universal opulence which extends itself to the lowest ranks of the people'.[38] The social inequalities which arise from the division of labour are defended on the same grounds as those used subsequently by Ricardo, namely, that 'the accommodation of a European prince does not always so much exceed that of an industrious and frugal peasant as the accommodation of the latter exceeds that of many an African king.'[39] Smith attributes the division of labour to a natural human propensity 'to truck, barter, and exchange one thing for another'.[40] This propensity to seek one's own advantage through exchange is constrained only by the limits of the market.[41]

As Smith describes the means by which productivity is increased and goods and services are distributed, he distinguishes between 'productive' and 'unproductive' labour and between 'opulent' and 'poor' nations and cities. He concludes that 'The proportion between capital and revenue . . . seems everywhere to regulate the proportion between industry and idleness. Wherever capital predominates, industry prevails: wherever revenue, idleness. Every increase or diminution of capital, therefore, naturally tends to increase or diminish the real quantity of industry, the number of productive hands, and consequently the exchangeable value of the annual produce of the land and labour of the country, the real wealth and revenue of all its inhabitants.'[42] In *The Wealth of Nations* the relationships between production, distribution, exchange and consumption are interpreted in a manner and to an end quite at variance with Marx's analysis, but the emphasis on production is similar. Marx denied, however, that these relationships, as they existed under capitalism, were immutable or that they were in any way a reflection of 'inviolable natural laws on which society in the abstract is founded'.[43]

Smith and Marx both wrote at times when social services, as we understand them today, did not exist — apart, that is, from charitable enterprises. In our time the proliferation of social services seems to provide *prima facie* evidence of the existence of a separate institutional entity, which can be termed the social market. If the social market is taken to include all those welfare goods and services which are allocated by reference to criteria of need rather than effective demand, it should properly be located in the sphere of distribution rather than production. It can of course be argued that social services are also productive forces, insofar as they contribute to greater economic efficiency. It is doubtful, however, whether the claims of the social market to institutional autonomy could be defended for long on such utilitarian grounds.

In short, if we argue from the position of either Smith or Marx, the social market can be seen to function as an agency of distribution, but its material scope and normative autonomy will always be prescribed by the nature of the productive forces operating in the economic market. Smith and Marx both offer a theoretical framework for the analysis of social policy in relation to the wider society, but the logic of their respective approaches consigns social policies to a very subordinate role.

Yet the emphasis which both authors place on production within the economic market has great relevance to students of social administration who may be tempted to differentiate what can be called the values of the economic market from those of the social market and to concentrate their attention upon the latter. The social market may perform certain handmaidenly functions in relation to the economic market, but it is in the last analysis an agent of distribution rather than production. In a subject like ours it is tempting to forget that wealth and hence welfare have to be produced before anything can be either distributed or redistributed.

This error of emphasis can begin very early in the historical study of the relationship between industrialization and social policy. The rise and survival of capitalism cannot be explained by reference to the poor law, and capitalism can no more be judged by reference to the poor law than Christianity by reference to the Spanish inquisition. Marx himself was foremost in recognizing the unprecedented capacity of capitalism to produce wealth, even as he indicted the human damage it might cause in the act of creation.[44]

In seeking to understand the ways in which social welfare is enhanced — by whom and for whom — we must make use of theories which help us to understand better the relationship between the social and the economic market. Both classical economic theory and Marxist theory can be used to this end. The normative content of the first insists that the two are indivisible and that the free play of the economic market is the best way to enhance welfare. Marxist social theory sought to demonstrate that the economic institutions and values of capitalism are destructive of welfare and that social policies can never be more than ameliorative, since their ends and values are always subordinated to and reflective of the competitive ethos.

Colonial reformers and free trade

Of all the great industrializing nations of the nineteenth century, Britain came nearest to realizing the internationalist ideals of free trade and *laissez-faire*. Yet the logic of mercantilism offered a viable alternative prospect of international influence through the purposive acquisition and exploitation of colonies. The conflict between these two doctrines was temporarily resolved in the first half of the nineteenth century — before Marx published *The Communist Manifesto* and long before Marxism became an influential doctrine.

Both *laissez-faire* and mercantilism were compatible with the rise of a capitalist mode of production but *laissez-faire* was far less compatible than was mercantilism with the development of collectivist welfare policies. The rise of welfare collectivism in Britain was to become associated with the subsequent revival of protectionist economic policies which owed much to the mercantile tradition. This relationship can be stated in more negative terms — the gradual loss of confidence in the capacity of a free economic market to enhance individual welfare was attended by a growing conviction amongst the citizenry that the state ought to play a more active role in the collective provision of welfare. As the terms of welfare obligation and entitlement at home became more generous protectionist trading policies became more popular. The protracted series of events through which these issues were resolved merit some attention because they help us to understand more clearly why British social policies developed as they did. In subsequent chapters I shall extend the analysis by comparison with other countries.

As it happened, the crucial years in the formation of Britain's imperial trade policies were those in which the doctrines of free trade were rapidly gaining political ascendancy. The turning-point occurred just before the repeal of the Corn Laws in 1846. By that date the imperial alternative to free trade was in temporary eclipse. In setting out the case against the retention of the colonies the leading free traders, Cobden, Bright and Goldwin Smith, argued that in any event separation was inevitable as well as necessary. First, the status of being a colony was inherently degrading and offensive to liberal principles.[45] Secondly, expenditures on colonial defence were already high and were certain to go on rising, because colonies were a major cause of war. Thirdly, these costs of colonial defence fell upon the ordinary citizen and thereby necessarily diminished his welfare. Fourthly, the counter argument that the colonies provided free land for emigrants from the mother country was tendentious and irrelevant. The majority of British emigrants went to the United States and not to the colonies. After separation this pattern would probably be maintained, but separation would not in itself deter those who wished to go to the colonies. Once granted independence, the former colonies would continue to trade with Britain, since it would be in their interests to do so. The lobby for the repeal of the Corn Laws was thus complemented by a far more wide-ranging campaign for the general liberalization of trade and the separation of the colonies from the mother country.

During the 1830s these free trade views were opposed by a small but influential group of colonial reformers, which included Lord Durham, Charles Buller, Sir William Molesworth and Gibbon Wakefield. Durham's unpredictable temperament was one of the factors which were to deny him the highest political office, but he served as Lord Privy Seal in Grey's ministry of 1830 and played a key role in drafting the 1832 Reform Bill. In 1838 he became Governor General of Canada and undertook an investigation of the serious discontent which continued to trouble the colony after the risings of 1837 in Upper and Lower Canada. Durham prepared a major report, published in 1839, which recommended the union of the two provinces and the adoption of a new set of principles on which might be based the future governance of the colonies. These principles directed, first, that through the institution of cabinet government a colony might be granted autonomy with regard to its internal affairs and, secondly, that British interests should continue to be protected by the maintenance of imperial authority in four main areas of policy, which were 'the constitution of the form of government, the regulation of foreign relations, and of trade with the mother country, the other British colonies, and foreign nations, and the disposal of the public lands'.[46]

Under the Union Act of 1840 the provinces were united, and Canada was granted responsible government. Durham, however, died before the year was out, and when Lord Elgin assumed the governor-generalship in 1846 he was given powers to implement the remaining recommendations of the 1840 Commission as he saw fit. By this time, however, not only were free trade doctrines in the ascendant, but even those who favoured the retention of the colonies feared that undue control by the metropolitan country might drive the white colonial settlers to secede. Fieldhouse argues that after 1848 'the British never stood on diarchy, for if they had done so, they would have forced ambitious colonial statesmen to opt for independence. The British preferred to throw out of the window all that they once thought vital to their own interests in a colony in order to retain at least some formal connexion with it.'[47] This meant in the case of Canada that two of the four major principles recommended by the Durham Commission were swiftly abandoned. Imperial preferences were given up during and after 1846, and with the repeal of the Navigation Acts in 1849 Britain also surrendered its control of colonial shipping.[48] In 1852 the control of the 'public' lands was transferred to the Canadian government. Thereafter these two major policies were followed in the other colonies upon the granting of responsible government.

What determined whether or not a colony was granted responsible government? It was unlikely to be granted if the colony in question served a direct and particular metropolitan interest, for example as a military garrison or a penal settlement. Small or poor colonies would not qualify; neither would those without a majority white population.[49] In practice the dominant criterion was a racial one. Other overseas possessions might be granted not responsible, but representative government, or they might be governed as crown colonies or, as in the case of India, as viceroyalties. Responsible government was granted between 1842 and 1890 to the Australian states, New Zealand, the Cape Colony and Newfoundland, and with this status went control over trade and public lands.

The decline in the influence of the colonial reformers is explicable partly by the effective lobbying of the Manchester school and partly by the fact that free trade was becoming the most advantageous policy from Britain's point of view. In its enjoyment of massive industrial and naval power Britain was able to contemplate the prospect of a great peace, while other nations remained highly sensitive to the reality or imminence of conflict. The American Civil War and the rise of Prussia in the 1860s were to justify these fears.

Yet another factor which may have contributed to the mid-century demise of imperial policies was the eclipse of the colonial reformers as an effective pressure group. Durham had died in 1840, and Buller in 1848, both of them in early middle age. Wakefield had been debarred from Parliament as a result of youthful indiscretions, and the greater part of his subsequent career was spent abroad, away from the centres of metropolitan influence. Molesworth died in 1855 at the age of forty-five. With the loss of these men, much of the direction and impetus went out of the movement for colonial reform in Britain.

While it cannot be argued that the defeat of the colonial reformers had any direct influence on the course of social reform at home, the success of the free trade movement is evidence of the growing influence of *laissez-faire* doctrines in their popularized forms among policy-makers and influential members of the general public. This is the period to which Dicey refers when he writes of the popular acceptance of classical political economy 'as a science containing very definite and certain principles, from which were logically deduced conclusions of indisputable and universal truth'.[50] One of the fundamental principles of this doctrine was that minimal governmental interference in trade was the best way to enhance social welfare. In this respect free trade can be seen as the positive counterpoint to the deterrent policies which dominated poor relief during the 1840s and 1850s.

Burrow makes a point of further relevance regarding the complementary nature of certain aspects of utilitarian thought and political economy in the enhancement of human happiness. He observes that 'Much of the appeal of classical political economy for utilitarians lay in the fact that it provided in its own sphere what in the psychological sphere proved so difficult to obtain — namely, a means of determining what people wanted in an exactly measurable way. The price mechanism offered in the objective sphere of social life precisely what the Benthamite calculus failed to do in the subjective and inscrutable area of psychology . . . a numerical index of relative wants.'[51]

In keeping with the philosophical and economic spirit of the time it was inevitable that the role of government in the relief of destitution would remain a negative one. The new poor law was designed to force labourers to act positively on their own behalf. Yet for a brief period there had been a prospect that sponsored emigration and the settlement of the surplus poor in the colonial public lands might add a new and positive dimension to the enhancement of social welfare. In default of any government-sponsored initiative emigration became predominantly the concern of private enterprise, and the main flow of emigrants was towards the United States rather than the British colonies. The major intervention of government in this sphere, coming belatedly in 1842, took the form of the Passenger Act, which was designed to put a stop to some of the many malpractices which had become associated with the transoceanic shipment of paupers by private enterprise. The subsequent Passenger Acts, passed between 1847 and 1855, have rightly been described as representing a major stage in the development of effective regulatory practices in modern government.[52] In terms of the pursuit of welfare, however, these Acts were a reaction against the excesses of the private market. A more positive role for the government in emigration policy was effectively precluded once the control of the colonial public lands had been allowed to pass under the jurisdiction of the new colonial governments.[53]

The British transition to free trade was a gradual one, and its stages were dictated, according to Fuchs, 'step by step, according to the concrete necessities of English industrial life at the time of its introduction'.[54] Given the advantages in industrial development and resources which Britain then possessed in relation to other nations, this was a doctrine which was evidently attractive to the manufacturing classes. It was also a doctrine to which they were anxious to win converts abroad. Nonetheless the confidence of the free traders was such that they were fully prepared to see Britain converted to free trade on a unilateral basis, if necessary, since protectionist nations would only end up by raising their own costs of living, should they retaliate by erecting tariffs.

Despite these dire predictions this is exactly what the majority of other independent nations were already doing. Furthermore as soon as the colonies achieved the status of responsible government they also began to opt for protection rather than free trade and the regulation rather than the free movement of migrants. In 1859 Canada passed a major tariff law, which was designed to attract 'skilled settlers' and to nurture 'infant industries',[55] and thereafter Canadian trade policy became increasingly protectionist. In Australia all of the new states eventually adopted tariffs — once again in the interests of nurturing home industries — and the raising of wage levels by protecting their workers against the competition of cheap European labour. Very similar policies were adopted by New Zealand and the Cape Colony, after they had been granted responsible government.

These trends were viewed with some alarm by the minority of colonial reformers who survived in British political life. Throughout the years between 1850 and 1870, however, separatism in either its 'active' or 'reluctant' forms dominated government policy and large sections of influential public opinion. It also became, as Bodelsen points out, the policy favoured amongst the leading permanent officials at the Colonial Office. Sir James Stephens, who served as Permanent Under Secretary during the period 1836-47, achieved the reputation of being an early supporter of the interests of indigenous peoples and he sought to protect their interests against prospective colonizers.[56] Both Sir Frederick Rogers, who succeeded Stephens during the years between 1847 and 1871, and Herman Merivale were separatists. It is therefore not surprising that under the terms of the Colonial Laws Validity Act of 1865 it was laid down that laws passed by colonial legislatures 'should be void only in so far as they were clearly repugnant to an Act of the British Parliament'.[57]

The most significant exception to these trends in British colonial policy was the case of India, in which cotton duties were abolished. India became the temporary salvation of a Lancashire cotton industry which was already struggling to survive in an increasingly protectionist world. Lacking the status of responsible government, India had no choice in the matter. As Fuchs duly observes, 'A resolution of the English House of

Commons, on August 30th 1877, declared that the cotton duties in India . . . were, in their nature, protective; they were therefore in contradiction with the sound principles of trade policy, and should be abolished as soon as the condition of Indian finances permitted.'[58] Thus, with the exception of India, Great Britain came to offer the world 'the remarkable spectacle of a country, anxious to convert all other nations to Free Trade, and yet unable to introduce it to its own colonies'.[59]

In his brilliant contemporary study of the British free trade movement Fuchs explores the complex interaction of international altruism and scarcely concealed self-interest which sustained this policy until the end of the nineteenth century. Fuchs's own biases are clearly expressed. He suggests that Cobden 'well knew how to cloak the special interests of England in the garb of a philanthropic cosmopolitanism and of an ideal aspiration after the welfare of mankind'.[60] The same free traders who successfully campaigned for the repeal of the Corn Laws opposed trade union combination and the Ten Hour Bill. As it proved, the passing of that Ten Hour Act was the price paid for the repeal of the Corn Laws.

Despite the association of free trade with a general hostility to governmental intervention the popularity of free trade as a doctrine steadily increased within many sectors of the working class. The actual effect of free trade on their living standards, however, depended on a number of related factors, including wages. As Marx observed in his *Discourse on Free Trade*,[61] within the terms of Ricardian wage theory 'every means of cheapening . . . the means of subsistence of the workers was bound to accrue to the advantage of the manufacturers,'[62] 'and the poor would be better off so long as both wages *and* the price of corn remained high, since a little economy on bread would allow the purchase of other commodities'.[63]

Nonetheless many members of the working class were won over to free trade not because of moralistic appeals to internationalism but because of the real and immediate attractions of cheaper food. In this respect there emerged a temporary coincidence of interests between workers and manufacturers. The economic and social casualties of free trade were the farmers and agricultural labourers.[64] In reviewing the subsequent progress of free trade policy Fuchs noted the difficulties in assessing its impact on living standards, apart from 'the continuous displacement of agriculture by other branches of economic production'.[65] The increasing reliance on grain imports from Russia (especially in the periods 1866-70, 1871-5 and 1886-90), the United States and India had a disastrous effect on English agriculture.[66]

The peculiarities of the British free trade system were such that some sections of the working class benefited significantly more than others. Under the terms of the Gladstone tariff of 1860, protective duties, that is to say, duties on goods which were also produced at home, were removed. Pure revenue duties — those on goods which were not produced at home such as tobacco, tea, spirits and coffee — were, however, retained, and Fuchs argued that by 1890 Britain was raising about a quarter of its national revenue by such duties, a far greater proportion than that raised by any other major power.[67] The net effect of these duties was the imposition of taxes on the customary luxuries of the poor. Fuchs concludes, however, that it was the skilled rather than the unskilled members of the working class who were more positively disposed to free trade, because it enabled them to 'consume an increasing amount of cheap bread, cheap sugar, and the other cheap means of subsistence and enjoyment'.[68]

The decision to repeal the Corn Laws was also, as Burnett remarks, a 'conscious decision against self-sufficiency', and 'by the eve of the First World War British farmers supplied only half our meat and a mere one-fifth of our wheat requirements.'[69] The most remarkable feature of the free trade movement was the confidence which inspired it, a confidence in Britain's capacity to win out in a competitive world and a conviction that international peace rather than war between nations would prevail and endure. At the time of the repeal of the Corn Laws Britain had already lost one overseas empire and was well on the way to acquiring another. In an earlier work I argued that the adoption of the poor law principles of 1834 represented 'one of the few occasions in the history of English social policy on which theory was allowed to take normative wings and find a legislative perch'.[70] The complement to and indeed the rationale for this theoretical flight were embodied in the decision to adopt and maintain free trade policies, throughout a period during which every other emerging industrial power was becoming more protectionist, and during which the acquisition of a second empire was providing both the means and the incentive for Britain to do likewise.

From the 1870s onwards the trend towards protection gathered momentum throughout Europe and the United States as well as in the self-governing colonies of the British Empire. It was the raising of tariffs outside the Empire, however, which most seriously affected Britain. The MacKinley Act of 1890, for example, had a particularly adverse effect on the British tinplate, cutlery and textile industries. By 1889 the American market was taking nearly one-eighth of the total value of British and Irish exports.[71] Among the six major markets for British exports during the period 1860-90 the United States accounted on an average for 15.8 per cent of the total, France for 10.4 per cent, India for 9.9 per cent, Germany for 8.4 per cent, Australia for 6.1 per cent and Holland for 5.6 per cent. All these countries, with the exception of India, had adopted protection.

It was the onset of the Great Depression in world trade between 1873 and 1896 which more than any other event destroyed the general mood of optimism which had sustained Britain's confidence in free trade policies. Despite the brief periods of intermittent recovery this confidence was never to be regained. The rise of new industrial systems in the United States, Germany and France was depriving Britain of its privileged position in the international market. Every one of Britain's major industrial competitors was resorting to protection in order to survive the economic depression and quicken its rate of industrial growth.

Hinsley suggests that this general 'reversion to protectionism was more than offset by the constantly widening opportunities in international trade', and that Britain's continuing commitment to free trade only served to encourage protectionism elsewhere. The trend towards protectionism in Europe continued throughout the last quarter of the century in Russia, Spain, Italy, Germany and France.[72] At the same time it is possible to note throughout Europe an impetus not only towards protectionism but towards social reform and a more vigorous commitment to imperialism.[73]

Polanyi argues that the one form of protection reinforced the other and was conditional on it. Agricultural protection forced up the price of food, so that trade unions clamoured for higher wages and welfare legislation. Industrialists demanded protective tariffs to meet these demands. It was becoming clear, as Robinson remarks, that 'the case for Free Trade as a benefit to each nation could not be made out. The weak spot in the analysis was in overlooking the implications of the assumption of universal perfect competition . . . any one nation, within the conditions of the equilibrium model, may be better off with a smaller volume of trade at higher prices of exports in terms of imports than at the Free Trade position.'[74] Robinson goes on to observe that 'In the pre-1914 world Great Britain had everything to gain . . . and very little to lose' in a free trade world, and that 'Marshall, the old fox, had known perfectly well that it was all a question of national self-interest' but had chosen to hide away his reservations in a 'rather boring appendix to the *Principles of Economics*'.[75]

It is important to recognize the extent to which even Britain fell short of the ideal state of *laissez-faire* commended by the Manchester school. The liberalization of trade never went so far that protection was completely abandoned at home. As late as 1870 there were still seventeen dutiable imports.[76] Apart from these internal restrictions British trade had to contend with an increasing number of protected markets, as the century progressed. Given the central role of the City of London in the world money market, there was for a time a genuinely international free trade in capital. It was indeed vitally important for the working of the British economy that these exports of capital should be paralleled by opportunities to export paupers. For a relatively brief period there was an almost international market in labour, but this situation was changed by the increase in the number of nations which were imposing migration controls. Within Britain the internal movement of labour was also regulated by the sanctions of the poor law.

The Great Depression of the 1870s was to mark the beginning of the decline of free trade as the dominant British economic doctrine. In addition, although there was a brief revival of the full severities of the new poor law during this decade, the remaining years of the century were ones in which the advocates of more generous policies of social welfare were to find unexpected support amongst the imperialist and protectionist elements of both major political parties. In reviewing the major economic trends of the period between 1870 and the First World War Ashworth attaches greater importance to changes in real income per head than to price movements. He concludes that 'Despite the qualification that must be made about its later years the impression of the whole period from 1870 to 1914 is one of great economic advance.'[77]

A contrary view is taken by Hobsbawm. He recognizes that 'So far as the working people are concerned, it [the Great Depression] cannot compare with the cataclysm of the 1830s and 1840s, or the 1920s and 1930s', but he goes on to propose that 'If "depression" indicates a pervasive — and for the generation since 1850 a new — state of mind of uneasiness and gloom about the prospects of the British economy, the word is accurate.'[78] Hobsbawm draws attention to the adverse impact of the Great Depression upon the living standards of the poor and the confidence of the business community. Thereafter, he notes, we enter a period characterized by intensified political activity on the part of the working classes and exemplified in the formation of a Marxist International, and an increasing disposition on the part of business interests to call 'on the state not only to give [them] a free hand, but to save [them]'. Other leading industrial nations were now firmly committed to protection, but, although Britain remained free trade, its government and people were now looking anew at their empire as a possible source of salvation.[79]

References

[1] Adam Smith, *The Wealth of Nations*, Vols I and II, Everyman Edition, Dent Dutton, 1937.

[2] Lichtheim, op. cit., p. 51.

[3] John Hicks, *A Theory of Economic History*, Clarendon Press, Oxford, 1969, pp. 161-2.

[4] Jacob Viner, 'Power versus Plenty as Objectives of Foreign Policy in the Seventeenth and Eighteenth Centuries', in D. C. Coleman (ed.), *Revisions in Mercantilism*, Methuen, 1969, p. 71.

[5] Joseph A. Schumpeter, *History of Economic Analysis*, Allen & Unwin, 1963, pp. 251-2.

[6] See M. R. James, *Social Problems and Policy during the Puritan Revolution, 1640-1660*, George Routledge & Sons, 1930, pp. 275 et seq.

[7] Charles Wilson, 'The Other Face of Mercantilism', in D. C. Coleman (ed.), op. cit., p. 125.

[8] ibid., p. 127. See also James, op. cit., p. 276.

[9] Charles Wilson, 'The Other Face of Mercantilism', p. 128.

[10] Schumpeter, *History of Economic Analysis*, p. 270.

[11] James, op. cit., p. 243.

[12] ibid., pp. 275-6.

[13] ibid., p. 276.

[14] ibid., p. 286.

[15] Charles Wilson, 'The Other Face of Mercantilism', p. 128.

[16] ibid., p. 132.

[17] ibid., p. 133.

[18] Hicks, op. cit., p. 162.

[19] Charles Wilson, *England's Apprenticeship, 1603-1763*, Longmans, 1965, pp. 60 et seq.

[20] loc. cit.

[21] Karl Polanyi, *The Great Transformation: The Political and Economic Origins of Our Time*, Beacon Press, Boston, 1968, p. 135.

22 ibid., p. 134.

23 David Ricardo, *The Principles of Political Economy*, Everyman Edition, Dent Dutton, 1929, pp. 54-5.

24 A. W. Coats, 'The Classical Economists, Industrialisation and Poverty', in Institute of Economic Affairs, *The Long Debate on Poverty*, IEA Readings 9. London, 1972, pp. 146-7.

25 C. A. Bodelsen, *Studies in Mid-Victorian Imperialism*, Glydendalske Boghandel-Nordisk Forlag — KJØ Benhaven, Kristiana, London and Berlin, MDCCCCXXIV, p. 35.

26 Carl Johannes Fuchs, *The Trade Policy of Great Britain and Her Colonies Since 1860*, Macmillan, 1905, p. 178.

27 ibid., p. 179.

28 Eric Roll, *A History of Economic Thought*, Faber & Faber, 1973, p. 227.

29 See Charles Wilson, *England's Apprenticeship*, pp. 337-57.

30 Karl Marx, *Grundrisse*, Penguin Books in association with New Left Review, Harmondsworth, 1977, p. 156.

31 See Polanyi, op. cit., pp. 139 et seq. and pp. 249 et seq.; Joseph Schumpeter, *Capitalism, Socialism and Democracy*, Allen & Unwin, London, 1961, pp. 77 et seq.; and Adam Smith, op. cit., Vol. I, p. 138, where Smith observes, 'To expect, indeed, that the freedom of trade should ever be entirely restored in Great Britain is as absurd as to expect that an Oceania or Utopia should ever be established in it. Not only the prejudices of the public, but what is much more unconquerable, the private interests of many individuals, irresistibly oppose it.'

32 A particularly clear and helpful account of the concept of praxis is to be found in Poggi's *Images of Society*, pp. 94 et seq., from which the reference to Simmel is also taken.

33 Karl Marx and Frederick Engels, *The German Ideology*, Part I, Lawrence & Wishart, London, 1970, p. 53. Marx and Engels go on to argue that 'Out of this very contradiction between the interest of the individual and that of the community the latter takes an independent form as the *State*, divorced from the real interests of individual and community' (ibid.). In *Capital* Marx explores at greater length the destructive impact of capitalism on the family, suggesting that the resultant breakdown of traditional role relationships 'is building the new economic foundation for a higher form of the family and of the relations between the sexes' (*Capital*, Vol. I, Dent, London, 1946, p. 529).

34 Marx, *Grundrisse*, pp. 87-8.

35 ibid., pp. 89-90.

36 ibid., pp. 99.

37 ibid., p. 96.

38 Adam Smith, op. cit., Vol. I, p. 10.

39 ibid., p. 11.

40 ibid., p. 12.

41 ibid., p. 13.

42 ibid., p. 301.

43 Marx, *Grundrisse*, p. 87.

44 See Marx, *Capital*, Vol. II, Ch. 22, pp. 636 et seq. See also K. Marx and F. Engels, *Manifesto of the Communist Party*, Foreign Languages Publishing House, Moscow, 1959, 'The bourgeoisie, during its rule of scarce one hundred years, has created more massive and more colossal productive forces than have all preceding generations together. . . . What earlier century

had even a presentiment that such productive forces slumbered in the lap of social labour?', pp. 51-2.

[45] Bodelsen, op. cit., p. 37.

[46] Quoted from D. K. Fieldhouse, *The Colonial Empires: A Comparative Study from the Nineteenth Century*, Weidenfeld & Nicolson, London, 1865, p. 257.

[47] ibid., p. 262.

[48] ibid., p. 263.

[49] ibid., p. 258.

[50] Dicey, op. cit.,

[51] J. W. Burrow, *Evolution and Society: A Study in Victorian Social Theory*, Cambridge University Press, 1970, pp. 72-3.

[52] See Oliver MacDonagh, *A Pattern of Government Growth 1800-1860*, MacGibbon & Kee, London, 1961.

[53] Bodelsen, op. cit., p. 21.

[54] Fuchs, op. cit., p. 178.

[55] ibid., p. 241.

[56] Bodelsen, op. cit., p. 48.

[57] David Thomson, 'The United Kingdom and Its World-Wide Interests', Ch. VIII in J. P. Bury (ed.), *The New Cambridge Modern History*, Vol. X, *The Zenith of European Power, 1830-1870*, Cambridge University Press, London, 1967, p. 355.

[58] Fuchs, op. cit., pp. 272-3.

[59] ibid., p. 227.

[60] ibid., p. 18.

[61] Quoted in Fuchs, op. cit., p. 12.

[62] ibid., p. 10.

[63] ibid., p. 12.

[64] Polanyi, op. cit., p. 183.

[65] Fuchs, op. cit., p. 172.

[66] ibid., p. 196.

[67] ibid., pp. 13-15.

[68] ibid., pp. 202-3.

[69] John Burnett, *A History of the Cost of Living*, Penguin, 1969, p. 192.

[70] Pinker, *Social Theory and Social Policy*, pp. 60-1.

[71] Fuchs, op. cit., p. 74.

[72] F. H. Hinsley, Introduction to F. H. Hinsley (ed.), *The New Cambridge Modern History*, Vol. XI, *Material Progress and World-Wide Problems, 1870-1898*, Cambridge University Press, London, 1970, pp. 7-10.

[73] Werner Coze, 'The German Empire', in Hinsley (ed.), *Material Progress and World-Wide Problems*, p. 264.

[74] Joan Robinson, *Economic Philosophy*, Penguin, Harmondsworth, 1964, p. 63.

[75] ibid., p. 64. The 'boring appendix' to which Robinson refers is in Alfred Marshall, *Principles of Economics*, Macmillan, London, 1907, pp. 767 et seq.

[76] Hinsley, Introduction to *Material Progress and World-Wide Problems*, p. 8.

[77] William Ashworth, *An Economic History of England 1870-1939*, Methuen, London, 1960, p. 244.

[78] E. J. Hobsbawm, *Industry and Empire: An Economic History of Britain Since 1750*, Weidenfeld & Nicolson, London, 1968, pp. 103-4.

[79] ibid., pp. 106-8.

7 The Collectivist Reaction

Imperialism and social reform

In mid-nineteenth-century Britain there was a conservative reaction against the excesses of the 1834 Poor Law Amendment Act which influenced welfare policy long before either imperialism or socialism became effective political forces. The paternalistic welfare policies of successive Tory ministers can be seen as attempts to mitigate the sufferings of those who were forced to seek their own welfare in the economic market of the 1840s and 1850s. This reaction was given coherence and a clearer sense of broad political purpose by Disraeli. In making the Conservatives the 'patriotic party' he recognized the need to recover a sense of national unity. The wounds of class conflict could be healed by social reform at home and imperialism abroad. We should, however, note that Disraeli's Crystal Palace speech of 1872 came four years after the publication of Charles Dilke's *Greater Britain*, in which very similar views were put forward.[1]

Dilke was elected to Parliament as a Liberal in 1868 and quickly acquired the reputation of being a radical reformer and a man who was likely to achieve the highest office. Between 1882 and 1885 he served as President of the Local Government Board and he was perhaps the ablest man ever to hold that office. Dilke was Chairman of the Royal Commission on the Housing of the Working Classes between 1884 and 1885, but his ministerial career was suddenly brought to an end when he was cited as co-respondent in a divorce case. In 1886 he lost his parliamentary seat, and, although he returned to the House again in 1892, he never recovered his former position and prospects.

Dilke nevertheless exerted a measure of influence on the political and economic thought of his time as an expert on colonial affairs who wrote from the perspective of a highly unconventional liberal imperialist. He was a free trader in economic policy, having close links with the Manchester school, yet he was able to understand and sympathize with the protectionist policies of the self-governing colonies. He was also paradoxically both a colonial separatist and an imperialist, dedicated to the cause of Empire and to policies of sponsored migration. Dilke's vision of Empire took the form of a confederation of independent states, united by common 'Saxon' heritage and culture. It was a vision which encompassed not only Britain and the Empire but the United States of America. He saw nothing incompatible between the independence of sovereign states and the idea of confederation. The one principle complemented the other, since 'Many of our emigrants who flock to the United States are attracted by the idea that they are going to become citizens of a new nation instead of dependent upon an old one.'[2]

Between 1880 and 1910 both major parties had their imperialist lobbies which were urging the need for social reform in the interests of national efficiency. There was, however, a fundamental conflict of principle, which prevented a coalition of interests between the Tory and Liberal imperialists. While Joseph Chamberlain's Tariff Reform League was protectionist, Rosebery's Imperial Federation League stood for free trade. Their common interest in social reform failed to provide a sufficient basis for a new party of national efficiency.[3] It was the conflict between the principles of free trade and protection — a conflict deemed to be of crucial relevance to the nation's welfare — which prevented the formation of a coalition. Among the Fabians there was another group of imperialists which included the Webbs and Shaw. Through their discussion group, known as 'The Co-efficients', they sought to gain influence among the liberal imperialists. Although the making of social policy was left largely to Lloyd George and other radical members of the Liberal Party between 1905 and 1914, the reform movements of the time were greatly assisted by a flood tide of patriotic sentiment, which was both intellectually and popularly respectable.

The association between patriotism and social reform is manifest in the writings of many of the most influential social scientists of the period, including Benjamin Kidd and Karl Pearson.[4] Kidd is now an almost forgotten social theorist, yet his major work, *Social Evolution*, enjoyed widespread popularity between 1894 and 1914, and he was considered to be an intellectual successor to Spencer in English sociology.[5] Kidd's revision of social Darwinism was strongly reformist and anti-socialist. He argued that both social Darwinists and Marxists underestimated the potentialities for co-operation rather than competition or conflict which existed in capitalist societies. For Kidd the answer to internal conflict was necessarily to 'complete the process of evolution in progress by bringing all people into the rivalry of life, not only on a footing of political equality, *but on conditions of equal social opportunities'.*[6] Kidd was one of the first apostles of embourgeoisement. He saw the growth of population as the greatest threat to social reform, which he thought could best be countered by schemes of sponsored emigration. His hopes of internal harmony were, however, complemented by a belief in the inevitability of conflict between nations. Domestic social reforms would 'raise the position of the lower classes *at the expense of the wealthier classes',*[7] leaving them better equipped for competitive enterprise within their own society and ensuring that the whole community would share a sense of common purpose in the international struggle for survival. Kidd also believed that the recovery of religious belief would help in bringing about consensus within the nation.

The writings of Karl Pearson represent another attempt to revise social evolutionist theory. Pearson, who was much admired by the Webbs and Shaw, propounded a strange blend of socialism and racialist theories. He believed in socialism at home and imperialism abroad. He argued in favour of a socialist society in which allegiance to and respect for the state would be 'the most sacred principle' of community organization.[8] He believed that the creation of socialism in a nation depended on a sustained and scientific programme of selective breeding and environmental improvement. He was obsessed with fears of racial deterioration and the danger of 'inferior' races and sub-groups within races becoming an insupportable burden on the 'superior' in the struggle for survival.

Kidd, who was opposed to socialism, was even more appalled by Pearson's highly idiosyncratic vision of a socialist society. In *The Science of Power* Kidd describes Pearson's observation that 'Socialists have to inculcate that spirit which would give offenders against the State short shrift and the nearest lamp-post' as the expression of a 'pagan ethic'.[9] Kidd went on to compare Pearson's version of the socialist state with Bernhardi's glorification of the military state of Hohenzollern Germany.[10] His own view of the civilizing mission of the West with regard to the Empire was grounded in the more pacific traditions of Christianity. The established churches were also disposed to equate the cause of Empire with a civilizing mission. While their missionaries carried the spirit of religious altruism to India's sunny shores, there were nonetheless minorities in all political parties who readily identified themselves with Pearson's remark that 'No thoughtful socialist . . . would object to cultivating Uganda *at the expense of its present occupiers* if Lancashire were starving.'[11]

There were also working-class socialists such as Blatchford who claimed to be 'Britons first and Socialists next'.[12] Blatchford ridiculed the 'cosmopolitan friends who are so cosmopolitan that they admire everything but their own, and love all men except Englishmen'.[13] He argued in defence of agricultural protection on the familiar grounds that becoming 'a defenceless nation' in time of war was 'a rather stiff price to pay to get a farthing off the loaf'.[14] Blatchford was reluctantly anti-Boer during the South African war but a vigorous advocate of preparation for war with Germany in the years before 1914. The outbreak of war in 1914 was to reveal how shallow were the roots of international working-class solidarity amongst the European proletariat. In his study of Salford life between 1905 and 1914 Roberts observed that throughout these years of working-class militancy 'the ultra patriotic mass remained intensely loyal to the nation and the system as a whole'.[15]

Towards the close of the nineteenth century the causes of protection, imperialism and social reform gained support among sections of the academic community. William Cunningham and Sir William Ashley, for example, were enthusiastic supporters of Joseph Chamberlain's programme for tariff and social reform. They were both influenced by the work of Schmoller and the other German 'socialists of the Chair' and influential in advocating a mercantilist alternative to the still dominant doctrines of free trade.

Joseph Chamberlain's Tariff Reform League stands out as the most dramatic and sustained attempt to combine the objectives of imperial federation and social reform in one political programme. Chamberlain first entered Parliament as a Liberal. In the early years of his political career he worked closely with Dilke, as a member of the radical caucus, in the interests of electoral reform, free education and old age pensions. After his break with the Liberal Party over the Irish question in 1886 he served in Salisbury's cabinet as Colonial Secretary between 1895 and 1900 and in this capacity was able to foster a new spirit of imperial purpose in government policy. However, the imposition in 1902 of a new tax on imported corn caused Chamberlain to resign office in the following year. He favoured a preferential tariff system, which discriminated between Empire and foreign foods. Chamberlain was also convinced that the established sources of government revenue were now insufficient to meet the costs of long overdue social reform. A preferential tariff would broaden the basis for taxation without necessarily raising the cost of living for the poor. The Tariff Reform League was founded in 1903 to advocate Empire federation and protection based on imperial preference. Chamberlain's subsequent campaign both embarrassed his own party and evoked the opposition of Rosebery's group of Liberal imperialists, who favoured free trade.

The Tariff Reform League drew attention to the increasing threat to British economic prosperity of foreign competition. Britain's major competitors, the United States, Germany and France, had all successfully built up their industrial power with the aid of tariffs and were now exploiting the British markets, which were still largely unprotected. The League wished to impose a tax on foreign food imports and a general 10 per cent tariff on all imported manufactured goods. These policies were to be balanced by a reduction of duties on tea and sugar and a generally preferential treatment of Empire produce. Chamberlain admitted that protection might result in dearer bread but he argued that against this cost must be set the prospects of greater job security, and better social services such as old age pensions which would be partly paid for from tariff revenues. Shortly after the formation of the League an anti-tariff manifesto was published; its signatories included fourteen professors and lecturers in political economy, among whom were Edgeworth, Marshall, Smart and Bowley.

In the election of 1906 the Unionist Party was heavily defeated, although the only Unionists to escape significant losses were the tariff reformers. The initiative for social reform in Campbell-Bannerman's new Liberal cabinet passed to the radical members who had never been strongly imperialist. The Fabians, having gone to much trouble to cultivate a special relationship with the Liberal imperialists, subsequently found themselves at a disadvantage in seeking to influence social policy. The position of the Fabians was not significantly improved after Asquith succeded Campbell-Bannerman in 1908 as Prime Minister and Leader of the Liberal Party. By 1910 the Tariff Reform League was a spent political force. Nonetheless a vigorous sense of imperial destiny was now a force in British politics, and, although free trade doctrines appear to have maintained their intellectual ascendancy in government circles, their demise had only been postponed.

Opposition to tariff reform had been strongest in those industries such as cotton which were heavily dependent on the importation of cheap raw materials. Consequently the debate about protection and free trade created serious divisions within the Conservative Party, which looked to counties like Lancashire as traditional centres of loyalty. Chamberlain was never able to convince his critics that it would be possible to exempt raw materials from duties — or even to provide a satisfactory definition of a raw material for purposes of taxation. Furthermore, the Liberal Party had been quick to point out that giving imperial preference to colonial food producers meant taxing the food imports from other countries.[16] The tariff reformers had sought to counter the appeal of cheap food by focusing attention on the dangers of industrial depression and unemployment under free trade. Their electioneering slogan of 'Tariff Reform Means Work for All' emphasized the connections bet - ween welfare and economic policy as well as those between welfare and better social services.

Given the strength of free trade sentiments within both the Liberal Party and the small parliamentary Labour Party, the prospects for tariff reform in the short run depended upon the future electoral success of the Conservatives. But the Liberals were to remain in power until 1922. During the early years of this Liberal ascendancy the Conservatives continued to equivocate on the question of tariff reform. In the 1910 election Balfour tried to placate the Unionist free traders by suggesting that the issue should be resolved by a referendum. When Balfour retired in 1911 he was succeeded as party leader by Bonar Law, who favoured tariff reform. Bonar Law rejected the idea of a referendum but was persuaded to say that 'a Conservative government would not impose taxes on imports of food until after a general election on the issue'.[17] Thereafter the divisions of opinion within the Conservative Party remained for another decade.

The world economic order, which stood on the brink of dissolution in 1914, was in internationalist terms a remarkably open one. It rested on a system of exchange which was based on gold and within which currencies were freely convertible. Despite the growth of protection trade could still move relatively freely between nations. Citizens were able to travel without passports between countries despite the growth of immigration controls on permanent settlement. The First World War effectively ended this internationalist era. It destroyed the economic framework and the illusions of peace and prosperity which had sustained the credibility of free trade in Britain by making manifest the latent power and violence of national interests. The exigencies of war also compelled Asquith's coalition cabinet to introduce tariff controls as an emergency measure in 1915. These controls, which became known as the McKenna duties, took the form of a $33^1/_3$ per cent tax on all 'luxuries' and a wide range of specific duties on many other commodities. These duties were continued after the war on an *ad hoc* basis although they were to be temporarily lifted by Snowden — an enthusiastic free trader — in 1924.[18] Between 1921 and 1925 new Acts of Parliament were passed extending protection to various key industries.

Yet the years between 1919 and 1929 were a period during which a serious attempt was made at restoring Britain's economy on the basis of free trade and the gold standard. Between 1919 and 1922 Lloyd George's coalition cabinet of Liberals and Conservatives remained ostensibly free trade despite the extension of protection to certain key industries. By June 1921 unemployment passed the two million mark, only a few months after Lloyd George had extended the unemployment insurance scheme to the majority of manual workers. In the election of 1922 the Conservatives under Bonar Law returned to office after sixteen years. When Law resigned in the following year he was succeeded by Baldwin, who decided to go to the country on a programme of tariff reform. The Conservatives were opposed by the Liberal and Labour Parties, which remained free trade. Although the Conservatives won the most seats in the election of December 1923, Baldwin declined to form a government without a mandate for tariff reform. Asquith, as Leader of the Liberals — now the smallest of the three major parties — decided to support a minority Labour government under Macdonald. During the Labour Party's brief term of office between January and November 1924 Snowden, as Chancellor, followed a staunchly free trade policy. His decision to abolish the McKenna duties lowered the cost of living for many poor families but deprived the public works programme of urgently needed funds.[19] At the same time the level of unemployment benefits was raised, and uncovenanted benefits were made a right, although, as Lloyd observes, this meant that 'in practice . . . officials at the Labour Exchange interrogated the applicant and decided whether to give him anything.'[20]

The Conservatives under Baldwin fought the November 1924 election on a free trade programme, which was the only basis on which Baldwin could hope to have a united party. The Conservatives won 419 seats against 151 for Labour and 40 for the Liberals, who were now a party in decline and riven with dissension. Having turned against protection, the new government prepared for a return to the gold standard as the best way to restore international trade and prosperity. In 1925 Britain ostensibly returned to the gold standard. In effect, however, the old system could not be fully restored, because Britain could no longer sustain it without the support of foreign depositors. The new gold exchange standard functioned for 'purely international purposes'.[21] As Taylor remarks, 'The half-hearted gold standard was a symbol of post-war restoration. To outward appearances, all trouble past, all passions spent: free trade, the gold standard, stability at home and abroad. Underneath, an unformed belief was growing that men now counted more than money.'[22]

Despite the government's pursuit of a programme of domestic social reform in pensions, housing and education the problem of unemployment remained unsolved. It existed largely within the older industries which were losing their export markets. The arguments in favour of cutting wages in order to lower prices rested on the false assumption that the goods produced in these older industries could still be sold if only their price were low enough. In other sectors of the economy real wages were rising. These difficulties were compounded by the fact that Britain had returned to the gold standard in 1925 at too high a parity, which placed her major exporting industries under an additional handicap. The government's attempt to resolve the crisis included tacit support for the mine owners' proposal to cut wages and lengthen the working week. The failure of the General Strike was followed by a period of industrial peace, but the causes of the conflict remained unresolved.

In the election of 1929 the Conservatives remained a free trade party, and Labour emerged as the largest parliamentary party, with 288 seats as against 260 for the Conservatives and 59 for the Liberals. When the short-lived Labour government broke up in 1931, it was succeeded by a National government, led by Macdonald. In the face of the mounting economic crisis the old loyalties to free trade were at last breaking down. In September 1931 the National government abandoned the gold standard, and, under pressure from its Conservative supporters, it went to the country in search of a 'doctor's mandate'. By now the Conservatives were firmly committed to protection. Labour fought as a free trade party. Lloyd George refused to support the National Government and Samuel took over the leadership of the Liberals. The Conservatives and Nationalists won 521 seats, Labour 52 and the Samuelite Liberals 33.

Looking back, one can see that throughout the 1920s the conversion of the business community to protection was so gradual that neither Bonar Law nor Baldwin could carry sufficient members of their own party or win over enough Liberal voters to make the Conservatives the protectionist party until after the economic disasters of 1929-30. In the case of the Liberal Party Lloyd George had been moving away from free trade as early as 1922. After the Liberal Party split he had retained control over the party funds, which he did not use until the 1929 election, when he supported over 500 candidates and campaigned on a programme of massive public works, while avoiding a clear commitment on the issue of free trade and protection. Lloyd George's campaign was supported by Keynes, who was also moving towards a protectionist position. It would have been clear at the time, however, that an expansionist public works programme of the kind favoured by Lloyd George and Keynes could only have succeeded if imports had been restricted. But the Liberals were the historic party of free trade in Britain, and there was no possibility of reunification on any other basis.

The Labour Party was also officially a party of free trade. Tariffs, and especially food tariffs, were viewed as 'evil devices to lower working-class living standards'.[23] Yet by 1930 Mosley had come close to persuading the party conference of that year to adopt a tariff programme. His motion was lost by 1 million to 1¼ million votes. Marquand also records that in January 1930 Macdonald 'shocked Snowden by remarking casually during a debate in the House that the best way for Labour to win the next election would be to campaign for a three-point programme, consisting of no reductions in the social services, a "forward" policy on unemployment and a 10 per cent revenue tariff'.[24] Marquand goes on to note that Keynes, 'a life long free trader . . . announced his conversion to protection in his evidence to the Macmillan committee in February'.[25] Keynes's protégé, Hubert Henderson — who had assisted Lloyd George in drafting his 1929 election programme — was also active in his role as joint secretary of the Economic Advisory Council, devising an Industrial Reconstruction Fund. This scheme was to be financed from the 'proceeds of a 10 per cent revenue tariff' and spent on 'capital investment and on helping to meet the deficit on unemployment insurance'.[26]

The political supporters of protection came together in the National government of November 1931. Both the Samuelite and Simonite Liberals in company with Snowden actually agreed to support protection on a temporary basis. In 1932 the Samuelites (with Snowden) left the government, but the National Liberals under Simon remained. Lloyd George — now converted to a version of Keynesian economics — was isolated in opposition, with a party of four.[27] Power now lay with Baldwin and Chamberlain, who were now firmly committed to protection and imperial preference.

Throughout the 1920s the imperialist lobby had continued to press the case for imperial preference. Yet the conference of Dominion prime ministers which met in London in 1921 produced few positive results. The Dominions were no longer interested in an international division of labour which relegated them to the role of primary producers. They had infant industries of their own to protect. The British government for its part was unwilling to impose taxes on foreign food in order to give preference to Dominion farmers. After the 1931 election Chamberlain, as the new Chancellor, introduced his protectionist measures imposing duties on a wide range of imports. The Import Duties Act of 1932 raised tariffs, leaving only about 25 per cent of imports free of duty. Most of these exempted imports were Empire goods.

At the Ottawa Conference of 1932 another attempt was made to create a Commonwealth free trade area. The outcome was a very limited system of bilateral trade agreements between Britain and the Dominions. Yet neither Canada nor Australia, as the major Dominions, was willing seriously to jeopardize its growing trading connections outside the Empire. The Ottawa Agreement Act of 1932 fell far short of the ideals of Amery, Beaverbrook and the other Tory imperialists. So long as the Dominionists were unwilling to endanger their industrial prospects and Britain remained unwilling to tax its supplies of cheap foreign food, there was no basis of mutual interest on which to found an imperial trade policy.[28] Chamberlain's commitment to protection was a matter of expedience rather than principle. He saw it as the best policy by which Britain could rebuild its economy before returning to free trade. He also recognized the importance of tariffs as a means of raising revenue, which he proceeded to employ, while cutting direct taxes. His budgets were consequently 'truly reactionary. They reversed the trend towards direct taxation which had been going on for nearly a century.'[29]

Taylor goes on to observe that 'Protection was carried by the Conservatives who claimed to believe in free enterprise. It was opposed by Labour, whose programme demanded a planned economy. Now no great principle was at stake. The idea of protection had long been accepted — for the sick, for the aged, for the unemployed. It was a comparatively trivial extension of this principle when ailing industries were protected also.'[30] Under Chamberlain there was a noticeable growth in British trade with the member nations of the Empire, although 'the total of this trade was every year a diminishing proportion of British trade as a whole'.[31] Agriculture was subsidized. Some major reductions were made in the productive capacity of older industries through the application of the quota system, but the radical reform of British industry did not take place.

This extension of the protectionist principle from the social to the economic market was to have anything but trivial implications for Britain, as comparison with Germany indicates. In Germany protection was adopted as a positive policy in order to create a new industrial system. It was a gesture of confidence that helped to make Germany a major industrial power by 1914. In Britain protection followed a loss of political confidence. It expressed a desire to buy time in which to preserve the *status quo* rather than to plan for a radical economic transformation. As for the Empire, the discovery of its potentialities came too late. Cross offers three main reasons for the failure of the ideal of Empire. First, the growth of national consciousness in the white Dominions and latterly in the Indian sub-continent removed the basis of economic reciprocity on which an Empire free trade system might have been built. Secondly, apart from brief jingoistic episodes Britain failed to develop a consistent and coherent imperial policy. Far from exploiting the Empire, Britain acquired much of it by accident and then destroyed its own strategic credibility by involvement in two European wars. Thirdly, after 1945 Britain was to abandon its remaining sense of imperial destiny in the face of the growing power of the new imperialisms of the United States and the USSR.[32]

In retrospect it seems remarkable that commitment to free trade in Britain survived the Great Depression of 1873-96 and the First World War and lasted until the economic collapse of

1931. Hobsbawm gives three main reasons why the doctrine managed for so long to outlive its apparent usefulness. First, the depression of 1873-96 did not last long enough to bring the system into total discredit. (It should also be noted that the volume of British exports was actually increasing again during the early years of Chamberlain's tariff reform campaign.)[33] Secondly, it was 'not until the basic export orientated industries of the late nineteenth century collapsed after the First World War, and the domestically orientated industries became decisively important', that the adoption of protection became a political possibility. Thirdly, free trade was good for city financiers even though it was bad for British industry. The slump of 1931 destroyed the 'single web of world trading and financial transactions whose centre was London and the £ Sterling. . . . Even then it was not Britain that abandoned it. It was the world that abandoned London.'[34]

The end result was the adoption of increasingly mercantilist policies under a Conservative administration throughout the 1930s. Apart from the unemployed the standard of living of the majority of the working population actually improved during this period. It was a period of gradual economic growth and some modest extension in social service provision.[35] Furthermore it was a period free from the depredations of inflation. Poverty amongst a sizeable minority of the population remained, however, a seemingly intractable problem. It was most evident in large families, whether or not the father was employed, amongst the unemployed, and in families which were inadequately insured against the contingencies of sickness, disability, loss of the main earner and the onset of old age. Unemployment, however, was the issue which dominated the debate about economic and social policies throughout the 1930s and which Keynes believed would have to be resolved if capitalism were to survive.

Laissez-faire and free trade were internationalist doctrines based on economic market values and a theory of individual and collective interests which rendered welfare altruism an irrelevant concept. Within this frame of reference there was no significant role for collectivist policies of social welfare. With the demise of free trade the Utopian element disappeared altogether from capitalist thought and practice. Thereafter the internationalist aspects of capitalism became closely associated with imperialist doctrines which seemed to many of the critics of capitalism to be the very antithesis of universal brotherhood.

At the turn of the century, in looking back upon the great debate between free trade and protection, William Cunningham noted with some satisfaction that 'There remained no longer the old enthusiasm for free trade as the harbinger of a Utopia. The old principles of the bourgeoisie had been taken up by the proletariat and shaped to suit themselves. Socialism, like free trade, is cosmopolitan in its aims, and is indifferent to patriotism and hostile to militarism. Socialism, like free trade, insists on material welfare as the primary object to be aimed at in any policy, and like free trade, socialism tests welfare by reference to possibilities of consumption.'[36]

In a perceptive and challenging essay John Knapp argues that the extent to which particular nations held to the older mercantilist policies or adopted those of *laissez-faire* was determined by expediency rather than principle.[37] As Fuchs had argued eighty years earlier, free trade seemed to be the most effective way in which Britain could advance its own interests. The internationalism of the Manchester school was nothing more than an altruistic gloss on policies of national interest. It was the most effective form of imperialism which Britain could follow at the time. Knapp's thesis has much in common with that of Fuchs. Knapp argues that 'Nineteenth-century free trade was an abnormal form of disguised (if perhaps unconscious) mercantilism' and that the most significant feature of 'contemporary economic reality in the advanced western world' is the extent to which a 'reluctant mercantilism' continues to dominate economic policies.[38] He distinguishes between two major paradigms, or frameworks, for economic analysis; these rest on conflicting assumptions about the nature of economic and political motivation and the appropriate role of the state in the regulation of economic behaviour.

The first of these paradigms derives from neo-classical theory, which treats the 'desire for present and future consumption' as the 'dominant economic motive' and advances the thesis that, if economic forces are allowed to work without hindrance from governments, involuntary unemployment will prove to be *'impossible in the long run'*. The second approach is based on ultra-Keynesian theory, which treats the 'desire for survival, independence, power, prestige, distinction' as the dominant economic motive and advances the thesis that the regulation of economic markets by governments is both *'normal and rational'*,[39] as was 'the long and mercantilist period of pre-nineteenth-century capitalist history'. Knapp goes on to argue that 'The effect of the repeal of the Corn Laws was to trigger off a world-wide boom in highly-populated, fertile, overseas areas of migration. The effect for Britain was to bring about, precisely, the realization of the standard objectives of mercantilist policy: maximization — at least for some eighty years — of the scope for profitable domestic investment and for profitable exports.'[40] Knapp may have exaggerated the period of time during which Britain enjoyed the mercantilist benefits of its commitment to free trade. Nonetheless the thesis carries as much conviction with regard to the period between 1840 and the mid-1870s as it did when it was first set out at length by Fuchs in 1890.[41]

In Britain collectivist forms of welfare provision appeared at a relatively late stage of industrialization. These provisions were in part a response to the gradual, if partial, democratization of political life, the dangers of social conflict and a growing uncertainty regarding the capacity of a free economic market to meet essential welfare needs. In the eighteenth century Caribbean slavery had provided some of the primitive accumulation of capital necessary for industrial take-off in Britain. (The same methods, following the same mercantilist principles, were subsequently adopted by Stalin over a century later.) As mercantile capitalism and slave labour were superseded by industrial capitalism and wage labour, the colonies ceased for a time to matter.[42] It became more important to discipline the growing army of wage labourers at home. The new poor law was introduced a year after the abolition of slavery under the British flag. As long as the new system of free trade appeared to be an effective way of enhancing economic welfare, the *laissez-faire* arguments against collectivist welfare intervention carried conviction. The free market was the welfare society.

The other leading industrial nations, the United States, Germany, France and, later, Japan, were acutely aware of the mercantilist realities on which national prosperity depended and they recognized the potential benefits of Empire in a hostile world. There is no doubt that many of the smaller British colonies were economic liabilities, but this was not true of India; its value to the British economy was clearly recognized by free traders, who treated it as an exceptional case. The nascent Indian textile industry was destroyed so that Lancashire might be saved. By the time of the outbreak of the First World War India was probably financing 'more than two-fifths of Britain's total deficits'.[43] It may well be argued that the possession of

India and its exploitation on largely mercantilist lines constituted a fourth reason for the survival of free trade policies long after the acquisition of Empire and the adoption of explicitly imperialist policies by Britain. The First World War accelerated the process of relative industrial decline which the Great Depression and the rise of new competitors had begun, and the Second World War boom brought that process to the edge of disaster.

Keynes and Beveridge

The European nations which began to industrialize late in the nineteenth century did so under the shelter of protectionist economic policies. In the cases of Prussia, France, Russia and Italy, government was far more extensively involved in economic policy than was the case in Britain. Free trade was a distinctively British doctrine, and *laissez-faire* had no great appeal to nations which were belatedly entering into competition with the 'workshop of the world'. It was no accident that Bismarck's Germany became the first welfare state in Europe, since it was natural and logical for a government already involved in economic policy to become, as expediency required, a major agent of social policy. Even in Russia the early stages of industrialization coincided with the introduction of modest schemes of state-sponsored social insurance.

In Britain the belated adoption of Keynesian principles in economic policy signalled the revival of neo-mercantilist doctrines and helped to create a political climate after 1945 which was favourable to the extension of collectivist social policies. As early as 1930 Keynes had begun to re-evaluate the conditions under which protection would be a policy preferable to free trade and to argue in favour of various forms of state intervention, as means by which capital investment could be stimulated at home.

In contrast to the largely iconoclastic relationship which certain types of sociological theory have recently established with the study of social policies, Keynesian economic theory from the start provided the knowledge base which made possible the emergence of modern universalist welfare systems under capitalism. In formulating his *General Theory* Keynes looked back to once discredited mercantilist doctrines and took from that tradition certain insights which had great relevance to the development of social policies.

In the penultimate chapter of *The General Theory* Keynes suggests that the mercantilists were right in attaching so much importance to a monetary theory of interest, and he goes on to argue that protectionist policies designed to secure a favourable balance of trade in one country need not be incompatible with the equally important task of enlarging the volume of international trade and securing the benefits of an international division of labour. He then challenges the classical argument that protection cannot cure unemployment, referring to his own earlier societies, where the state was not directly involved in investment, the scope for home investment was determined by the domestic rate of interest, and the amount of foreign investment by the size of the favourable trade balance. Under these circumstances the balance of trade depended mainly on variations in the inflow or outflow of precious metals which were then the only direct way of increasing home investment. He notes, however, that, if the domestic rate of interest falls so low that investment is raised to the point at which, in turn, a high employment level pushes up wage costs to a level which unduly raises the cost of exports, then the balance of foreign trade will suffer. There is also the risk that the domestic rate of interest can fall so low that foreign lending is over-stimulated and will consequently be followed by an outflow of precious metals. Keynes also reminds us that trade restrictions can provoke counter-measures which will result in a seriously adverse balance of trade. He concludes therefore that 'There are strong presumptions of a general character against trade restrictions unless they can be justified on special grounds.'[44] Keynes recognized nonetheless that a favourable balance of trade helped to maintain employment because it constituted a form of investment.[45]

In place of the traditional mercantilist preoccupation with bullion and the traditional *laissez-faire* preoccupation of the City with 'the technique of bank rate coupled with a rigid parity of foreign exchanges',[46] Keynes proposed the creation of a system of flexible exchanges and international co-operation which would stimulate investment and employment opportunities. He argued that a managed currency 'would permit a greater stability of the domestic price level than could be achieved under the gold standard, combined with short-term stability and long-run flexibility of foreign exchange rates'.[47] As a wartime economic adviser to the government, Keynes played a vitally important role in helping to establish such an exchange system, initially in the creation of an international clearing union and sub-

sequently after that union was brought within the terms of the
Bretton Woods agreement in the setting up of the International
Monetary Fund and the International Bank for Reconstruction
and Development.

Keynes outlines the key tenets of mercantilist thought —
using Heckscher's definitive study of the subject — in order to
demonstrate its *practical* relevance to his own theory.[48] First,
the mercantilist writers were well aware that 'If an excessive
liquidity preference were to withdraw the influx of precious
metals into hoards, the advantage to the rate of interest would
be lost.' Neither did they believe that 'there was a self-adjusting
tendency by which the rate of interest adjusted itself at the
appropriate level'. Secondly, they were equally aware of the
danger that 'excessive competition may turn the terms of trade
against a country'.[49] Thirdly, the mercantilists were perceptive
enough to recognize that the propensity to save is always
stronger than the inducement to invest. Finally, they were
clearly committed to using economic policy as a means to gaining national advantages, even to the point of provoking war. Yet
the *laissez-faire* theorists, Keynes goes on to suggest, whilst
believing that an internationally fixed gold standard was a means
of promoting peace, failed to see that it was just as likely to
provoke conflict between nations. 'In truth', he concludes, 'the
opposite holds good. It is the policy of an autonomous rate of
interest, unimpeded by international preoccupations, and of a
national investment programme directed to an optimum level
of domestic employment which is twice blessed in the sense
that it helps ourselves and our neighbours at the same time.' If
the mercantilists were unable to solve the problem, which they
recognized, the classical economists ignored it to the extent that
they managed both 'to overcome the beliefs of the "natural
man" and, at the same time, to be wrong'.[50]

Keynes ends his chapter on mercantilism by paying tribute to
a doctrine which recognized that far from the rate of interest
being self-adjusting there is a chronic tendency for the rate of
interest to rise too high, unless it is regulated by government.
He reminds us that even Adam Smith was sensitive to the danger that high rates of interest made it more likely that savings
would be absorbed in the payment of debts rather than by
investment.

In the last chapter of *The General Theory* Keynes explores
further the book's practical political implications. He begins
by stating that the 'outstanding faults of the economic society

in which we live are its failure to provide for full employment and its arbitrary and inequitable distribution of wealth and incomes'.[51] He argues that higher direct taxation is conducive to an increase in the propensity to consume and therefore to the creation of more employment opportunities. A greater degree of income equality in this respect makes for greater general prosperity and a growth in real wealth. Next, a lower rate of interest will not be a disincentive to saving, because 'The extent of effective saving is necessarily determined by the scale of investment . . . provided that we do not attempt to stimulate it in this way beyond the point which corresponds to full employment.'[52] The victim of such policies would not be the entrepreneur but the *rentier*. Although Keynes emphasizes throughout *The General Theory* the vital role of entrepreneurship in the creation of wealth, he was equally convinced that private initiative must be complemented by the active involvement of the state in economic policy.

In summary, therefore, his thesis pointed towards three major policy innovations, namely, that 'The State will have to exercise a guiding influence on the propensity to consume, partly through its scheme of taxation, partly by fixing the rate of interest, and partly, perhaps, in other ways.' These 'other ways' included a more generous provision of social services, public investment programmes and co-operative enterprises sponsored jointly by public and private bodies. He did not believe that nationalization was necessary for the realization of these broadly mercantilist ends. He was, however, firmly committed to the view that the survival of capitalism was contingent on a much more positive alliance between the state and private enterprise, even leading to 'necessary measures of socialism', which could be 'introduced gradually and without a break in the general traditions of society'.[53] The precondition of that survival was the end of mass unemployment. Dillard suggests that 'Although it would be misleading to call Keynes a "mercantilist", his position on some important issues is much nearer the mercantilist than the classical position.'[54] As Hansen observes, Keynes's sympathy with mercantilism was of a conditional and pragmatic kind. He was never a protectionist in a narrow beggar-my-neighbour way. Towards the end of his life, as the prospects of closer Anglo-American co-operation seemed likely to become a permanent feature of the post-war world, Keynes became increasingly optimistic about the possibility of a multilateral trading world.[55]

The mercantilist elements in Keynes's thought were drawn from a distinctively British version of that doctrine which goes back as far as the seventeenth century. In writing about English economic policy at that time Wilson suggests that it reflected 'an increasingly effective blend of two elements: the interests of private individuals and groups, and the interest of the State'. It therefore represented 'a middle way between the lack of a central policy to be found in the Dutch Republic . . . and the economic authoritariansim of a state like [Colbertian] France'.[56] Keynes recognized that the enhancement of welfare was contingent partly on a reconciliation of the sovereign interests of the state with those of private entrepreneurs and partly on compromise between the patriotic interests of particular states in the creation of a more stable trading world.

Keynes was neither a free trader nor a protectionist in an unqualified sense, since he did not believe that either policy was necessarily and invariably conducive to high employment. In his view full employment was a precondition of freer trading policies, and trading policy should be dictated by the state of the home economy. There were circumstances under which tariffs were preferable to unemployment, when it became more important to reduce unemployment by protection, even if this resulted in higher unit costs of production. Where full employment prevailed, it would pay to reduce unit costs of production by means of free trade policies.

Keynes categorically rejected totalitarian remedies for the problem of unemployment, whether Marxist or Fascist. He believed that individualism, tempered and restrained by a measure of statutory regulation, could solve the problems of unemployment and inequality without any countervailing loss of efficiency, freedom or international harmony. It was the old system of *laissez-faire* which provoked such ruinously competitive struggles for a share in the diminishing volume of world trade. I have set out at greater length than might be thought necessary some of the practical policy implications which Keynes believed to follow from his thesis because I wish to remind readers of the intellectual debt which social policy owes to his theoretical work. Students who take the trouble to read half as much of Keynes as they are encouraged to read of Marx will quickly find out the extent of that debt. As Keynes himself observed, 'Marxian socialism must always remain a portent to the historians of Opinion — how a doctrine so illogical and so dull can have exercised so powerful and enduring an influence over the minds of men, and through them, the events of history.'[57]

Keynes remained a liberal, but one who rejected *laissez-faire*. Like the earlier mercantilists, he could see no evidence to support the view that a natural harmony existed and guided the free play of economic forces. Some measures of social control were necessary if capitalism was to survive. He recognized that many features of capitalism were unlovable — in particular the practices of *rentier* as distinct from entrepreneurial capitalism — but he was equally convinced that it was preferable to any other economic system. Like Beveridge he included the idea of freedom in his idea of welfare.

If Keynesian economics made possible the creation of a welfare state under capitalism, the Beveridge Report provided the form and substance of its social policies. According to Harris, Beveridge's own intellectual odyssey from a free market position to a commitment to social planning owed little or nothing to the influence of Keynes. In the early 1930s, when Keynes was announcing his conversion to a modified version of protectionism and recommending the imposition of tariffs on imports and bounties on exports, Beveridge was urging a revival of free trade policies.[58] He advanced the traditional free trade argument that food tariffs were a regressive tax on the poor. He sought the remedy for unemployment in a greater degree of wage flexibility, which in practice meant wage cuts, and he criticized the extension of uncovenanted unemployment benefits, on the grounds that such a policy encouraged trade unions to resist such cuts. In contrast, although Keynes did not favour increases in wages, he was strongly opposed to wage cuts and favoured more generous social service provisions as the best means of supplementing low wages.

Harris tells us that Beveridge was highly critical of Keynes's *General Theory* with regard to both its method of enquiry and its conclusions. He disliked its high degree of abstraction and argued that 'if wages were raised and interest rates lowered as Keynes proposed . . . then saving would cease and the price of labour would henceforth be totally independent of labour demand.'[59]

Nonetheless by the mid-1930s Beveridge was beginning to favour some degree of collective planning. He was converted to the case for family allowances, partly because, like Keynes, he recognized that subsidies of this kind might help to keep down wage demands.[60] His conversion to the Keynesian approach to the problem of unemployment did not occur until after the publication of his own report.[61] Harris suggests that the Webbs and G. D. H. Cole might have been instrumental in bringing about this change of mind. The extent of Beveridge's conversion to collectivist social planning is shown clearly in *Full Employment in a Free Society*,[62] in which he argues in favour of adjusting the level of production to the total supply of labour, increasing the powers of state to regulate the movement of industry and labour and relying more extensively on budgetary controls.

There is, however, one dramatic contrast to be drawn between the respective public roles of Keynes and Beveridge in the critical years between 1944 and 1950. This was a period during which Keynes, until his death in 1946, was involved in the making of policy, first as an adviser to the wartime Coalition government and subsequently to the post-war Labour administration. In contrast Beveridge was adopted as a Liberal candidate and served for a few months as the Member of Parliament for Berwick before being defeated in the general election of 1945. It can be argued that there was a logical connection between his own recovery of collectivist convictions and their revival in one section of the Liberal Party at that time. Alternatively one may speculate — as many British voters must have done — about how much of Liberal thought remains in those who are so committed to collectivism that they no longer believe in free trade. As Colin Clark tartly observed, 'The Liberal Party, or what was left of it, also changed its mind on this subject — at any rate an important group in the Party did so. Lord Beveridge once explained to me that he regarded Free Trade as an essentially anti-liberal idea.'[63]

Keynes also remained a Liberal, but he was never a candidate for parliamentary office for the Liberal or any other party. Instead he continued working for the Attlee administration as an economic adviser, just as he had worked for the wartime coalition. In his last years he achieved, with Hugh Dalton as Chancellor, a working relationship and understanding that Beveridge never seems to have arrived at with any of his political masters. Dalton paid him a particularly touching tribute in his memoirs. Commenting on the death of Keynes in 1946, Dalton writes, 'He had supreme talent and many-sided genius. . . . Would that through 1946 and 1947 he had still advised me on the balance of payments, the sterling balances, still cheaper money and much else!'[64]

Taken together, we can see that Keynes and Beveridge contributed the major frameworks of theory and policy prescriptions on which the post-war British welfare state was built. And
each of these great men in the course of his intellectual development encompassed and resolved to his own satisfaction the
great issues of debate, choice and compromise between individualism and collectivism, between free trade and protection,
between classical economic theory and mercantilism. The outcome of their thought and of the adoption of so many of their
policy prescriptions was a diminution in the autonomy of the
free market and a significant increase in the regulatory powers
of the state in the sphere of social and economic policy. This
outcome can in no way be described as a crude reassertion of
the old mercantilist doctrines, but its rationale can best be
understood by reference to that tradition of economic and political thought.

Although the contributions of Keynes and Beveridge exercised a profound influence on the three largest political parties
their own loyalties lay with the Liberal Party, which had been
in decline throughout the inter-war years. Their respective associations with the Liberal Party, however, followed markedly
different courses. Keynes was very active as an adviser to the
Liberal Party until 1931, after which his direct and effective
association ceased. Beveridge did some work for the Party in
the early 1920s, but, according to Harris, he took great care to
maintain a neutral advisory role. He did not join the Liberals
until 1944. Throughout this period some Liberals served in the
succession of National and War cabinets, but without Lloyd
George their influence on the development of social policy was
minimal and undistinguished.

The achievements of the Conservatives in social reform during
the 1930s were modest ones, but they added something to the
foundations of the welfare state laid by the Liberals in the twi-
light of the free trade era. It is questionable whether a free trade
Liberal government during the 1930s could have functioned at
all as an effective instrument of social reform. We know from
the record that the Labour government could not do so. Commitment to free trade was an electoral liability which the
Liberal Party could never hope to shake off without ceasing to
be a Liberal Party. The tenacity with which the Labour Party
held to the same doctrine can hardly be explained in terms of
its compatibility with socialism. It is better understood by reference to the historical association of free trade with cheap food

and clothing.

The growth in influence of Keynesian economic thought between 1936 and 1945 provided a new framework for economic policy within which successive post-war Labour and Conservative governments were able to develop programmes of collectivist social reform which were neither distinctively socialist nor distinctively capitalist. In social policy we began a new period of mercantile collectivism in which there was no place for a reforming Liberal Party, because there was no place for free trade. Keynes was influential and active as a government adviser until his death in 1946. Beveridge's brief term as a member of Parliament ended in 1945, and, though he lived for another eighteen years, he never again recovered a position of direct political influence.

References

[1] See Robert Blake, *The Conservative Party from Peel to Churchill*, Eyre and Spottiswoode, 1970, pp. 130 and 270; and A. P. Thornton, *The Imperial Ideal and its Enemies*, Macmillan, London, 1963, p. 21.

[2] Charles Wentworth Dilke, *Greater Britain: A Record of Travel in the English-Speaking Countries during 1866 and 1867*, Vols I and II, Macmillan, 1868, Vol. II, p. 156. See Vol. II, Ch. VI, for a summary of Dilke's views on protection and free trade.

[3] A. M. McBriar, *Fabian Socialism and English Politics, 1884-1918*, Cambridge University Press, 1962, pp. 119-45; and B. Semmell, *Imperialism and Social Reform*, Allen & Unwin, London, 1960, p. 73.

[4] See Benjamin Kidd, *Social Evolution*, Macmillan, London 1894; and Karl Pearson, *National Life from the Standpoint of Science*, A. & C. Black, London, 1905.

[5] See D. Wiltshire, *The Social and Political Thought of Herbert Spencer*, Oxford University Press, Oxford, 1978, p221.

[6] Kidd, *Social Evolution*, p. 227.

[7] ibid., p. 233.

[8] Karl Pearson, *The Ethic of Free Thought*, T. Fisher Unwin, London, MDCCCLXXXVIII, p. 306.

[9] Benjamin Kidd, *The Science of Power*, Methuen, London, 1919, pp. 81-2.

[10] See General Friedrich von Bernhardi, *Germany and the Next War*, Edward Arnold, London, 1914.

[11] Karl Pearson, *Socialism and Natural Science*, p. 111.

[12] Robert Blatchford, *My Eighty Years*, Cassell, London, 1931, p. 199.

[13] *The Clarion*, 28 October 1889, p. 37, quoted in Semmell, op. cit., p. 225.

[14] Quoted in Lawrence Thompson, *Robert Blatchford: Portrait of an Englishman*, Victor Gollancz, London, 1951, pp. 112-13.

[15] Robert Roberts, *The Classic Slum: Salford Life in the First Quarter of the Century*, Manchester University Press, 1971, p. 69.

[16] T. O. Lloyd, *Empire to Welfare State: English History 1906-1967*,

Oxford University Press, London, 1970, pp. 5-6.

[17] ibid., p. 37.

[18] Sean Glynn and John Oxborrow, *Interwar Britain: A Social and Economic History*, Allen & Unwin, London, 1976, p. 136.

[19] Lloyd, op. cit., p. 131.

[20] loc. cit.

[21] A. J. P. Taylor, *English History 1914-1945*, Penguin, Harmondsworth, 1975, p. 287.

[22] loc. cit.

[23] David Marquand, *Ramsay Macdonald*, Jonathan Cape, London, 1977, p. 556.

[24] ibid., p. 555.

[25] loc. cit.

[26] loc. cit.

[27] Lloyd, op. cit., pp. 177-8.

[28] Colin Cross, *The Fall of the British Empire, 1918-1968*, Paladin, London, 1970, p. 194.

[29] Taylor, op. cit., p. 412.

[30] ibid., p. 411.

[31] ibid., p. 421.

[32] Cross, op. cit., p. 367.

[33] Semmell, op. cit., p. 86.

[34] Hobsbawn, *Industry and Empire*, pp. 206-7.

[35] See Glynn and Oxborrow, op. cit., pp. 33-51, for a review of general trends in economic growth and living standards; and Bentley B. Gilbert, *British Social Policy 1914-1939*, Batsford, London, 1970, for an analysis of social policies.

[36] William Cunningham, article on free trade in *Encyclopaedia Britannica*, eleventh edition, 1910-11.

[37] J. Knapp, 'Economics or Political Economy', *Lloyds Bank Review*, 107, 1973, pp. 19-43.

[38] ibid., p. 19.

[39] ibid., pp. 36-7.

[40] ibid., p. 39.

[41] Fuchs, op. cit.

[42] Lichtheim, op. cit., pp. 49 et seq. and p. 62.

[43] Quoted in Hobsbawm, *Industry and Empire*, p. 123, and footnotes 37i-xxi.

[44] John Maynard Keynes, *The General Theory of Employment, Interest and Money*, Macmillan, London, 1960, p. 338.

[45] Dudley Dillard, *The Economics of John Maynard Keynes*, Crosby Lockwood & Son, London, 1963, p. 281.

[46] Keynes, *The General Theory of Employment, Interest and Money*, p. 339.

[47] Dillard, op. cit., p. 285.

[48] E. Heckscher, *Mercantilism*, Allen & Unwin, London, 1955.

[49] Keynes, *The General Theory of Employment, Interest and Money*, pp. 341-5.

[50] ibid., pp. 349-50.

[51] ibid., p. 372.

[52] ibid., p. 375.

[53] ibid., p. 378.

[54] Dillard, op. cit., p. 280.

[55] Alvin H. Hansen, *A Guide to Keynes*, McGraw-Hill, New York, 1953, pp. 226-7.

[56] Charles Wilson, *England's Apprenticeship*, p. 57.

[57] John Maynard Keynes, *Laissez-Faire and Communism*, New Republic, New York, 1926, pp. 47-8, and quoted in Dillard, op. cit., p. 322.

[58] Harris, op. cit., pp. 317 et seq.

[59] ibid., p. 331.

[60] Beveridge Report, p. 342.

[61] Harris, op. cit., p. 429.

[62] W. H. Beveridge, *Full Employment in a Free Society: A Report*, Allen & Unwin, London, 1944.

[63] Colin Clark, 'What's Wrong with Economics', *Encounter*, 55, 1958, p. 22.

[64] Hugh Dalton, op. cit., p. 108.

8 Social Change and Social Policy in Russia before the Bolshevik Revolution

Introduction

The development of social and economic policies in Russia before the Bolshevik revolution offers an interesting context for examining the relationships between social change and social welfare. It also enhances our understanding of what happened after 1917, since most students of social welfare could be forgiven for assuming that there was no social policy — in any of the various accepted meanings of that term — before the Bolshevik revolution.

The vast land mass of Russia in Europe can be divided between the arctic tundra regions of the far north, an immense central region of forest, mixed forest and wooded steppe, and the southern steppeland which was known as the black earth region. The Russian climate imposes stringent limits on the productivity of even an efficient agricultural economy. In the mid-northern and central regions the length of the winter is such that all the field work must be completed within a period of from four to six months. The rainfall is most adequate in the north-western parts, where the soil is poorest. A large proportion of the peasantry supported themselves through a mixed economy of subsistence farming, cottage industries and the exploitation of wildlife.

Only in the southern black earth regions were the soil and climate so good as to encourage individual rather than collective modes of farming, since the longer periods of spring and autumn made it unnecessary to rely on large, readily available family teams. Much of this land was occupied by foreign invaders until the eighteenth century, and one result of the process of conquest by which these regions were recovered was that they passed largely into the hands of the state, the church, the nobility and other large-scale landlords.

The history of Russia in the eighteenth and nineteenth centuries is, among other things, a history of colonization. Inefficient modes of farming led to frequent exhaustion of land and the compulsory or voluntary migration of peasants to the south and

to the east into Siberia. Throughout this period there was at first
a steady increase in population, and in the last decades before
the revolution this growth reached dramatic proportions. In
1750 Russia had a population of roughly 18 million and by
1850 it had risen to 68 million, including about 10 million new
subject peoples. The census of 1897, however, recorded a population of 124 million, and by the time of the outbreak of the
First World War it had risen to no less than 170 million.

The economic dilemma of Russia is briefly summarized by
Richard Pipes, when he observes that 'Russia's rate of population growth during the second half of the nineteenth century
was the highest in Europe — and this at the very time when its
grain yields were Europe's lowest.'[1] The problem of feeding
such a large population was compounded, first, by the fact that
85 per cent of the population were still peasants and, secondly,
by a government policy of encouraging the export of grain in
order to earn foreign currency for belated industrial investment.
Thirdly, the reserve of virgin land in the best central and southern provinces had been taken into cultivation by the 1880s.
Fourthly, the beginnings of industrialization were sufficient to
destroy the cottage industries on which so many peasants sub-
sisted at a time when their rents were rising sharply, but were
insufficient to provide alternative forms of employment.

Political and legal institutions

The Russian state was and remained until 1917 an autocracy.
The Tsar appointed all ministers, and there was no cabinet
system or even a prime minister in any constitutional sense.
There was a 'Committee of Ministers', with a president who
possessed only nominal powers. In practice each minister
dealt directly with the Tsar. Unless the Tsar was endowed with
prodigious energy and conviction, each ministry formulated its
own policy with little regard for matters such as over-all policy
co-ordination. A Council of State prepared, examined and recommended legislation to the Tsar. The Tsar also had a 'Personal
Chancellory', divided into three sections — a private secretariat,
a legal section and the political police, the latter exercising immense power. The Orthodox church was an agency of the state
controlled by the Holy Synod, whose senior official, the Procu-
rator, was appointed by the Tsar.

Prior to 1905 the powers of the Tsar were described as 'autocratic and unlimited'. In that year some nominal limitations on
his authority were inserted into the fundamental laws, which

were revised between 17 and 30 October and the opening of the first Duma in April 1906. These fundamental laws placed some technical limitations on the Tsar's power. In theory the Tsar governed in concert with a reconstituted Council of State, which served as a legislative upper house, and the Imperial Duma, which functioned as a legislative lower house. In practice the Tsar retained almost complete power, in a form described euphemistically as 'a limited monarchy under an autocratic emperor'. As Pipes remarks, 'The patrimonial monarchy best defines this type of regime', in which 'the rights of sovereignty and ownership' were virtually indistinguishable. The country was organized on the lines of a 'giant royal estate'.[2]

With regard to the nature of the tsarist political system further insight can be gained by even a brief survey of its legal institutions. The Code of Laws established under the Speransky reforms of 1826-32 was concerned mainly with political offences. The laws of 1832 made any attempt to change the existing political order — as well as any failure to report such activities — punishable by death or exile (cf. Soviet RSFSR Code of 1927). The Third Section of the Imperial Chancellory which was established in 1826 was responsible for both the necessary political surveillance *and* the protection of widows and orphans. (The Third Section was replaced in 1880 by a central political police.)

Throughout the 1850s and 1860s there was a sustained campaign on the part of liberal reformers for the introduction of open court proceedings, due process and trial by jury. These objectives were secured through the judiciary reforms of 1864. Until that date there had been no legal profession recognized as such in Russia, and the state had not initiated legal proceedings, except when political offences were concerned; neither was there any separation of powers between a judiciary and the other branches of state administration. Criminal and civil trials were started on the initiative of the injured party.

The power of the sovereign after 1864 remained such that in practice it remained impossible to draw a distinction between imperial decrees, laws and administrative rulings — or between constitutional, criminal and civil aspects of law. Furthermore the traditional practice of passing laws on a confidential basis continued after 1864, so that the central bureaucracy went on adding to its already impressive range of powers.[3] After the assassination of Alexander II in 1881 a series of new decrees vested immense authority in a new corps of State Governors, who could dismiss any elected councillor or appointed official on the grounds that he was 'untrustworthy'. Almost every aspect of professional and commercial life was subject to regulation by the political police, whose responsibility it was to issue certificates of trustworthiness to members of the general public. All social policy initiatives and the practice of voluntary social work were so regulated. For example it was necessary to have police approval in order to become a fund raiser, or a visitor of the sick or a school governor.[4]

Internal migration was also regulated, by a system of passports which was vigorously defended by the Tsar's senior adviser, Pobedonostev, on the grounds that passports served as 'a graphic and visible certificate of personality'.[5] In the last year of the tsarist regime the police authorities entered the field of trade union activities, sponsoring their own movement, which undertook a variety of friendly society and mutual aid activities. Although the political police were ubiquitous they were not always efficient or consistent in their practices. It may be noted for example that Lenin's mother continued to draw until her (natural) death her government civil service pension after one of her sons had been executed and another two sent to prison.

Social stratification

A distinctive feature of the system of social stratification in Russia down to the revolution was the small size and political ineffectiveness of the middle class. For the greater part of the nineteenth century Russia remained a country without effective commercial institutions. The lack of an adequate monetary or legal system also greatly inhibited the development of a native capitalist class. The last census before the emancipation took place in 1859. Of the total population of 60 million the landed nobility and gentry accounted for about 1 million. There were another 11 million burghers, independent Cossacks, tradesmen, factory workers and professional people. The remaining 48 million were made up of 25½ million state peasants who were bound to the land but were not serfs and 22½ million proprietary peasants who were individually bound to the land and to private landlords.[6] A key distinction between state and proprietary peasants was that the former paid a higher tax but did not pay rent or perform labour duties. Some proprietary peasants paid rent and some gave their labour on an individual or corvée basis to their landlords. During the 1840s an increasing number of serfs were allowed to move to the towns, where they set up as petty traders or hired workers. Some of these formed *artels* or labour associations for the purposes of mutual aid and the collective payment of taxes. The peasantry were the first occupational group to experience the effects of radical social change when their legal status was transformed by the Emancipation Act of 1861. The traditional peasant family was a joint family of several related households, and the normal rural community was made up of between fifty and sixty people.

In the case of Russia we must chart a process of social change in which the traditional forms of self-help and mutual aid, based on local village communities, were eventually transformed into agencies through which modernization was imposed on a recalcitrant and conservative peasantry. In pre-revolutionary Russia the village commune, or *mir*, as a social institution, dominated the daily lives of the peasantry, who in 1859 accounted for 80 per cent of the total population.[7] Amongst the peasantry it was a generally accepted belief that although the nobles controlled the land they held it only in trust from the Tsar, who was himself accountable to God for the welfare of all the Russian people. This popular belief had no basis in law but it derived from a time when the nobility held their land in feudal tenures. The feudal distinction which Russian peasants were apt to make between ownership of persons and ownership of property was aptly expressed in their traditional saying, 'We are yours, but the land is ours.'[8] The peasant defined his welfare in terms of his relationship to the land, which he enjoyed and shared collectively. A tendency to conceive of welfare as a collective enterprise had always been an important feature of Russian culture and it was to remain so until and after the Bolshevik revolution. Although this disposition was common to both rulers and ruled, there was never agreement as to the form which the collective enterprise ought to take or the economic and social ends which it should serve.

Family and commune

The mir consisted of all the peasant householders of a village. They formed a village assembly which elected a village elder who was also a tax collector. Since the majority of peasants were serfs, the mir functioned under the patrimonial jurisdiction of the local land-owning noble. Nonetheless the final allocation of lands assigned by the noble was carried out by the village assembly. This periodic allocation of strips of land, and of various collective tasks, was the first major function of the mir. Decisions, once taken, were accepted as binding by all villagers. As Wallace observed, 'The peasants are accustomed to work together in this way, to make concessions for the communal welfare, to bend unreservedly to the will of the mir.'[9]

The purpose of periodic land reallocation was to ensure as far as possible that family land holdings would take some account of variations in the size and composition of individual households over time. In this respect the mir functioned as a kind of 'primitive labour association'.[10] The mir, however, also served as a collective unit for purposes of taxation. This shared responsibility for taxation in which the entire commune was collectively responsible for each of its individual members was not abolished until October 1906. Thus the possession of land was inseparably connected with the payment of taxes. Those who paid taxes were entitled to a share in the land.[11] In an administratively and economically backward society like Russia the mir was a relatively simple and effective unit of taxation.

The amount of tax levied, however, took little account of the quality of the land. The total sum required of a mir unit was based on the number of its male peasants, or 'revision souls'. There were periodic censuses to revise the number of such names, but adequate allowances were not always made for the births and deaths which occurred between revisions. As the censuses were taken infrequently and irregularly, the system of taxation could work either to the advantage or to the disadvantage of a mir, depending on the vagaries of population change in the periods of time elapsing between censuses.

This system of communal land holding in which strips were periodically re-partitioned and taxation was based on land tenure discouraged innovation in agriculture and inhibited the movement of population. Since the mir was bound to pay a collective tax, based on the assumption of a stable population, its members discouraged and frequently prevented emigration. Any individual who wished to migrate had first to obtain an internal passport, and this would not be granted without the consent of his village assembly, his local proprietor and the police. In the event of a peasant being allowed to leave his village he remained legally responsible for payment of his share of taxes. Failure to pay could result in the loss of his internal passport and a summary return to his village. Thus the continuity of the mir was based in part on a system of control similar in some respects to the Acts of Settlement. The key differences were that the Russian peasant was sanctioned not if he applied for relief but if he failed to pay his taxes, and that this action could be initiated not only by an alien official or persons of superior social status but also by his fellow villagers.

The serf therefore lived under a variety of restrictions upon his personal liberty but he could not be sold except in so far as the land to which he was tenured could be bought and sold. Before emancipation a master was empowered to intervene in the affairs of the commune, and there is evidence that this often occurred. The serf was also subject to the collective will of the mir although he shared in the exercise of that will on equal terms with other members of the village community.

In return for this degree of subjection the serf could enjoy, on a humanely and efficiently run estate, a measure of economic security, albeit at a very low level of subsistence. Although his own obligations to the master might be ill-defined, a serf might equally benefit by taking advantage of similarly vague but customary privileges such as the grazing of his cattle and the gathering of fuel on the master's domain. In times of famine, epidemic or other forms of adversity a good master would provide succour to his serfs.[12] Similarly the serf could turn to his own villagers for aid during the normal adversities of illness, accident and old age. The mir expressed a way of life in which economic efficiency — and merit — were alien concepts. Dependency amongst one's fellow equals could not be degrading, since the very fabric of daily life was woven on a frame of mutual interdependence.

It is necessary to draw a distinction between the Russian *dvor*, or joint family system, and the *mir*, or commune. The legal status of the joint family was never made clear, and not until the reform of 1906 was it possible to 'define the position of the members of the joint family in their relations to the house elder and to family property'.[13] It was customary procedure, however, to vest the right to hold land in the peasant household (*dvor*) and not the individual. Whilst the mir was a popular institution giving common if customary rights to grazing land and mutual aid in adversity, there is much evidence to show that the joint family system was widely resented. The 1861 Emancipation Act intensified such resentments insofar as it preserved the principle of collective ownership and vested collective ownership of the allotment land in the house elder, as the head of the peasant family, whilst weakening at the same time traditional forms of mutual aid based on the commune.[14]

Russian peasants had a long tradition of surviving by cunning

and superficial servility. A large number would willingly have
left the land but lacked the means to do so. There is little evidence that the peasantry shared that collective spirit which was
so much esteemed by reactionaries and revolutionaries alike. In
the main they showed an equal indifference to the romantic
adulation of the Slavophil nationalists and the calls to class
warfare of the radical agitators. Tolstoy showed prescience
when he wrote in 1865 that 'The Russian revolution will be
directed not against the Tsar and despotism, but against the
ownership of land.'[15] And the peasant, equating land with
welfare, sought property not in order to share it collectively
but in order to possess it individually. We can only speculate
upon the extent to which the peasantry were committed to
collectivism as a way of life. Nonetheless there is evidence that,
as the older system disintegrated under the processes of social
and economic change, a new class of kulak peasants began to
emerge. Many of the socialist revolutionaries 'learned to their
dismay that the peasant saw nothing wrong with exploitation
as such; he merely wanted to be the exploiter instead of the
object of speculation!'[16]

Viewed from the perspective of the government, however,
the village commune was the major instrument through which
social control was exercised. In a geographically vast and administratively undeveloped nation the commune was the means
by which taxes and dues were levied, the movement of labour
controlled and some sense of national unity preserved. It was
only the belated realization that the national greatness and
sovereignty of Russia could not survive without economic
development which compelled the regime to accept the need
for a series of economic reforms, reforms which began with
the emancipation.

If the village mir provided the institutional framework for
control from above it also expressed a complex network of
exchange relationships between equals, so far as its members
were concerned. It would, however, be difficult to describe
these relationships as exchanges between 'givers' and 'receivers'.
The peasants performed a variety of services for their proprietors
and paid their taxes to the government. They did so with a large
measure of resentment and an even greater sense of injustice. In
theory at least they received protection and securities of various
kinds. It is doubtful whether they were motivated by a desire
to achieve a state of equivalency in these relationships. From
what little we know of peasant attitudes and expectations, they

would gladly have withdrawn from all these associations with outside agencies — apart from commercial transactions. Most commentators note the long-enduring and popular peasant belief that when the Tsar finally learned of their suffering and poverty he would recover the land from the nobles and give it back to his own loyal servants.[17] The peasants lived in a circumscribed world, where the notion of altruism stopped short within the limits of personal acquaintance, kinship and common ownership of land. Governments levied taxes and conscripted their young men, the proprietors extracted their customary dues, and the distinction between members and strangers endured on the basis of geographical isolation, immemorial custom and, more often than not, bitter experience.

Reformers and revolutionaries

The mir represented a compromise between individualism and collectivism and had long been a focus of both conservative and radical interest.[18] During the 1840s Slavophil writers such as Khomyakov and Samarin romanticized Russian village life, describing it as a model for the future regeneration of their country. It is difficult to summarize the basic tenets of the Slavophil movement. Most of its writers shared a common hostility towards Western forms of rationalist thought and were deeply committed to the Eastern Orthodox religion. Ivan Kireevski, a founding member of the movement, traced the distinctive qualities of Russian society from the mir and its attachment to Orthodoxy. On the basis of these institutions, Russia, he believed, was potentially the most democratic of societies, and its salvation lay in the abolition of serfdom and the preservation of a unique national culture based on a regenerated form of communal life. Samarin wrote of the commune as 'a noble phenomenon of harmoniousness, a joint existence of rational beings'.[19] Like Samarin the other Slavophil writers emphasized the moral rather than the material components of social welfare. They argued, in almost Durkheimian terms, that the central issues of social life were moral rather than economic and political in nature.

In their intense patriotism the Slavophil writers of the 1840s argued that the village commune was a form of social organization morally superior to any Western institution. They contrasted its collectivism and mutual aid with the ruthless competitiveness of capitalism. Many of the early Russian populists and socialists shared the belief of the Slavophils that capitalism could be avoided and poverty alleviated in Russia by a strengthening of the commune as a social institution.[20]

Populist doctrines enjoyed the period of their greatest influence in the 1860s and 1870s. Their central political objectives were 'social justice and social equality', which they considered to exist 'in essence' in the peasant commune.[21] Populist theory derived its intellectual traditions from the socialism of Saint-Simon, Fourier and Proudhon. Despite the tendency of many populist writers to romanticize the Russian peasants, some of them were clear-headed enough to understand that the peasantry wanted 'to be fed and clothed, to be given physical security, to be rescued from disease, ignorance, poverty and humiliating inequalities. As for political rights, votes, parliaments . . . such programmes merely mocked their misery.'[22]

The clearest and most convincing exposition of populist doctrine is to be found in the work of Chernyshevsky. His pragmatic approach to the social problems of the time and his regard for evidence endow him with some of the qualities of an early English Fabian. Chernyshevsky wished to preserve the rural commune and also to apply it in modified forms to industrial life. He was, however, unequivocally hostile to capitalism as a mode of production and argued, like the Slavophils, that the only way in which capitalism could be bypassed in Russia was through a strengthening of the commune as a combination of individual and collective property holdings.[23] Chernyshevsky recognized that social amelioration and especially the relief of poverty ought to precede rather than follow radical political change. He favoured reform by persuasion and a willingness to meet from the start the peasants' desire for land, 'food, shelter and boots'. Unless their voluntary co-operation could be secured, Chernyshevsky predicted, the course of social change would end in both the destruction of the commune and the appearance of new forms of centralized tyranny.[24] He rejected the more extreme revolutionary doctrines, which so often entailed the sacrifice of immediate welfare interests to long-term collective goals. The strength of the commune lay in its capacity to reconcile the claims of individual and collective welfare interests. The primary requisite, however, was a spirit of co-operation, since 'without good will and voluntary agreement, nothing useful can really be done for the good of man'.[25]

Other populists such as Belinsky shared this hostility towards capitalism. Like Herzen and the other early Russian socialists they believed that 'social justice and social equality' already existed 'in

essence' amongst the peasantry.[26] Emancipation and the necessary overthrow of the tsarist tyranny would enable the peasant
to realize his truly democratic and altruistic nature.

Sustained by this upsurge of libertarian idealism, many of these
intellectuals, the 'repentant gentry', sought out the peasants in
the countryside in order to persuade and educate them. They
were met by 'indifference, suspicion, resentment, and sometimes
active hatred and resistance'.[27] The populists were among the
first to learn that 'It was the imported radicalism and the group
interest of the intellectuals that clashed with the spirit of the nation and not the Tsarist monarchy, which on the contrary had a
strong hold upon the vast majority of all classes.'[28] Berlin refers
to Kravchinsky's experiences of peasant apathy which he recounts in a letter to Vera Zasulich, describing how 'Socialism
bounced off people like peas off a wall.'[29]

A major consequence of this rebuff in the years following
emancipation was the decline of populism as an intellectual
force with any semblance of popular following. The leading
theorists and activists abandoned their hopes for a revolutionary
movement based on democratic support. The democratic and
decentralizing tradition survived, but the nihilists were typical
of a new kind of revolutionary, committed to terrorism and
'characterized by an embittered elitism which stressed the right
of a superior individual to act independently for the welfare of
humanity'.[30] In an illuminating essay, 'The World of Raskolnikov', Frank describes Dostoyevsky's *Crime and Punishment*
as an epilogue to the decline of populism. Raskolnikov's crime
was 'planned on the basis of a Utilitarian calculus' and posed
for Russia's radical intelligentsia a choice between 'a doctrine
of love and a doctrine of power'. With a characteristic pithi-
ness that might have done credit to Beatrice Webb, the Nihilist,
Pisarev, suggested that Raskolnikov's peculiar mental state and
violent conduct might have been attributable to malnutrition.[31]

The abolition of serfdom

Nearly all the major reformist and revolutionary movements,
despite their many doctrinal differences, agreed that the mir, as
a unit of communal organization, must be preserved. Paradoxically they shared this view with some of the more conservative and tsarist officials, who considered the mir to be a natural
and inoffensive form of local democracy, ideally suited to the
needs of peasant folk. For some time it had seemed that the
emancipation of the serfs and the preservation of the mir were

incompatible objectives. The mir was seen by radicals and conservatives alike as a bulwark against capitalism. There was,
however, another feature of Western Europe which haunted the
consciousness of the more conservative Slavophils and of many
proprietors, officials and nobles. This was the fear that the
creation of a free economic market in Russia would
generate an abnormal degree of competitive individualism in
social life and bring about the emergence of a landless proletariat. A general emancipation of the serfs which destroyed or
weakened the mir would inevitably create a problem of pauperism on an unimaginable scale. In the event it was this view
which prevailed when emancipation became a reality. The mir,
it was argued, had to be preserved because it was the only
available and acceptable social institution which could provide
even a rudimentary framework of social welfare and security
for the peasant.

The first clear statement of the Tsar's intention to examine
the problem of serfdom came with the publication of the terms
of the Peace of Paris of 1856, which ended the Crimean War.
The issue of emancipation had been a subject of intense and
often clandestine debate in Russia for a very long period. When
the Act of Emancipation was eventually signed on 19 February
1861 its provisions reflected the many devious compromises
which had been reached after years of negotiation. The Act
liberated all the serfs (apart from those owned by the state and
the imperial family, who were freed under a later statute) and
replaced the authority of the proprietor by a new form of
communal self-government based on the old institution of the
mir. The land to be allotted was vested in the mir, which was
now to enjoy a very high degree of local autonomy. The mir
also became the agency through which yearly dues were paid
to the proprietor in money or labour. The government undertook to provide loans for those who wished to buy or redeem
their lands. The two major criticisms of the Act were that in
general the cost of these redemptions was too high, while the
average size of the allotment was too small to ensure subsistence
and payment of the redemption dues.

Emancipation and land reform also came to serve a more
general economic purpose. 'It became quite clear,' observes
Gerschenkrov, 'by the end of the century that Russia could
only pay for the required volume of foreign investment by increasing its volume of agricultural exports. The peasant was to
bear the burden by increasing production and paying more

taxes.'[32] Emancipation would provide new economic incentives to improve his lot.

But the peasant had also lost in more immediate and profound ways. In place of traditional exchange relationships based on often ill-defined customs and usages the peasant was now required to pay for all the supplementary amenities, such as the use of implements, access to grazing and fuel gathering from the proprietor's land, which once he had been able to take for granted. The freed peasant was now becoming involved in a market economy and a new set of relationships based on a monetary nexus. As Wallace noted during his provincial travels, 'Nothing is now to be had for *gratis*. The demand to pay is encountered at every step.'[33] Perhaps the bitterest resentment was felt concerning the obligation to pay redemption dues for land which, according to the peasants' traditional beliefs, had always been in their possession.

Emancipation, as it began to undermine the traditional frameworks of mutual aid, also failed to prevent the emergence of pauperism. The gradual decline in living standards in many parts of the countryside was complemented by an increasing demand for labour in the growing industrial areas. Yet the communal ties survived for a time, as did the obligation of individuals to pay their part of the collective taxes. While the mir remained, it was impossible to raise the level of agricultural efficiency, and the consequent poverty served as a further incentive to migration — an incentive always curtailed in some degree by communal loyalties and obligations as well as legal restrictions. Men began to work in local towns on temporary contracts, returning to their families only for seasonal contingencies such as sowing and harvesting and in times of social distress. In this way 'a class of hybrid — half peasants, half artisans — was created and the formation of a town proletariat was greatly retarded.'[34]

Both the reform of agriculture and the division of labour and specialization necessary for efficient industrial production were delayed by the survival of the mir. The attempt to the tsarist government to resolve the long-standing anomaly of serfdom can easily be criticized as an ineffective compromise between the claims of modernity and those of tradition. An alternative view would be that as a measure of social reform the joint objective of emancipation and the preservation of the mir required a quality of vision and a degree of administrative skill which were simply beyond the competence of an inefficient and corrupt bureaucracy. The legislative intention was, however, more progressive in its design than many critics have been willing to concede. Its realization would almost certainly have defeated the wit and will of any other European government at the time. The other missing component was a genuinely free market in labour of the kind that accelerated the industrialization of Western Europe.

The way in which the issues of emancipation and the future of the village commune were resolved had a vitally important bearing on the welfare of the Russian peasant. The village commune was the only source of mutual aid to which the peasant could turn in adversity. Comparative analysis forces us to abandon or modify what have in many cases become our own traditional and sometimes narrowly drawn definitions of what constitutes a social service or a state of social welfare. The ideal of preserving the village commune in tsarist Russia was not to be realized, but the notion of community based on mutual aid and co-operation has survived as a major theme in the debate about social policy and the relationship between formal and informal agencies of social welfare.

Local government reform and voluntary effort

The more able of the Tsar's ministers were fully aware of the long-standing administrative inadequacies of the regime. They recognized that emancipation would in time weaken the traditional systems of local control. One of the Tsar's most competent and liberal administrators, N. A. Miliutin, was appointed chairman of a new commission charged with the preparation of a draft plan for local government reform. Miliutin was dismissed before the plan had been completed but not before he had exercised a considerable influence on its design. The law of 1864 created a new system of *zemstvos*, assemblies at both provincial and district levels, which owed much to Miliutin's original scheme. In the villages the mir became the basis of local political assembly from which the heads of households elected delegates to a new local government unit, the *volost*, which was responsible for a small group of neighbouring villages. The volost members, in turn, selected an electoral assembly which nominated delegates to a district zemstvo. At this level of local administration the zemstvo was composed of landowners, townspeople and peasant representatives, each separately chosen by a complex system of indirect elections and a property-based suffrage. At the third level of local government were the provincial zemstvos, whose members were also chosen by a similarly complicated electoral procedure. In practice the peasants could rarely afford to attend the annual meetings of the provincial assemblies.

These new zemstvos, or assemblies, were made responsible for the provision of a wide range of local public and social services, including poor relief, hospitals, elementary education, the encouragement of voluntary aid, public sanitation, roads and the promotion of better agriculture. They were financed by a local rate levied primarily on the land.[35] Wallace describes the zemstvos as 'a kind of local administration which supplements the actions of the rural communes, and takes cognisance of those higher public wants which individual communes cannot possibly satisfy'.[36] Although the nobility dominated almost every aspect of the new system, apart from the internal affairs of the mir, a remarkable degree of harmony appears to have prevailed in many districts between the nobles and peasants who served as delegates.

A complementary reform of municipal administration in the larger towns was introduced during 1870. The members of the new town councils were indirectly elected through a system of class voting based on the taxation register. Wealthier householders enjoyed a disproportionately generous representation. The duties of these new town councils were very similar to those of the zemstvos but were far less conscientiously discharged. In 1892 this system of municipal government virtually reverted to a more direct form of central control. Councillors were thereafter compelled by law to attend meetings once they had agreed to serve.

It is difficult to obtain reliable information concerning the welfare activities of the local zemstvos. Wallace thought that by the end of the century the better local assemblies had done much to improve medical services. He noted that 'In the towns there are public hospitals, which generally are — or at least seem to an unprofessional eye — in a very satisfactory condition.'[37] In some districts the doctor undertook tours of the local villages. Pares also describes the enthusiasm and 'missionary devotion' with which liberal, radical and revolutionary members of zemstvos worked together on public health and educational programmes.[38] Wallace was, however, deeply critical of the lunatic asylums which he visited, comparing the conditions in one such institution with 'the worst regions of Dante's Inferno'.[39] At the same time Pares was full of praise for the asylums which he visited, noting their permissive and kindly treatment of inmates. He describes an early experiment in running a mental hospital near Moscow on an 'open door' principle which he thought was a success, adding ruefully, however, that 'It involved a tremendous strain on the attendants and when I visited it, one of the doctors had himself gone mad.'[40]

In the villages the level of welfare provision appears to have been extremely modest. One account of village life near Voronezh in the 1890s refers to a system of boarding out for infants and the markedly high incidence of syphilis which prevailed among the foster parents. Malaria was another endemic disease in this region, and most of the houses were infested with vermin. The peasants rarely made use of the few free hospital beds available in the town.[41]

Troyat also describes what appears to have been an extensive boarding-out system in the early nineteen-hundreds. He recounts the way in which the Moscow Foundling Hospital hired 'many' peasant women who had abandoned their own infants in the villages to earn some money by nursing other people's babies. Again reference is made to the high incidence of syphilis amongst both babies and nurses — and also to the high rates of illegitimacy in the towns. The foundlings stayed in the hospital on average for three to four weeks, after which they were vaccinated and boarded out, sometimes at considerable distances, without any subsequent supervision.[42] The Moscow Foundling Hospital was the largest institution of its kind in the world, with an average daily population of 2,000. It received an annual state subsidy of £100,000, most of which was levied on the sale of playing-cards. Troyat refers to the existence of approximately 2,500 charitable institutions throughout the country, the largest of which was the Administration of the Institutions of the Empress Marie. This charity had been established in 1797 to provide asylums for the handicapped, the sick and the orphaned.

During the reigns of Alexander II and Alexander III there were increases in the number of children attending schools, but a strict supervision of curricula in both schools and universities was maintained by the government. About 20 per cent of the cost of primary education was met by government subsidy and another 23 per cent by the local zemstvos. The village communities had to meet a third of the cost, and the remainder was made up from parental fees. The census of 1897 recorded regional variations in the incidence of illiteracy ranging from 89 to 45 per cent in the countryside and from 64 to 37 per cent in the towns. In 1884 primary education in the villages was placed under the control of the church, the effect of which was probably to widen the disparity in both the quantity and the quality of educational provision between town and country.

It seems clear that, despite the efforts of some of the more progressive zemstvos to extend welfare services and public relief, they were unable to make significant advances, owing to a chronic shortage of funds. Rimlinger remarks that 'The zemstvos' budgets for 1900 allocated 1.5 million rubles for public assistance and the municipalities allocated about 3 million. According to one estimate, modestly adequate care of the needy in zemstvo provinces would have required 300 million rubles; the zemstvos, however, spent only 4.5 millions.'[43] The worst miseries of material deprivation were perhaps alleviated by the mutual aid system of the mirs. Nonetheless in the periodic famines which occurred between 1870 and 1900 these limited resources proved totally inadequate and were not always readily supplemented by the central government.

It is possible that the significance of these reforms has been overshadowed by the fact that Russia remained a complete autocracy, with ultimate power vested in the Tsar. Nevertheless a genuine measure of localized democracy had been achieved, and, at least in theory, the new structure of local government was not markedly inferior — or less democratic — to the ones which prevailed at the time in Britain, France, and Germany. The system remained relatively unchanged until 1890 and might have continued to grow in maturity and competence, but for a series of events which checked the slow course of democratization in Russia.

One of the delayed consequences of the assassination by terrorists of Alexander II in 1881 was the almost total subordination of the zemstvos to a new system of local governors, or land-captains, introduced by his successor, Alexander III, on the advice of Pobedonostev. The terrorist activities of revolutionaries like Nechayev, Zasulich and other members of the various secret societies had found their natural victim in the one liberally disposed Tsar who was prepared to contemplate limited reform.

Wallace and most other contemporary authorities agree that by 1912 'the achievements of the zemstvo had not lived up to reformist expectations'. Educational and medical services remained totally inadequate despite commendable progress in some districts. It is difficult to see how the rate of progress could have been otherwise. Russia simply lacked the taxable capacity, the administrative expertise and the economic efficiency to undertake an adequate programme of social reform. Even the modest budgets of the zemstvos had added to the already intolerable burden of taxes, which fell almost exclusively on the peasantry. Without the support of the central authority there was no prospect of using the system of taxation as a means of redistributing wealth. Even the reforming ministers such as Witte and Stolypin saw the main functions of imperial taxation as those of financing industrial growth and reducing still further the volume of consumer demand among the peasants.

The imperial officials frequently obstructed the reforming schemes of progressive zemstvos because they feared that any consequent increases in local taxation might curtail or compete with the imperial levies.[44] Wallace points out that by the end of the century the zemstvos were spending about 43 per cent of their total revenue on health, welfare and education. He criticizes their relative neglect of public service spending on the improvement of roads and agriculture, which he argues would most directly enhance peasant welfare. He suggests that the zemstvo members had generally invested too much hope in the long-term effects of educational reform.

The condition of the people

The evidence of peasant impoverishment was often confusing and open to various interpretations. The worst arrears of taxes occurred in the richer black earth regions, areas of which were becoming exhausted by bad farming methods. In such districts the peasants had long been accustomed to supplementing their incomes by other forms of wage labour. Nonetheless the most efficient peasants were able to pay off their redemption dues and to add to their lands by purchase. And between 1865 and 1909 the number of depositors in the government savings banks had risen from 72,000 to over 6 million. Over a quarter of the deposits (£120 million) were believed to belong to the rural population.[45]

It is probable that the head of a peasant household was paying roughly a quarter of his income in imperial taxes, after deducting grain for his own domestic purposes. In addition to this he paid local and indirect taxes. Wallace suggests that this was a tolerable burden only 'if the peasant families could utilize productively all their time and strength'.[46] If the evidence of trends in redemption payments, land sales and savings can be relied upon, at least a minority of the more efficient and fortunate peasants were prospering. The Peasant Land Bank did excellent business between 1882 and 1902, advancing over £40 million for the purchase of land at 7½ per cent interest. It is worth noting for comparative purposes that at about the same time there were former citizens of tsarist Russia among the millions of emigrants seeking to protect and enhance their own welfare by joining claim clubs in the countryside and mutual aid societies in the cities of the USA.

During the 1880s the process of industrialization, funded largely from foreign capital, began to get under way. Between 1860 and 1913 the number of wage earners increased from 4 million to 18 million, although the latter figure still included 4½ million agricultural labourers.[47] By 1900 the trend towards a class of landless labourers, in both town and country, had passed the point of no return. This development destroyed any realistic hope of attaining the welfare ideals of the populists. Some idea of the condition of the small urban proletariat can be gained from the reports of Factory Inspectors and surveys carried out by the Union of Zemstvos and Towns. Some retrospective work based on the census of 1918 is also revealing and thought to be reliable. According to Florinsky 'The average monthly earnings of an industrial worker was computed at something like 22 rubles or about 11 dollars.'[48]

One of the major causes of this extraordinary low level of average earnings was the continuing agrarian crisis. Briefly, a complex system of remittance payments had grown up between town and country. Migrant workers frequently left their kin behind but returned home when they themselves were sick, disabled, retired or unemployed. They left their families behind because it was impossible to support them in the cities, and living was cheaper in the villages. But this artificial survival of the extended family in the country removed one of the potential pressures on employers to pay a genuine family wage in the towns.[49]

At the same time the more liberal of the Tsar's ministers were more concerned to help the urban workers than the peasants. They recognized that the future economic prosperity of Russia depended upon industrial growth and like their conservative peers they also feared the consequences of urban political unrest. Throughout the 1880s a series of labour statutes were passed under the direction of N. K. Bunge, the Minister of

Finance. These new laws prohibited the factory employment of children under the age of twelve and imposed an eight-hour working day for young persons betweeen the ages of twelve and seventeen.[50] Under the first Labour Code of 1886 an attempt was made to check the arbitrary imposition of fines and dismissal by employers, who were also required under this statute to provide free medical treatment for their workers. As a result of these reforms Bunge lost popularity with the industrialists and was dismissed. The factory inspectorate set up in the 1880s proved to be an efficient and honest group of officials. Szamuely remarks that Russian labour legislation was relatively progressive in comparison with that of most other industrializing nations of the period.[51] Subsequent reforms included restrictions on the length of the working day for adults in 1897, provision against industrial accidents in 1903 and a Health and Accident Act in 1912. Much of this later legislation was based on the German insurance scheme. Although it allowed a measure of workers' participation, the range and scale of provisions were modest and applied in practice only to workers employed in the larger factories.[52] According to Milligan 'Only 20 per cent of industrial workers were covered by the acts of 1903 and 1912, and 'they did not extend to invalids, the old, or the unemployed'.[53]

In our review of the structure and functions of the Russian mir, the process of emancipation and the complementary introduction of local administrative reforms, we may note how in Russia the question of land reform dominated all other issues of social welfare. Matters such as the creation of modern forms of social service were of relatively marginal importance not only in what was achieved by the government but also in what was expected by the mass of the population. As late as 1917 80 per cent of the Russian population were still peasants for whom the ultimate form of welfare was the possession of land. It was, however, increasingly recognized within both government and opposition circles that the long-term solution to the land question and the state of the peasantry lay in the industrialization of the Russian economy. The Bolshevik revolution was not an event that rudely interrupted a century of intellectual torpor and political inactivity in tsarist governmental circles. It came, rather, at the end of three decades of intense intellectual debate and a series of dramatic policy decisions regarding economic reform.

The beginnings of economic reform

The response made to these social and economic dilemmas by

the reforming ministers of the Tsar was a combination of limited social reforms and a more radical economic programme of forced industrialization. The best of these ministers, Count Sergius Witte, was greatly influenced by the German mercantilist economist, Friedrich List. In List's work Witte found the economic doctrine to complement his patriotism and his belief that economic institutions and activities had a value not only in themselves but in the service of the overriding political interests of the state. Russia, he was convinced, could only industrialize effectively with the protection of an adequate system of tariffs. Free trade was an indulgence which could be enjoyed only by those nations which were economically strong enough to win the battles of international competition.

After a brief period of service as Minister of Communications, Witte was appointed Minister of Finance in 1892. This appointment gave him the opportunity to put his theories to the test. During his subsequent terms of office, between 1892 and 1903, Witte carried forward with prodigious energy the economic reforms started by his predecessors, Bunge and Vyshnegradsky.

In so many ways Witte typified all the paradoxes of the reforming Russian conservative. Though intensely patriotic, he was prepared to finance industrialization from foreign loans and the ruthless taxation of his own people. While he was totally committed to economic and educational reform he was equally hostile to political reform. He believed in a free movement of labour but not of manufacturers, and in the liberty to take economic risks but not to vote. His goal was the economic transformation of Russia from a backward agrarian society into a first-rank industrial nation with a greatly extended sphere of political and economic influence. In the absence of a developed and enterprising middle class Witte decided that the costs of industrialization would have to be met from foreign loans paid for by higher domestic taxation and increased grain exports.

These schemes were complemented by the restoration of the gold standard, the reform of the tax system and a general raising of tariffs. Between 1869 and 1876 the scale of *ad valorem* duties had averaged less than 13 per cent. Between 1895 and 1899 the average rate rose to 33 per cent.[54] As a consequence of Witte's tariff reforms more foreign manufacturers set up businesses within Russia. Although protection was popular with small groups of Russian businessmen and certain patriotic groups it generated great hostility amongst both agrarian conservatives and social reformers. As von Lane comments, 'Both the tariff and the gold standard antagonized all who put agriculture and popular welfare first in their scale of social and political priorities.'[55] In the period between 1905 and 1912 tariffs were to average 'the fabulously high rate of 30-38 per cent of the total value of imports', compared with the then prevailing rates of 5.7 per cent in Great Britain, 8.4 per cent in Germany and 18.5 per cent in the United States of America.[56]

Witte was, however, indifferent to such hostility, even though it grew more intense as his taxation policies became more savage. The rate of indirect taxation of goods such as tobacco, paraffin, matches and sugar was sharply increased. The sale of highly taxed spirits was made a state monopoly, and Jews were forbidden to hold licences for the sale of liquor. High levels of taxation became the device by which the volume of grain exports was increased. Between 1860 and 1900 'the average annual export of grain rose from under 1½ million to over 6 million tons.'[57] Throughout this period there were outbreaks of famine in some of the richest farming areas; even in good years the average peasant lived at or below a subsistence level, while the export of 'surplus' grain broke new records. The peasant, however poor, was obliged to sell the greater part of his own produce — or labour — in order to pay his taxes.

The wider issue of general backwardness was being resolved largely at the expense of inefficient peasants. It is significant that Witte was prepared to support limited social reforms which would benefit the urban working class, as when in 1897 he agreed to impose new restrictions on the length of the working day for adults and juveniles.[58] For the peasant there could be no such mitigation.

The best solution to rural poverty was the abolition of the mir, since this would also remove a major obstacle to increasing the rate of industrial growth and productive efficiency. Witte looked forward to the creation of a more mobile labour market, which would reduce the surplus rural population and increase the supply of urban wage labourers. His agricultural reforms included a reduction in the loan charges of the Peasants' Bank in 1894 and the postponement of redemption dues in 1896. More systematic attempts were made to encourage internal migration — especially to Siberia — during the 1890s, and, after a series of government enquiries, collective responsibility for taxes was abolished in 1903. Industrialization, however, depended upon improvements in the quality as well as the quantity of urban labour. Witte's attempts at educational reform were largely frustrated by Pobedonostev, who still controlled primary education through the offices of the Holy Synod. Nonetheless he did succeed in influencing the development of technical education, which remained under secular control. He showed far less imagination and concern with regard to the welfare aspects of industrialization. These unconsidered problems became evident during the economic slump of 1899-1903 and the delay in recovery caused by the outbreak of the Russo-Japanese war. As the volume of unemployment rose, so did the incidence of often violent strikes and severe police repression. These conditions created ideal circumstances for the revival of militant revolutionary activity. These political legacies of Witte's economic reforms were inherited by his successor, Stolypin.

The ill-organized terrorism of the 1870s had been one kind of radical response to the political apathy of the peasants and the unyielding attitudes of the tsarist regime. There was, however, another kind of reformist response, which took advantage of the limited reforms which were carried out in local government after 1864. In the new provincial and local zemstvos liberal intellectuals, experts and professional men, as well as reformist nobles, began to acquire for the first time some direct acquaintance with the actual needs and expectations of the poor. The reforms of 1890 provided further administrative scope within which these reformers could achieve a measure of confidence based on practical experience and some modest local successes.

There is some evidence to suggest that during the 1890s the exclusive hold of radical extremists on the Russian revolutionary and reformist movements was temporarily weakened. The exponents of violence had been discredited because they had failed to achieve their own objectives and had frequently prejudiced the prospects of limited reform. Not until the economic recession of 1899-1903 and the political disasters and crises of 1905-6 were the revolutionaries able to reassert their policies with conviction and the prospect of some popular support.

By this time, however, many of the old populists had become convinced that capitalism could not be prevented. Nonetheless it was possible that a wide range of social reforms might still be extracted from the capitalists, if not by persuasion then by militant strike action. Some of these radicals became Mensheviks in the new Social Democratic Labour Party, but others stayed closer to the populist tradition within their own Social Revolutionary Party.[59] Lenin became intensely hostile towards these 'legal Marxists' who were willing to support programmes of social reform with limited welfare objectives and little regard for long-term political goals.[60] Nevertheless Lenin was to encourage the Bolsheviks in their exploitation of the new social insurance committees, established under the 1912 laws. Shortly before it was banned, *Pravda* regularly published articles explaining how workers could claim their maximum benefits and committee representation under the new legislation. The Bolsheviks even went so far as to publish a second paper 'devoted entirely to the question of social insurance'.[61] Lenin, however, was concerned with objectives of a more profoundly subversive nature than a successful welfare rights campaign. In the meantime he was content to use the new welfare committee structure for his own purposes, while opposing the 1912 provisions on grounds of principle. The Bolsheviks objected to capitalistic insurance schemes which operated on a contributory and contractual basis. They argued that under socialism such services were the inalienable right of citizens, who would receive their benefits as 'a gift from the state' in return for work.[62]

The campaign for constitutional reform

During the crucial years of 1905-6 both the issues of land reform and improvements in the welfare of the urban proletariat were subsumed under the growing campaign for constitutional reform. The demands facing the Tsar and his new senior minister, Stolypin, were explicitly political in their nature. Even the more moderate liberals who served in the zemstvos were losing patience. In 1904 the Tsar was petitioned by a large group of zemstvo delegates to agree to the establishment of a nationally elected assembly. There was even a measure of support for these proposals from the Marshalls of the Nobility, and — on largely tactical grounds — Witte also favoured concessions. The events of Bloody Sunday, defeat in the war with Japan, the formation of a Peasants' Union, a further wave of urban strikes and the combination of employers to resist wage demands all contributed to the Tsar's reluctant decision to accede to the demand for an elected Duma. It was to be a purely consultative body.

In 1903 Witte had been 'promoted' to the post of President of the Committee of Ministers but he resigned during 1905, after losing the confidence of the Tsar as a result of his attempts to conciliate the reformers. Under the terms of the new Fundamental Laws, as revised by Witte, Stolypin was in effect Prime Minister of Russia. Stolypin had acquired a reputation for severe and summary forms of justice, as a provincial governor.

He claimed that he was a constitutionalist but not a parliamentarian and immediately set about demonstrating what he meant by this. His immediate objective was to secure an obedient and subordinate Duma, and he played a key role in securing the dismissal of the first and second assemblies of that body by a skilful if dishonest manipulation of the Fundamental Laws.

The first Duma, which was assembled and dissolved in 1906, 'included the cream of the liberal intelligentzia' and 'the best peasant members', chosen 'without any thought of politics or parties'.[63] Sustained by a sense of 'national indignation', its members appealed to the Tsar for an extension of parliamentary and social reform, including a constitutional settlement of the land question through the redistribution of landed estates. After some weeks of prevarication and confusion the Tsar dissolved the assembly and called for new elections. There were outbreaks of terrorism throughout the country which included the bombing of Stolypin's own home, the death of twenty-seven of his servants and the injury of his daughter. Stolypin responded by establishing 'field courts-martial' and a determined counter-insurgency campaign.[64]

The second Duma, which lasted only from 6 March to 16 June 1907, was even more hostile than the first and explicitly socialist in its demands, which included the end of police repression and the expropriation of landed estates.

Stolypin was undoubtedly a man of subtler and more complex character than might be inferred from popular historical accounts of the Bolshevik revolution. He was certainly capable of ruthless and brutal action in defence of the political *status quo*. Yet he was viewed by many conservatives as a dangerous radical. He was well aware of the need to implement new social legislation, which would enhance the living conditions of the urban poor. He came to the second Duma prepared to offer the prospect of extensive social reforms as well as a new land policy. His proposals included a promise of greater religious toleration; legal reforms to ensure and extend civil rights; a review of the tax system; a reorganization of local government including the establishment of zemstvos in border provinces; the introduction of new educational reforms including compulsory elementary education; and a scheme for social insurance and medical care. It was a remarkable performance for a man whose home had only recently been destroyed by terrorist bombs, which killed most of his personal staff and servants and crippled his daughter.

The assembly responded with a vote of no confidence. The left wing were not interested in either social reform or the land proposals. The liberal constitutionalists of the centre failed to support Stolypin, although he had in effect met the greater part of their own demands for constitutional reform. Some indication of Stolypin's cast of mind can be gained from his answer to the hostile reply of Tseretseli, the Social Democrat leader in the Duma. 'These attacks count on paralyzing the will and thoughts of the government. They all come down to two words directed at authority: "Hands up!" To these two words, sirs, the government with complete calm, with a consciousness of its uprightness can reply in two words: "You will not frighten us *(ne zapugaete)*".'[65] He followed up this challenge with the accusation that fifty-five of the Social Democrat members were plotting insurrection, and he demanded their indictment. The Duma prevaricated and was summarily dissolved. As soon as these immediate political challenges to the regime were disposed of, Stolypin turned his attention to formulating his own resolution of the land problem. His revision of the electoral laws produced a third Duma, more sympathetic to his views and obedient to his wishes.

The reform programmes of the political parties

Tsarist Russia was a police state in which the free expression of opinion was stringently controlled. Censorship was strictly maintained, and after 1884 the universities and other educational establishments were very closely supervised. Student demonstrations in 1895 and 1899 had been sternly suppressed. The majority of the population were illiterate, and the expression of popular sentiment in the countryside found its most dramatic form in sporadic outbursts of violence and arson. Nonetheless it is very difficult indeed to estimate how representative these outbreaks were of general peasant feeling, and the same must be said of the manifestos and tracts of various political opposition groups and individual writers. The Peasant Union, formed in 1905, eventually came to claim a membership of over 200,000.

Trade unions were made illegal under the 1874 penal law, strikes were ruthlessly suppressed, and everyday life in the factories was closely supervised by the police. In 1902 a group of professors at Moscow University, in collaboration with the police authorities, established a 'Society of Mutual Help of Workers in Mechanical Production', which organized patriotic rallies and occasional social calls on the Minister of the Interior. The activities of this society were swiftly curtailed after it became infiltrated by militants. A new law of 1906 legalized trade unions, and, although strikes remained illegal, their incidence increased rapidly.[66] In 1914 approximately 1½ million workers participated in some form of strike action.

The balance of representation in the first and second Dumas does, however, provide some guide to the key issues raised in official debates regarding land reform and, to a lesser extent, social policies. The predominance of reformist and radical interests is significant, when account is taken of the property-owning basis of the franchise and the indirect mode of election. Nonetheless some allowance must be made for the fact that the more radical left-wing parties boycotted the first Duma and participated in the second, while the third Duma, which first met in November 1907, was elected on a more restricted franchise, thus greatly reducing the number of left-wing members.

It must also be stressed that in both the first and second Dumas there was never one single party which secured any kind of representation approaching a majority. There were a number of ill-defined coalitions and a sizeable group of uncommitted peasant delegates. Neither assembly lasted long enough to permit the emergence of working coalitions, and, had they done so, their scope for decisive policy-making would have been minimal. Under the Fundamental Laws of 1906 the Tsar and the Council of State retained more than enough power to veto any undesired legislative initiative. The Tsar also appointed and dismissed all ministers and retained effective control over the budget. The government was empowered to initiate its own legislation in the form of decrees and ignored, when necessary, its constitutional obligation to submit such decrees for the retrospective approval of the Duma. In this sense it could be said that the main concern of the first two Russian 'parliaments' was to secure the establishment of a true parliamentary government.

We can briefly recount the domestic policies of the main political parties and groupings which were active in 1905. On the far right there was a monarchist party, hostile to all change, and the Union of Russian Men, which was both strongly Slavophil and anti-Semitic. This Union had affinities with the still more conservative Union of the Russian People. From the fringes of these parties were drawn the recruits to the 'Black

Hundreds' and other anti-Semitic groups. The first Duma contained no more than half a dozen representatives of the extreme right, but in the second and third Dumas about 50 of the 520 delegates came from this sector.

The Octobrists were a conservative party, favouring cautious measures of land and social reform. Their membership was strongly nationalistic and generally opposed to a more generous treatment of other minority ethnic groups. The Octobrists were supported by many of the zemstvo reformers, some land-owners and businessmen, and the more progressive officials. They were a small minority of about forty in the first two Dumas but in the third Duma they became the largest single party. The left Octobrists were strongly committed to the extension of social insurance, tax reform and more generous economic assistance to the peasants.

The Constitutional Democrats, or Kadets, were slightly to the left of the Octobrists and also drew support from the zemstvo movement. The Kadets were committed to constitutional reforms such as universal suffrage and a range of social reforms very similar to those of the Octobrists. Their land programme was, however, more radical. They favoured the compulsory purchase of land from the nobles, who were, however, to receive fair compensation under the Kadets' reform programme. (In election campaigns some of the left Kadets went so far as to promise free distribution of land to the peasants.) The Kadets were the largest single party in both the first and second Dumas but lost half their seats in the third.

The Social Revolutionaries, or SRs, were the political inheritors of one radical element in the old populist tradition. Their land programme was strongly focused on the peasants. It was based on the traditional peasant belief that no individuals had the right to own land. The Social Revolutionaries were in favour of total expropriation and the vesting of all land in elected local authorities, which would allocate plots of land to individual peasants on the basis of 'labour ownership'. Land owners were not to be compensated but would be allowed public assistance during the period of their readjustment! For the Social Revolutionaries the expropriation of land was the final stage of socialism.[67] They were in favour of reviving the commune and resisting capitalism, detesting Stolypin's reforms as a device for infecting the peasantry with a desire for private property. In industrial areas the Social Revolutionaries wished to apply the commune principle in the form of small *artels*, or community workshops.

Among the Social Democrats the Mensheviks were in favour of 'municipalizing' all land and vesting it in local authorities, which were to administer it on behalf of the peasants. They were suspicious of too much central control. Lenin and the Bolsheviks wanted outright nationalization of the land as part of a long-term socialist programme. Nonetheless Lenin was quite prepared to support the Social Revolutionary programme of instant land redistribution since he believed that after the overthrow of tsarism a bourgeois regime would be established. During this period the 'petit bourgeois' mentality of the peasantry would generate policies likely to intensify class conflict between rich and poor peasants. Lenin drew a distinction between Stolypin's systematic attempt to sponsor the mobility of a minority of the stronger peasants and what he described as the 'American' way of open and ruthless competition. 'In this case the peasant predominates, becomes the only type of agriculturalist, and evolves into the capitalist farmer.' In contrast to Stolypin Lenin was prepared to back the 'losers', placing his trust in the revolutionary potential of an alliance between the poorest peasants and the urban proletariat.[68] The strength of this alliance might under certain conditions be sufficiently powerful to carry the revolution direct to socialism, without a bourgeois interlude.

The public debates and programmes of the various Social Democrat factions were contingent upon their uncertainty as to the kind of revolutionary regime which might succeed the overthrow of tsarism. At their Stockholm conference the Menshevik resolution on 'municipalization' had carried the day. In political terms these proposals seemed likely to be less popular with peasants than the Social Revolutionaries' plan, which was based on the argument that 'The essence of socialism turned not on methods of production but on equal distribution.'[69] Although Lenin was disposed to support this scheme for tactical reasons, he considered it to be in fundamental conflict with the long-term aims of a communist revolution. It would create new problems which would have to be dealt with at a later date.

The Bolsheviks responded in a similar way to the limited measures of social insurance introduced by the government and favoured by other reformist opposition parties of the right and the centre. As we have already noted, Lenin urged his supporters to infiltrate the new insurance committees and assist the workers in maximizing their benefits. But in contrast with his reticence regarding the ultimate objectives of Bolshevik land policy, Lenin publicized the party's own scheme for social security reform at every possible opportunity.

Lenin's main social and economic analysis of the peasants is contained in two of his works, *The Development of Capitalism in Russia* (published in 1899) and *The Agrarian Question in Russia* (published in 1908). He broadly distinguished three main groups of peasant — the Kulaks, or richer peasants owning over fifty acres of land, the Seredniaks, or middle peasants owning between thirty-five and fifty acres, and the Bedniaks, the poorest group owning less than thirty-five acres. Lenin estimated that the Kulaks accounted for 12 per cent of the rural population and owned 31 per cent of the land. The middle peasants made up 7 per cent of the rural population and owned 7 per cent of the land. The poorest peasants thus constituted 81 per cent of the total but owned only 35 per cent of the land. The large land-owning class, which amounted to less than 1 per cent of the population, owned 27 per cent of the land. Lenin argued that between 1861 and 1900 the average size of peasant holdings had been falling as the rural population grew. He was convinced that the stratification of the peasants into classes was already under way. The revolutionary process ought therefore to begin by the incitement of the entire peasantry to destroy the old system. In the second stage the poor peasants would be mobilized against the Kulaks, gradually winning over the middle group. The final stage should be one in which the Kulaks were voluntarily persuaded of the economic and ethical advantages of co-operative farming.[70]

At the most critical stage in the revolution the Bolsheviks proved to be the only party which did not vacillate on the land question. It was Lenin who single-mindedly held the party to one clear and unequivocal objective.

Consequences of the Stolypin reforms

A disturbing feature of the waves of violence and unrest which occurred in 1905-6 was the evidence of a fairly widespread peasant involvement. As a consequence an increasing number of proprietors began to see some truth in the old populist assertion that the mir was in essence a socialist institution. Stolypin's land policy was based on the belief that the best hope of regaining the loyalty of the peasants was to offer them not the benefits of a philanthropic social market but the simple economic incentive of private ownership. The over-all objective remained the same — to transform Russia into a major industrial power with the minimum of political change. The agricultural reforms of 1906, supplemented by later modifications, were of a more radical nature than those of 1861. They were based on plans prepared during Witte's term of office, but in timing their presentation Stolypin was mindful of the need for the government to take a decisive initiative in a period of crisis. The first of the three main laws set up land commissions to implement the reforms. Almost all the arbitrary powers of the land-captains introduced in 1890 by Pobedonostev were abolished. All residual tax obligations of a collective nature were ended.

The purpose of the reforms of 1906 was to encourage the extension of genuine private ownership and to create a new class of 'yeoman farmers'. Peasants were now allowed to buy, sell and mortgage property. In the communes where re-partition of land was no longer practised the land was distributed amongst the members. In the re-partitional communes any householder could apply to purchase his strips of land in full hereditary ownerships. There were additional incentives to consolidate strips into single units. Peasant banks were established and loans made available to individuals rather than communes. By 1917 at least 50 per cent of all peasants' land would be held in full, hereditary tenures.

Stolypin's explicit intention was to undermine the traditional egalitarianism of the mir, to create a class of wealthy peasants, to raise levels of agricultural efficiency and also to encourage labour mobility, including the voluntary emigration to Siberia of both successful and unsuccessful peasants. The greatest migration occurred from the Ukraine, where the poverty of the rural wage-workers was most extensive. These economic reforms constituted Stolypin's 'wager not on the needy and the drunken but on the sturdy and the strong'. They caused Lenin greater alarm than the more generally popular attempts to introduce social reforms such as the improvement of factory conditions and the implementation of insurance schemes.[71] There is little doubt that Lenin was correct in fearing that a belated reliance on the capacity of a freer economic market to enhance the welfare of the peasantry still had an outside chance of abating social unrest and delaying the prospect of revolution. Some members of the nobility found encouragement in this prospect. The reformers who attended the First Congress of Representatives of Nobles in 1906 drew comfort from the hope that 'the extension of property rights amongst the peasants will increase their attachment to what is their own and their respect for what belongs to others'.[72] As a consequence of these reforms the foundations of a Kulak class were consolidated in the country-side.

The development of co-operative peasant enterprises was also encouraged. These co-operatives were mainly concerned with credit and savings schemes for equipment and fertilizers.[73] A major incentive was also given to a process of migration which had begun to gather momentum after 1889, with the introduction of state-assisted schemes. Between then and 1900 the number of migrants rose from 10,000 to 100,000 per annum.[74] Approximately 2 million households left the communes between 1906 and 1911, many of them moving to the Ukraine and the Caucasus.[75] The rate of migration to Siberia also increased during the same period.[76] In this Siberian emigration it is interesting to note that the collectivist tradition of peasant farming was most clearly preserved.

Under Stolypin's direction the third Duma had modified the original terms of the land reform. It replaced the scheme by which peasants applied individually to leave the mir with a system in which the entire commune voted. A two-thirds majority dissolved the commune. After the emancipation it became accepted practice for whole villages to emigrate *en bloc* to Siberia. Between 1906 and 1911 peasant migration became largely a co-operative enterprise, but it was capitalist rather than socialist in character. Extensive co-operative settlements occurred in the central areas around Omsk, which became during the Civil War a focus of anti-Bolshevik resistance, providing soldiers and supplies for Kolchak's armies.[77] The challenges and hardships of frontier farming in desolate areas preserved much of the old co-operative spirit of the mir, but the dominating spirit of these pioneers was one of collective enterprise in the pursuit of private gain and familial welfare.

Thus it may be argued that the most effective attempt to resolve the long-standing social and economic ills of Russia amounted to a programme of rigorous positive discrimination in favour of those who could prove, given the chance, their ability to survive and prosper in a freer labour market. This policy had been complemented by relatively peripheral social reforms, again directed specifically at allaying social unrest amongst the growing urban proletariat. The poorer peasants continued to suffer an almost unrelieved negative discrimination in the form of rigorous indirect taxation. The emancipated serf still paid imperial taxes to the Tsar, local taxes to the zemstvo and taxes to the mir and the volost. The mir had failed to provide a bulwark against either proletarianization or pauperization. Stolypin's reforms were a recognition of this fact and served to accelerate the flow of landless, poverty-stricken peasants into the towns or distant provinces.[78]

It was to the economic market rather than the social market that the reforming tsarist ministers looked for a restoration of prosperity and national concensus. For decades the populists had looked forward to the political awakening of the Russian peasant — all their hopes had been 'dominated by a single myth: that once the monster was slain, the sleeping princess — the Russian peasantry — would awaken and without further ado live happily ever after'.[79] Stolypin was to awaken the princess, not with the prospect of a political Utopia but with the promise of a property-owning autocracy and the prospect of prosperity for the swift and strong. The new class of Kulaks which Stolypin helped to create did not live happily ever after — but for a few years to come its members were perhaps to enjoy more material welfare than they had known before or were to know again in the bitter years ahead.

The Kulaks were not the only group to benefit from Stolypin's reforms. By 1915 'probably more than 7 million peasant families possessed hereditary private holdings', and between 1906 and 1912 the cash wage rates of agricultural workers improved, although the price of food also rose.[80] The promises of social reform were at least partially honoured. A free primary educational system was established, and the salaries of school teachers improved. The law of 1912 introduced a limited measure of social insurance and free medical care for some urban workers. During the tsarist government's last decade of peace it seems clear that the dramatic increase in zemstvo expenditures was encouraged by the Finance Ministry. Special treasury grants were made for educational and public health purposes, and Seton-Watson concludes that 'expenditure by local government on social services, though miserably small in comparison with needs, was increasing at a rapid rate.'[81]

Stolypin did not live long enough to witness the beginning of the social insurance scheme. In 1911 he was assassinated by a double agent of the Social Revolutionaries and the Imperial police. It is not clear on whose behalf this agent was acting. Stolypin was already beginning to lose favour with the Tsar and he had made many enemies among the more conservative ministers and officials of the government. His plans for further zemstvo reform had barely survived the bitterest opposition. In pre-revolutionary Russia 'conservatives' and 'radicals' alike seem always to have been relative terms.

These programmes of social and economic reform must, however, be considered in relation to long-established traditions of negative discrimination directed against various minority groups. This was the other major feature of Russian domestic policies which exercised a profound influence on the shifting tides of support and opposition which the regime encountered in the years prior to the revolution. The central government, and even more the provincial governments, never hesitated to invoke the crudest forms of nationalist prejudice and anti-Semitism as a means of social control. However humble and poor, the Russian peasant remained a Great Russian. At the bottom of an ethnic hierarchy the Jew was the ultimate victim of negative discrimination. The Jews benefited less than any other social group from the constitutional reforms of 1905-6. In the original proposals for reform submitted to the Tsar by his own commissioners they were to remain unenfranchised, although they did receive the vote under the final law.[82] None of the other discriminatory laws were removed, and there were further pogroms in 1905.

Throughout the 1890s other minority groups suffered persecution. Schools in the Baltic provinces and in Armenia were placed under Russian control. Lutheran, Catholic and Armenian churches were restricted in their activities, and their funds were occasionally appropriated by the government. The Finns suffered from similar attentions, including a more rigorous conscription policy. Moslem minorities were also affected. Stolypin intensified this programme of Great Russian nationalism. His revised electoral laws of 1907 not only excluded most of the left-wing parties but greatly reduced the number of delegates representing national minorities. Latvia and the Ukraine were areas of bitter resistance and repression during the 1905 uprisings. In the Ukraine the nationalist movement was particularly strong. This was a province in which the peasants, who were heavily dependent upon wage earnings, gained least from the abolition of redemption dues and the 1906 reforms. Most of the land was held in large estates, and the commune system had never been extensive.[83] In the Baltic provinces Stolypin allowed the German communities to reopen their schools but refused to do the same for the other Baltic peoples. The powers of the separate Diet granted to Finland in 1906 were greatly reduced only four years later.

Stolypin's extension of the zemstvo system into Poland was designed to give majority representation to the Russian peasant population. It was the Tsar's fear of alienating still further the loyalty of the Polish nobility that caused him to have doubts about the measure. Yet Stolypin's personal sense of nationalism was expressed in political rather than religious discrimination, and he was instrumental in securing, against powerful court opposition, a greater measure of religious freedom throughout the empire, even for the Jews.

The tsarist regime was thus characterized not only by massive disparities in wealth and opportunity but also by a hierarchy of negative discrimination in which Jews and national minorities were denied even the limited freedoms enjoyed by the ethnically Great Russian majority.

Social policies in the revolutionary period

The collapse of the tsarist government in February 1917 unleashed a popular demand for a land reform which would give the land to the peasants. Despite the efforts of the provisional government the peasants began expropriating the land — and land ownership was the traditional expression of their ideal of welfare. The final collapse of the armies was caused by mass desertions of peasants determined to get back to their villages in time to secure their share of the best land. By August 1917 over 1½ million soldiers had deserted.

The Bolsheviks under Lenin were the most vigorous agitators for the expropriation of land, taking as much care as possible, however, *not* to say to whom the land should subsequently be assigned. Their main radical rivals, the Social Revolutionaries, were more explicit — they did not favour private ownership but wanted to revise a modified commune system. Their assumption was that the Russian peasant was at heart a natural socialist and that the commune was an indigenous element of peasant culture. They neglected the fact that the commune had been created as an instrument of state control, originally as the institutional basis of serfdom, and after emancipation as a convenient unit for the levying of taxes and redemption dues.

The Bolsheviks were under no such illusions, and their views would have accorded with Barrington Moore's assertion that 'The demands of the Russian peasant were brutally simple: to get rid of the landlord, divide up the land, and of course to stop the war.' They would also have agreed with the view that 'The peasant had no abstract interest in feeding the towns. His organic conception of society stopped quite short of altruism. For him, "outsiders" were and are mainly a source of taxes and debt.'[84] The Bolsheviks were thus quite opportunistic about land reform. Even before their seizure of power in November 1917 they voted, at the Second Congress of Soviets, a land decree giving the land to the peasants — many of whom had already helped themselves.

All that we know of the peasants' subsequent response to the revolutionary demands of the Bolsheviks suggests that the majority of them were at best indifferent, and in the end openly hostile, to the needs of the wider community. The poorest class of peasant wanted land, food and an end to the war.[85] The revolution had given them the long awaited chance to satisfy their desire for land. They were willing to sell their agricultural products in return for something of value but they would not accept worthless money or respond either to pleas for altruism or to threats from the Red Army and the police.

The land question dominates the history of Russian social policy because in a subsistence economy the components of human welfare are defined in terms of elementary factors such as land and bread. Since the members of industrial societies rarely work the land on which they live, property takes the place of land in popular definitions of welfare, and, when expectations rise above the level of subsistence, there is a tendency to forget that 'The defence and salvation of the body by daily bread is still a study, a religion and a desire.'[86] In town and country alike attachment to a particular place and time is a sentiment of such intensity that it turns the gentlest of citizens into militant counter-revolutionaries, if they are threatened with dispossession or exile. The material loss of private property leads to a desolation of the spirit for which the principle of common ownership rarely compensates. It is as if, in their longing for a sense of location, people turn to private property as a defence against isolation and dependency. The very notion of institutionalization — or removal from one's own home — is synonymous with that of stigma, partly because it so often follows dependency but also because it describes a state of being without an identifiable personal habitat.

Commitment to the idea of collective ownership is, I suggest, a belief largely confined to a certain class of intellectual. If the tsarist regime created the largest minority group of unemployed and migrant intellectuals in Europe, the Russian revolution gave them a vocation and brought them home. These men and women had endured the uncertainty of exile, residing in lodging-houses and hotels and suffering periodic consignment to labour camps and prisons. They returned to Russia having less immediate affinity with the ordinary people than even the landlords and nobles. Indifferent to the natural yearnings of ordinary people expressed in the attachment to familiar locations, they were well prepared to serve as the expropriators of the smallholder and property owner and as the organizers of the greatest forced collectivization of property and deportation of labour in modern history.

Within a month of seizing power the Bolsheviks quickly set up an Extraordinary Committee for the Suppression of Counter-revolution, Speculation and Sabotage. In January they broke up by the use of armed force the Constituent Assembly, which was the only democratically elected body that had ever existed in Russia. By July 1918 the Social Revolutionary members had been expelled from the Soviets. They, in turn, responded by assassinating Uritsky, the head of the secret police, and nearly succeeded in killing Lenin. Thereafter the counter-terror was unleashed on the Social Revolutionaries and all other enemies of the Revolution. On the very eve of the Bolshevik revolution the Petrograd Soviet set out in the Resolution of their garrison a direct and simple statement of their broad objectives. The Resolution declared that 'The army demands peace, the peasants land and the workers bread and work.' It also demanded 'All power to the Soviets! An immediate armistice on all fronts! The land to the peasants! An honest and prompt convocation of the Constituent Assembly!'[87] The aims of Soviet social policy were thus stated in simple terms as a part of the revolutionary manifesto. The very basic and dramatic nature of these aims reflected the appalling circumstances in which they were drafted — against a background of violence, chaos and hunger.

It was clear that the majority of the civilian population and of the army wanted peace. Most of the Bolsheviks were hostile to the convocation of the assembly but could do nothing to prevent it. Similarly it was easier to promise bread and work than to provide either. The peasants had already seized the land and had done so in such a way that securing a supply of food for the towns was to become still more difficult. The immediate political survival of the Bolsheviks was, however, dependent upon their apparent capacity to give to the poor what they wanted — and upon their accession to the peasants' own definition of what constituted their best welfare interests.

The last revolutionary objective — 'All power to the Soviets!' — expressed the central long-term political objective of the Bolshevik Party. It was to determine the eventual nature of the land reform and the criteria by which all welfare goods and services were subsequently to be allocated. The only revolutionary objective which was both immediately attained and universally desired by the peasants was the expropriation of the land. Thereafter all the powers which were gathered to the Soviets came eventually to be used in the repossession of that land for the state.

The way in which social priorities came to be ordered and social needs defined derived some of its rationale from the basic tenets of the political theory of Marx and Engels. Since it was Lenin more than any other single individual who first translated this theory into practice, we may usefully refer to his thoughts on the subject. They are nowhere more clearly expressed than in *The State and Revolution*, which was written in July 1917. In this tract Lenin recapitulates Marx's view of the state under capitalism as 'the product and manifestation of the *irreconcilability* of class antagonisms'. The state is seen as 'an organ for the *oppression* of one class by another'[88] and universal suffrage as merely a means by which the bourgeois maintains his dominance. Once the proletariat seizes power, the bourgeois state is abolished, and the first task of the proletarian state which succeeds it is to suppress the bourgeoisie as a class. During this period of the dictatorship of the proletariat all the means of production are possessed 'in the name of the whole of society'.[89] This stage can only be achieved and preserved by violent revolution and the use of force in which the state becomes 'the proletariat organized as the ruling class'.[90] The subsequent 'withering away' of the proletarian state would 'obviously be a lengthy process'.[91] But the dictatorship of the proletariat would be a 'democracy for the people and not democracy for the moneybags', who would be crushed.[92] Communism would eventually render the state unnecessary, because there would no longer be any classes.

Lenin went on to reaffirm the argument set out by Marx in his *Critique of the Gotha Programme*, namely, that under socialism, the first phase of communist society, 'differences, and unjust differences, in wealth will still exist', although the exploitation of one class by another will be impossible, since the workers will own the means of production. 'Bourgeois right' will remain a criterion by which goods and services are allocated, 'as long as products are divided according to the amount of labour performed', but 'only in respect of the means of production'.[93] By this phrase Lenin meant that the means of production which were private property under capitalism would become common property under socialism. The role of the state is to preserve the institutions of common ownership and to 'safeguard equality in labour and equality in the distribution of products'.[94]

Thus we arrive at what is for our purposes a central welfare tenet of Marxist social theory. Under socialism — the first stage — it would still be necessary 'to calculate with the cold heartedness of a Shylock' the relative worth of each man's work and reward him accordingly. Beneath this 'narrow horizon of bourgeois right' a hierarchy of differential rewards and privileges would continue to exist, reflecting the unequal endowment of human beings. The role of the state would be to ensure that at least this condition of 'formal equality' was preserved through 'the strictest control . . . of the measure of labour and the measure of consumption'. But this control would be exercised 'not by a state of bureaucrats, but by a state of armed workers'[95] in which the officials would function simply as 'foremen and book-keepers'. Lenin goes on to describe socialism as a society which will have become 'a single office and a single factory, with equality of labour and equality of pay'.[96] The only requirement will be that all men and women should 'do their proper share of work'.[97] With the transition from socialism to communism society will move from a condition of 'formal equality to actual equality, i.e., to the operation of the rule "from each according to his ability, to each according to his needs" '.[98]

Under socialism the trade unions and all the other institutions of the working class would become instruments of state authority. Operating through the agencies of the Party, the workers themselves would decide on the relative worth of each man's work and the objectively correct ordering of welfare priorities. Work would be a moral obligation, and 'He who does not work, neither shall he eat.' Under socialism it would be difficult but not impossible to reconcile the claims of 'bourgeois right' — the need to stimulate economic effort — with the claims of social need among the whole community.

It was the historic role of the Party to discover and to determine objectively these labour values and social needs. Subjective definitions of these needs were unimportant. The decisions of the Party were based on assessments of how best to develop an industrial society as swiftly as possible, with the minimum delegation of power and the minimum amount of resistance. Lenin refers constantly to *armed* workers, and they are of necessity armed against enemies within and outside the first socialist state. The urban workers are the vanguard of the revolution, which can only be preserved and extended by conflict. Industrialization becomes a revolutionary imperative, not only because of the wealth it creates but because it is the source of revolutionary power. Industrialization not only increases the number of the proletariat, thus broadening the popular base of the regime, but it also creates the means by which armed struggle can be effectively waged. After the decision to build socialism in one country, industrialization remains the only possible means by which the revolution can be defended.

Thus, after the first stage of the revolution, the dominant criterion by which scarce goods and services were to be allocated became that of utility. Although this criterion was applied in the economic market, the economy was one based on common ownership and not private property. Thus a powerful set of economic rewards and sanctions was developed for ultimately political rather than economic ends.

Conclusion

The following factors would seem to be of relevance to our understanding of the scope and aims of Russian economic and social policies before the revolution of 1917 as well as the positive and negative institutional features of Russian society which influenced the making of these policies. First, the political system was autocratic, repressive and generally inefficient. There was no effective and continuous tradition of co-operation between central and local government. The lack of adequate legal institutions and process greatly inhibited the progress of orderly economic and social reform, and major legislative changes such as the emancipation created as many new legal anomalies as they resolved. The traditional resistance to almost every form of democratization made it impossible to create a viable parliamentary system within which conflicts could be accommodated. The parties of opposition were as much in conflict with each other as they were with the government.

Secondly, Russia remained throughout our period of study a predominantly peasant society, and the absence of a vigorous and innovative middle class inhibited economic and social reform. In default of such a class the objectives of economic reform and the pace and pattern of industrialization were largely defined and regulated by the government. Industrialization was imposed on a reluctant population as the willed objective of a small ruling élite. The way in which this was done and the purposes for which it was done were essentially mercantilist — national power rather than collective prosperity was the overriding consideration.

Conservatives, reformers and radicals alike were frequently indifferent, if not hostile, to the most widely shared aspiration of the peasants — which was to own the land. The policies of land reform and industrialization were carried out in such a way that a relatively small proportion of the population received, or seemed likely to receive, the benefits of positive forms of discrimination. The great mass of traditionally disadvantaged peasants were required to bear additional burdens and risks without benefit of social amelioration. At the same time a dangerously large and heterogeneous group of minorities continued to suffer traditional forms of negative discrimination which offended the criteria of both political justice and economic efficiency.[99] In a country as poor as tsarist Russia it was inevitable that industrialization and land reform would impose singular hardships on the mass of the population. The processes of change, however, were such that the traditional institutions of political and communal solidarity were undermined with relative determination and speed, without any comparable attempt being made to create alternative institutions of a protective nature.

The system of exchange relationships in Russian society became increasingly dominated by the values and expectations of a competitive economic market. In the societies of Western Europe the pace of industrial change was sufficiently rapid and uncontrolled to create a vast range of social problems, many of which were retrospectively dealt with by governmental legislation. In Russia industrialization took place in a society which lacked both democratic political institutions and efficient and honest administrators. The key legislative acts were concerned

not with retrospective social amelioration but with anticipating
the actual needs of industrialization, by the creation of a freer
labour market. The stresses and crises caused by the free play
of market forces in Western Europe were minor ones in comparison with those which were caused by the crude and sweep-
ing political decrees of the tsarist government. Emancipation,
the abolition of redemption dues, the ending of collective tax
liabilities and the land reform of 1906 were measures of enor-
mous crudity which would have created chaos and disaffection,
even if it had been possible to relate them, however approximately, to national and local labour needs. The entire process
depended upon the effective maintenance of political control
and the infinite capacity of the Russian peasant to endure hardship and uncertainty. A democratic alternative was never
seriously considered by the Tsar's advisers, although by 1906 it
would have been as much of a gamble as the course which
Stolypin decided to take. Even so the regime might have survived, and prosperity might have been more widely shared in
the long run, had the government kept its nerve in its war
with internal enemies and remained at peace with those outside.

Nonetheless the Stolypin reforms may have come nearer
to success than we will ever know. There was nothing inevitable
about the revolution of 1917, and it required a staggering
degree of ineptitude, obstinacy and suffering to bring down the
old regime.

In describing the condition of Russia prior to the First World
War the Webbs wrote that 'History records no clearer case
of an incapable autocratic ruler, with a degenerate aristocracy
and a hidebound and corrupt administration, blindly staggering
towards its doom.'[100] Stolypin had gambled on the possibility
that Russia might enjoy a further twenty years of peace. The
truly fatal administrative weaknesses of the regime became
apparent in the war. It could be argued that the political revolution began in the forests of Tannenberg. The subsequent destruction of the regular imperial army in the first year of the
war left both the tsarist and the provisional governments without credible means of military resistance or significant constituencies of political support and loyalty. The initiative and will
to win passed to the 'armed' workers and peasants who supported the Bolsheviks. This emphasis on military force becomes
apparent in Lenin's key writings during the period. The first
stage of the revolution ended in November 1917 with a small
company of Latvian conscripts evicting the Constituent As-

sembly from the Tauride Palace and with the murder of the Tsar and his family shortly afterwards at Ekaterinburg by a detachment of Siberian irregulars.

The Bolshevik revolution promised a new era of international brotherhood, but the fulfilment of that promise was contingent on the destruction of class enemies within Russia as well as the spread of revolution to other countries. Stalin, however, never equivocated in his determination to build socialism in one country, although he allowed communism to remain an international ideology throughout his lifetime. The Stalinist way to socialism was through enforced and rapid industrialization, extensive state control of every aspect of social and economic life, protective tariffs and the prevention of migration. The policies were mercantilist — albeit directed towards socialist ends — but they were also mercantilist in an essentially eighteenth-century context. In place of administrative efficiency and an innovative class of entrepreneurs Stalin relied on the use of terror, regimenting the compliant and exterminating the real and imagined enemies of the revolution.

In positive terms the immediate benefits of the revolution accruing to the Russian population were minimal. The majority of citizens suffered a sharp diminution in their living standards. The criteria by which social benefits were allocated proved to be highly selective. Savage policies of negative discrimination were adopted against dissident social groups. All the institutional bases for such resistance, the family, the commune and ethnic or religious groupings, were strictly controlled, sanctioned and modified, as necessary. A large minority of dissidents effectively lost all civic status. In place of these traditional bases of loyalty and obligation new institutional groupings were created, groupings based on the Communist Party, local street communes, comradely courts, youth organizations, collective farms and so on.

The early revolutionary attempts at transforming the legal and cultural basis of the family as a social institution were subsequently abandoned by the Soviet government in 1936. The family ceased to be derided as a relic of bourgeois society and was restored as an institution central to the needs and life of a socialist society. It was, however, to remain an institution subjected to the closest scrutiny and regulation by the Communist Party. The lives of its youngest members were integrated into the activities of the official youth movement. Priority was given to the development of social services concerned with

the care of expectant and nursing mothers and provision for
their infants when they returned to work. Divorce and abortion
were made more difficult.[101] These social policies were, however, only a part of a broader programme designed to improve
the functional relationship between familial and industrial life
and to make it a more reliable instrument for the transmission
of new political values.

The decisions to build socialism in one country and to give
total priority to rapid industrialization and the development of
military power were in effect decisions to postpone improvements in living standards for all but a minority of the population. Stalin's decision to place the aim of national security
above that of national welfare was primitive mercantilism without a trace of social conscience. As Nove observes, 'the new
men were remarkably indifferent to the welfare of the masses.'[102]
The peasants were forced into collectives 'in order to make
them the main basis . . . of the socialist version of primary
capitalist accumulation'.[103]

A new minority of highly privileged citizens was created and
its membership was decided by criteria of political loyalty and,
in special cases, economic utility. Since the regime lacked
widespread popular support, Soviet social services were used
for winning and preserving this loyalty; they were used also as
positive and negative instruments of labour discipline among
the masses. As Rimlinger concludes, 'No other country has
ever exploited its system of social protection in such a blatant
fashion.'[104] Workers in vital sectors of industry, especially
those with scarce skills, were given generous economic incentives
and welfare privileges. Malingerers and other 'hostile' citizens
were punished by the withdrawal of the most basic amenities.
Since the Party had subsumed all secondary associations under
its control, the trade unions were used for the administration
of these sanctions. This system of 'comradely courts' was a
novel form of community participation in which the workers
were required to discipline and supervise each other.[105]

As these processes of political discrimination became intensified during the 1930s, the economic market, already disrupted
by war and administrative chaos, was rendered incapable of
maintaining, let alone enhancing, standards of living. Failure to
meet even modest social expectations necessitated further
coercion and a still greater reliance on political criteria in the
allocation of what little welfare provision was available. It is
significant that the kolkhoz peasants remained largely excluded

from the benefits of the Soviet social security system until the Kruschev period of reform between 1956 and 1964.[106]

The fact that Soviet Russia has always been a one-party state ought not to obscure the extent to which the government has been able to transform public values and use various forms of community participation as means of social control. During the past decade there has been a vigorous campaign against 'parasites, vagrants and beggars', who by all accounts still constitute a major problem in Soviet Russia. We can only surmise that some of these vagrants and beggars are the victims of earlier political discrimination. The 'parasite laws' of 1960 empowered local associations such as street committees and resident associations to institute *ad hoc* public trials of such offenders.[107] The traditions of communal participation and control which derive from the pre-revolutionary mir now appear to be used in applying the strictest criteria of the economic market within a socialistic context.

In the post-Stalinist era the successful inculcation of a strictly utilitarian work ethic in the mass of the population has contributed to a more equable compromise between the claims of the political, the economic and the social markets. There have recently been significant improvements in levels of social welfare provision, and there is evidence to suggest that these welfare measures have done much to widen the basis of a genuine political consensus. In nineteenth-century Britain and America those who accepted the popular versions of *laissez-faire* asserted with confidence that no man need remain unemployed in a free economic market. Poor law officials were employed to teach that lesson to the idle. In Soviet Russia today it is asserted with equal confidence that under socialism unemployment cannot exist, and the belief is now sufficiently widely shared for local community associations to be entrusted with the task of teaching this lesson to the indolent.

References

[1] Richard Pipes, *Russia Under the Old Regime*, Weidenfeld & Nicolson, London, 1974, p. 13.

[2] ibid., pp. 21-3.

[3] ibid., p. 228.

[4] ibid., p. 307.

[5] Robert F. Byrnes, *Pobedonostev, His Life and Thought*, Indiana University Press, Bloomington and London, 1969, p. 64.

[6] Pipes, *Russia Under the Old Regime*, p. 144.

[7] Warren Bartlett Walsh, *Russia and the Soviet Union*, University of

Michigan Press, Ann Arbor, Mayflower, London, 1958, p. 227.

[8] Donald MacKenzie Wallace, *Russia*, Cassell, London, 1912 edition, p. 505.

[9] ibid., p. 139.

[10] ibid., p. 123.

[11] ibid., p. 126.

[12] ibid., p. 530.

[13] M. T. Florinsky, *The End of the Russian Empire*, Collier Books, New York, 1971, p. 179.

[14] See Pipes, *Russia Under the Old Regime*, pp. 162 et seq.; and Florinsky, op. cit., pp. 170 et seq.

[15] Quoted in Pipes, *Russia Under the Old Regime*, p. 156.

[16] ibid., p. 159.

[17] Wallace, op. cit., pp. 504-12.

[18] Isaiah Berlin, Preface to Franco Venturi, *Roots of Revolution*, Weidenfeld & Nicolson, London, 1964, pp. vii and ix; Graham Stephenson, *History of Russia 1812-1945*, Macmillan, London, 1969, p. 16; Carl Joubert, *Russia as It Really Is*, Eveleigh Nash, London, 1905; Henri Troyat, *Daily Life in Russia under the Last Tsar*, Allen & Unwin, London, 1961, pp. 102-3; and Wallace, op. cit., pp. 120 et seq.

[19] Quoted in Stephenson, op. cit., p. 132.

[20] Berlin, op. cit., pp. viii and xxix; Venturi, op. cit., pp. 147, 150 and 160; and Wallace, op. cit., pp. 143, 411 and 497.

[21] Berlin, op. cit., p. viii.

[22] ibid., p. x.

[23] Venturi, op. cit., p. 150.

[24] Berlin, op. cit., p. xxix; and Venturi, op. cit., pp. 147 and 160.

[25] Venturi, op. cit., p. 151.

[26] Berlin, op. cit., p. viii.

[27] ibid., p. xiii.

[28] Schumpeter, *Capitalism, Socialism and Democracy*, Allen and Unwin, 1961, London, p. 326.

[29] Berlin, op. cit., p. xvi.

[30] Joseph Frank, 'The World of Raskolnikov', *Encounter*, June 1966, p. 32.

[31] ibid. It is interesting to note that Dostoyevsky and Pobedonostev, one of the most powerful and conservative of the Tsar's ministers, became close friends during the last years of the author's life. On his death, Pobedonostev arranged a state funeral for Dostoyevsky and secured a government pension for his wife — see Byrnes, op. cit., p. 96.

[32] Quoted in A. Nove, *An Economic History of the USSR*, Allen Lane, London, 1969, p. 19.

[33] Wallace, op. cit., pp. 530 et seq.

[34] ibid., pp. 149-50.

[35] Stephenson, op. cit., pp. 107-8; and Walsh, op. cit., pp. 155-6.

[36] Wallace, op. cit., p. 560.

[37] ibid., pp. 85-6.

[38] Bernard Pares, *Russia*, Penguin, Harmondsworth, 1941, pp. 76-7.

[39] Wallace, op. cit., p. 87.

[40] Pares, op. cit., p. 77.

[41] Stephenson, op. cit., p. 16.

[42] Troyat, op. cit., pp. 102-7.

[43] G. V. Rimlinger, *Welfare Policy and Industrialization in Europe,*

America and Russia, John Wiley & Sons, New York, 1971, pp. 248-9. See also Bernice Madison, 'The Organization of Welfare Services', in Cyril E. Black (ed.), *The Transformation of Russian Society*, Harvard University Press and Cambridge University Press, 1960, p. 518.

[44] Wallace, op. cit., p. 570.

[45] ibid., pp. 536-8.

[46] ibid., pp. 548-9.

[47] Rimlinger, op. cit., p. 246.

[48] Florinsky, op. cit., p. 152.

[49] ibid., pp. 148-9.

[50] Walsh, op. cit., pp. 287-8; and H. Seton-Watson, *The Decline of Imperial Russia, 1855-1914*, Methuen, London, 1960, pp. 124-6.

[51] Tibor Szamuely, *The Russian Tradition*, Secker & Warburg, London, 1974, pp. 409-10.

[52] Rimlinger, op. cit., pp. 250-1.

[53] Sandra Milligan, 'The Petrograd Bolsheviks and Social Insurance, 1914-1917', *Soviet Studies*, XX, 3, 1969, p. 370.

[54] Seton-Watson, *The Decline of Imperial Russia*, pp. 109-10.

[55] Theofanis George Stavrou, *Russia Under the Last Tsar*, University of Minnesota Press, Minneapolis, 1969, pp. 127-35. See also Wallace, op. cit., pp. 660-2 and 670.

[56] Seton-Watson, *The Decline of Imperial Russia*, p. 287.

[57] Wallace, op. cit., p. 553.

[58] Seton-Watson, *The Decline of Imperial Russia*, p. 126.

[59] D. Treadgold, in Stavrou, op. cit., pp. 71-8. See also Solomon M. Schwarz, *The Russian Revolution of 1905*, Chicago University Press, Chicago and London, 1969, for an account of the involvement of both the Mensheviks and the Bolsheviks in workers' movements.

[60] R. Pipes, 'The Origins of Bolshevism', in R. Pipes (ed.), *Revolutionary Russia*, Harvard University Press and Oxford University Press, 1968, pp. 46-9.

[61] Milligan, op. cit., p. 371.

[62] Rimlinger, op. cit., p. 254.

[63] See Pares, op. cit., p. 81 and p. 22.

[64] Wallace, op. cit., pp. 725, 732-6 and 740-2; and Seton-Watson, *The Decline of Imperial Russia*, pp. 250-9.

[65] Alfred Levin, *The Second Duma: A Study of the Social-Democratic Party and the Russian Constitutional Experiment*, Archon Books, Hamden, Connecticut, 1966, p. 122.

[66] Seton-Watson, *The Decline of Imperial Russia*, p. 128. See also Schwarz, op. cit.

[67] Seton-Watson, *The Decline of Imperial Russia*, pp. 157 and 278-80.

[68] ibid., p. 279.

[69] E. H. Carr, *The Bolshevik Revolution 1917-23*, Vol. II, Macmillan, London, 1969, p. 19.

[70] Christopher Hill, *Lenin and the Russian Revolution*, Penguin, Harmondsworth, 1971, pp. 68 et seq.

[71] The expression used by Stolypin in explaining his policy objectives is given by Carr as 'The government has placed its wager, not on the needy and the drunken, but on the sturdy and the strong', Carr, op. cit., p. 22 (quoted from G. T. Robinson, *Rural Russia Under the Old Regime*, 1932, p. 194). There is an extensive literature of Stolypin's land reform policies. Carr provides an excellent summary of trends between 1906 and 1917 in

Ch. XV.
[72] Stephenson, op. cit., p. 93.
[73] Seton-Watson, *The Decline of Imperial Russia*, p. 276.
[74] Stephenson, op. cit., p. 85.
[75] Nove, op. cit., p. 22.
[76] A. Carr-Saunders, *World Population, Past Growth and Present Trends*, Frank Cass, 1964, p. 56, and Stephenson, op. cit., pp. 84-6.
[77] Pares, op. cit., p. 111.
[78] Carr, op. cit., pp. 21 et seq; and Hill, op. cit., pp. 66 et seq.
[79] Berlin, op. cit., p. xxviii.
[80] Seton-Watson, *The Decline of Imperial Russia*, pp. 273 and 276.
[81] ibid., p. 289-90. See also M. Miller, *The Economic Development of Russia, 1905-14*, 1926, pp. 139-46 and 168-70.
[82] Seton-Watson, *The Decline of Imperial Russia*, p. 243.
[83] ibid., p. 304-5.
[84] Barrington Moore Jr., *Social Origins of Dictatorship and Democracy*, Peregrine, Penguin, Harmondsworth, 1967, pp. 481 and 498-9.
[85] Pipes (ed.), *Revolutionary Russia*. See articles by Marco Ferro; G. F. Kennan; R. Pipes; and H. Seton-Watson. See also Nove, op. cit., pp. 30-1.
[86] Thomas Hardy, *Far From the Madding Crowd*, Macmillan, London, 1974.
[87] James Bunyan and H. H. Fisher, *The Bolshevik Revolution, 1917-18: Documents and Materials*, Stanford University Press, Stanford, 1965, p. 79.
[88] V. I. Lenin, *The State and Revolution*, Foreign Languages Publishing House, Moscow, 1951, pp. 14 and 15.
[89] ibid., p. 31.
[90] ibid., pp. 43-4.
[91] ibid., p. 134.
[92] ibid., p. 141.
[93] ibid., pp. 149-50.
[94] ibid., p. 151.
[95] ibid., pp. 154-5.
[96] ibid., p. 161.
[97] ibid., p. 160.
[98] ibid., p. 158.
[99] See Seton-Watson, *The Decline of Imperial Russia*, pp. 158-64, 243-4 and 303-9; Joubert, op. cit., pp. 84-137; and Byrnes, op. cit., p. 207.
[100] Sidney and Beatrice Webb, *Soviet Communism: A New Civilization*, third edition, Longmans Press, London, 1944, p. 439.
[101] Ronald Fletcher, *The Family and Marriage*, Penguin, Harmondsworth, 1962, pp. 34 et seq.
[102] Nove, op. cit., p. 367.
[103] Moore, op. cit., pp. 481 and 498-9.
[104] Rimlinger, op. cit., p. 245.
[105] See Rimlinger, op. cit.; Madison, op. cit.; and Robert Conquest, *Agricultural Workers in the USSR*, Bodley Head, London, 1968.
[106] Rimlinger, op. cit., p. 292.
[107] R. Beerman, 'A Discussion on the Draft Law Against Parasites, Tramps and Beggars', *Soviet Studies*, IX, 2, 1958; 'Laws Against Parasites, Tramps and Beggars', *Soviet Studies*, IX, 4, 1958; and 'The Parasite Laws', *Soviet Studies*, XIII, 2, 1961.

9 Community and Social Welfare in America before the First World War

The expansion and settlement of the United States offers an ideal historical context for an analysis of the relationship between social change and the development of social welfare practices. The building of new communities in the middle and far west preceded the creation of state legislatures and effective regulation by central government. Apart from self-help and mutual aid there was little assistance to be had. Furthermore the reluctance of the central government to intervene in social welfare matters was matched by a general hostility on the part of the new settlers to any undue government interference. Although there were some influential figures in American political life who favoured strengthening the powers and functions of the central government the traditions and beliefs of Jeffersonian democracy remained dominant throughout the greater part of the nineteenth century.

Political and legal institutions

Jefferson's view of good government was epitomized in his remark that it consisted of no more than 'a few plain duties to be performed by a few servants'. He feared the coming of industrialization and the time when free men might become subordinated to the growing public and private bureaucracies of the great cities. For Jefferson the ideal state of social welfare was to be found in a nation of independent farmers within which the manifest destiny of the American people might be realized.[1]

Embodied in this view of welfare was the idea of a 'covenant' between man and nature under the guiding hand of a Divine Providence inspiring the hope that in the new lands of the west a 'complete and uncorrupted' democratic way of life would be established.[2] It is significant that, from the very start of his political career in his home state of Virginia, Jefferson singled out education as the one social service which a democratic society must make freely available to its citizens. Despite his considerable influence and prestige Jefferson failed to realize this ambitious objective. The commitment to a faith in education remained, however, a distinctive feature of the traditions of Jeffersonian democracy in America. Later in the century even so intransigent a supporter of *laissez-faire* principles as William Sumner readily accepted the need for a free and universal education system.

In a succinct and illuminating comparative essay Richard Rose brings out some of the distinctive features of American democracy. As a system of government it was based upon a 'doctrine of popular sovereignty [which] places ultimate authority in the hands of the governed'.[3] The major institutions were those of the Presidency, the Congress, consisting of a Senate and a House of Representatives, and the Supreme Court. Within the terms of a written constitution extensive rights were granted to the individual citizen which enabled him to challenge — through the Supreme Court if necessary — the powers of government to infringe 'individual claims to privacy, liberty of the person, or freedom from self-incrimination'.[4] These rights, as Fine observes, were frequently exercised and 'It was in the Courts that the idea of *laissez-faire* won its greatest victory in the three and one-half decades after the Civil War and the *laissez-faire* views of academic and popular theorists and of practical businessmen were translated from theory into practice. Bar and bench joined forces in making *laissez-faire* an important element in constitutional doctrine and in establishing the courts as the ultimate censors of virtually all forms of social and economic legislation.'[5] Such interventions greatly inhibited the powers of the federal and state governments to raise taxes or loans for collective welfare purposes.

The courts not only protected but succeeded in extending the area of private rights that states could not 'arbitrarily invade; and at the same time . . . placed the narrowest possible interpretation on the admitted rights of the states to promote the general welfare through the exercise of police power.'[6] Rose also draws attention to the wide range of voting powers vested in the American citizen. The majority of office holders at federal, state and local levels — including some judges — were elected. Referendum voting on issues such as special taxes and loan raising was also a common practice.[7] The constitution therefore provided for a range and degree of public participation and community involvement that have had few historical parallels. Rose goes on to question whether these complex arrangements 'strengthen or weaken public sovereignty' or permit any electorally successful group to capture sufficient power to effect significant changes.[8]

Next, the balance of power between the federal government and the states was so ordered that the local authorities enjoyed a far greater degree of freedom from central control over their expenditures than was ever to be the case in the United Kingdom. Governmental powers were dispersed not only across the country but within Washington, so that national social policies were more difficult to formulate and, once formulated, to enforce.[9] The federal government has always had to offer financial incentives to the states, in most instances when it has been seeking the degree of co-operation necessary for unified policies or to redress regional inequalities. As Rose comments, 'Many welfare programmes established under federal law, such as aid to disabled workers or aid to dependent children, allow benefits to be fixed by state government.'[10] The consequent variations which occur between states are much greater than those tolerated in Britain.[11] These variations are a logical outcome of the wider dispersion of powers which have become institutionalized in the USA. Underlying these differences are some fundamentally different beliefs regarding the role of the central government. As Rose concludes, 'In Britain it is the freedom for combining together to use the collective institutions of government to secure common purposes, such as a national health service or strict town and country land-use planning. American values are individualist, and British values collectivist.'[12] In the case of the USA the dominant forms of mutual aid were established both in advance of governmental legislation and in regions beyond the range of effective governmental intervention.

Free enterprise and the pursuit of welfare

In contrast with Russia the United States was an open and socially mobile society which was created by emigrants drawn to it by the prospect of personal freedom and advancement. Whilst the modernizers of tsarist Russia struggled to dispense with an archaic system of land-holding and personal servitude, the United States laid claim to vast domains of sparsely inhabited territory. The emancipation of the serfs in Russia occurred during the same decade as the emancipation of black slaves in the United States. Each of these major transformations left its legacies of persisting injustice, inequality and resentment. In Russia the absence of a democratic tradition and the failure to develop democratic institutions prepared the way for violent revolution.

Collectivist doctrines had always constituted an important element in Russian culture, and the peasant had traditionally depended on the village mir for mutual aid and assistance in adversity. The survival of that institution greatly inhibited the free movement of labour during the greater part of the nineteenth century. In the United States the only comparable system — apart from the institution of slavery — was the provision for indentured labour under which some emigrants came to the eastern seaboard during the eighteenth century.

In the United States it is arguable that democratization hindered rather than helped the development of collectivist social services. The absence of a traditional land-owning class and the apparently limitless scope for self-help tended to foster attachment to the values of the economic market amongst new and old immigrants alike. During the greater part of the nineteenth century 'The poor in America considered themselves merely impoverished entrepreneurs, not as an independent class. Opportunity, not support, was their goal.'[13] For example even the majority of settlers who became wage labourers rather than independent farmers eventually formed their unions in the spirit of potential entrepreneurs rather than socialists.[14] The immigrants who survived were those who acquired most swiftly the qualities of self-help and independence which were to inhibit the growth of public social services in the succeeding decades.

By the middle of the nineteenth century the majority of white American males were enfranchised without regard to property qualifications.[15] Yet there was neither a democratic nor a paternalistic reaction against either *laissez-faire* doctrines or the poor law which America inherited from colonial times[16] and subsequently rendered still more deterrent in imitation of the English Act of 1834.[17] The major forms of statutory provision for the indigent had derived from British legislation. During the colonial period workhouses were built under 'colonial and state laws modelled on the English Elizabethan Statute of 1601'. Similarly, the itinerant poor were regulated under provisions based on the English law of settlement and removal of 1662.[18] After the Poor Law Amendment Act of 1834 the eastern seaboard states adapted their systems of relief to the new philosophy of deterrence. Workhouses and almshouses were built in greater numbers, and access to relief was generally curtailed.

What was missing from these local systems of poor relief was a central authority with its own inspectorate — like the Poor Law Commission established under the Act of 1834. The Commission survived the hostility of many parliamentarians, the majority of the guardians and the poor. It was subsequently transformed into the Poor Law Board in 1848 and merged into the new Local Government Board in 1871. Nothing comparable to this growth of central authority occurred in the history of American social policy. The deterrent philosophy of the new English poor law was adopted but not its administrative form. American poor relief remained highly localized.

Such evidence as we have suggests that it was the states and ports of the eastern seaboard which had to expand their poor law provision — both deterrent and protective — at greater speed after the 1830s. These were the states and cities standing first in line to receive a gathering multitude of the alien poor — especially of the destitute Irish. The Massachusetts legislature passed new laws in 1848 imposing heavier penalties on ships' masters who tried to evade bonding regulations. In 1847 the New York legislature passed an act requiring every ship's master 'to pay a fee of one dollar for every passenger he landed in the harbour'. In Baltimore the master had to meet the cost of caring for all sick immigrants landed and a similar scheme was adopted in New Orleans.[19]

Coleman describes the attempts made by the Massachusetts authorities during the 1850s to introduce a more deterrent regime into overcrowded workhouses and almshouses and to deport undesirable immigrants.[20] Hostility towards the increasing number of immigrants led to the growth of many nativist and anti-Catholic organizations and the rise of the Know-Nothing Party, which by 1855 had gained power in all but one of the New England states.[21] The party's influence at the national level was short-lived, but it continued to exert influence at local levels, supporting various attempts to reduce the inflow of undesirable immigrants.

After 1847 both Boston and New York began levying a head tax on all immigrants landing at their ports. Their right to levy such taxes or sureties on sick or aged immigrants had long been established. A Supreme Court ruling in 1849, however, declared that head taxes as such were illegal. It was right that bonds should be laid on 'the aged, the poor and the infirm' to continue their journeys out of the state and that the bonds should be forfeited if they stayed, but it was wrong to presume that all immigrants would become charges on the rates, when

the majority did pass through without trouble. Head taxes were
therefore ruled to be unconstitutional. Thereafter, as Coleman
observes, New York and Massachusetts 'worked a dodge
demanding not the payment of a tax but the execution of a
bond for all passengers, but kindly permitting the amount of
the bond, say several hundred dollars, to be commuted by a
once-for-all payment to be made on entry'.[22]

The desire to improve the economic and social well-being
of their families appears to have been the dominant objective
for the great majority of emigrants to America. The political
and religious freedoms to be enjoyed in the new country were
also a part of that well-being, but relatively few of the nineteenth-
century emigrants were political or religious refugees from their
own countries, and, for those who were, the future was in-
auspicious.

Hansen compares the relative successes of those who emigrated in groups and those who went as individuals or families.
A few of the groups which were religiously motivated survived
as unified settlements. Many of those who had been subjected
to political persecution were offered free passages by their
governments, but most of them 'preferred jail and martyrdom
at home'.[23] Hansen writes that 'Taken all together, the political
refugees who emigrated to America numbered only a few thou-
sand . . . and of those who had nothing to offer but their
reminiscences, Americans soon tired.'[24] Znaniecki and Thomas
also comment on the rapid demise and dissolution of politically
motivated groups of settlers. Hansen concludes that the great
majority of emigrants came from regions where 'business was
poor and the future of trade and agriculture unpromising. It
was the desire to improve their economic situation that attracted them.'[25] The politically or religiously motivated groups
failed in the main 'because they curbed the most important
single factor leading to success — individual enterprise. The
moral was clear: a single person or a family could be better
alone.'[26]

Self-help and mutual aid in the frontier communities

F. J. Turner in his 'frontier thesis' argued that western migration provided a 'safety valve' for the tensions and frustra-
tions of the new American cities[27] and that the availability
of frontier lands ensured the survival of local democratic
communites against both collectivism and competition.[28] There
are certain affinities between Turner's thesis and that of the

early Russian social and political theorists who looked to the village commune for moral salvation. Both were in the populist tradition. Turner comments on the family-centred individualism that was characteristic of the new immigrants. In one respect he saw this quality as 'anti-social', producing 'antipathy to control, and particularly to any direct control'. As was so often the case in the countries they had left behind, the new settlers viewed the tax-gatherer 'as a representative of oppression'.[29] Yet in order to enjoy the amenities of a civilized life — and also to attract more immigrants — the new communities had to provide some elementary social and public services. The availability of free land enabled these needs to be met for a considerable period without undue recourse to taxation. As Turner remarks, 'Provisions for reserving lands within the granted townships for the support of an approved minister, and for schools, appear within the seventeenth century and become a common feature of the grants for frontier towns in the eighteenth.' In subsequent decades this practice became the foundation 'for the support of common schools and state universities by the federal government'.[30]

These educational and religious institutions served a wider purpose in generating new patriotic loyalties and a sense of national identity. One effect of the frontier on the new communities, according to Turner, was the promotion of the values of democracy and self-help. Boatright, however, draws attention to 'the numerous ways in which the principle of mutuality finds expression in frontier life'. The experience of 'common danger and common poverty provided a strong corporate life'. Neighbours helped each other in times of sickness, death or other disasters. Each settler 'helped his neighbour with his cattle because he needed his neighbour's help. He nursed his sick neighbour because he himself might need nursing. It wasn't that he expected immediate or specific payment in kind. It was that . . . this sort of neighbourly co-operation was the frontier's answer to social security.'[31]

What the settlers did demand and eventually secure from the federal government was a measure of protection in the form of tariffs. They were also determined to dispossess the Indians of their lands, with or without the support of the central government. Initially this process began through the insidious effects of 'alcohol, disease, and dependence upon the implements of civilization'.[32] The sustained and systematic destruction of the buffalo between 1866 and 1873 completed this process by destroying the economic foundations of the Indian way of life. The assimilationist policies which were followed sporadically after 1887 as a result of the Dawes Act further enfeebled what remained of a separate cultural identity amongst the Indians. But by this time the final push to occupy what remained of the open lands was under way. By the early 1890s the era of the frontier was over.

In one respect the Turner thesis can be interpreted as a cursory but illuminating analysis of the relationship between social development and changing popular conceptions of social welfare. It is, however, necessary to piece together this theme from the various essays which Turner published during his life-time. The immigrants in the main were men 'who would not accept inferior wages or a permanent position of social sub-ordination when this promised land of freedom and equality was theirs for the taking'. They were prepared to endure inferior standards of living in order that their children might eventually 'enter into a heritage of education, comfort and social welfare' and it was 'for this ideal' that the pioneer 'bore the scars of the wilderness'.[33]

Competitiveness, tempered by degrees of mutual aid, and an attachment to the ideals of democracy and equality were seen by Turner as the distinctive qualities of community life on the frontier. These qualities began to pass away or to become sub-ject to modification 'with the end of the era of free lands'.[34] Turner could already discern that 'In the . . . arid plains . . . of the remoter west . . . all this push and energy is turning into channels of agitation . . . demanding an extension of govern-ment activity in its behalf.'[35] Turner was preoccupied with the collectivist influence of new forms of populist doctrine on the mid-western farmers in the 1890s. In part he attributed the growing influence of these doctrines to the increasing number of 'alien immigrants' who tended 'to lower the standard of living and to increase the pressure of population upon the land'.[36]

The cultivation of these marginal arid lands was fraught with additional risk and was creating a new class of capitalist farmers, who were paradoxically more disposed to seek the protection and support of the government. Legislation in the form of trans-port nationalization, special agricultural credit schemes and government-sponsored irrigation programmes was increasingly seen as 'an instrument of social construction'.[37]

Neither the welfare beliefs and practices of the American

settlers nor the subsequent form of government intervention fit readily into the analytical models which we use in the study of British social administration. The beliefs of the settlers cannot be understood in terms of unqualified egoism or altruism. Individualism was an important feature of the culture, but, as Turner argues, the settlers 'were not mere materialists. . . . They were idealists themselves, sacrificing the ease of the immediate future for the welfare of their children, and convinced of the possibility of helping to bring about a better social order and a freer life. They were social idealists.'[38] They were in effect familial altruists *par excellence*.

There are affinities with Weber in Turner's final comments, when he compares in passing the American and the Prussian experience of social betterment. The forms of government intervention demanded by the mid-western farmers were meant to stop far short of any direct intervention in family and local community life. The fundamental 'heritage of pioneer experience' was a 'passionate belief that a democracy was possible which should leave the individual a part to play in a free society and not make him a cog in a machine operated from above'.[39]

Turner did not despair of the survival of democracy and he did not believe that it was incompatible with industrialization. He believed that the American populist movement was liberal in its openness to new forms of democratic control but also conservative in its disposition to preserve as many of the older forms as was possible. He hoped that the most beneficial effect of frontier culture upon American capitalism would be to help it to develop along a middle way, avoiding the excesses of unrestrained competition and 'institutional regimentation' which were a part of the European experience. The moral authority of the middle way rested upon an appeal to patriotism and natural interest, since 'The distinction arising from devotion to the interests of the commonwealth is a higher distinction than mere success in economic competition.'[40] In the pursuit of this ideal Turner hoped that the new state universities of the middle west would play a major educational role, providing 'bulwarks against both the passionate impulses of the mob and the sinister designs of those who would subordinate public welfare to private greed'.[41]

Despite this expression of hope there are elements of geographical and economic determinism in Turner's thesis which conflict with even his conditional optimism. By the early 1890s the era of free land was over. The prospect of land had served in the past as a necessary restraint upon the selfishness of men and a wholesome antidote to their natural fears of insecurity and hunger. The possibly beneficial effects of greater industrial production are not explored at length by Turner, although this theme was later taken up by Charles Beard,[42] who argued that the capitalist 'plutocrats' of the eastern seaboard had misused the Supreme Court and the Constitution to limit state rights in the exercise of private power and the disposal of private property. Beard looked back to the period between 1896 and 1912, when, during the administration of Theodore Roosevelt, there had been a sustained attempt to find the middle way between capitalism and socialism, using the powers of the executive to improve 'the general standard of life, labour and education'.[43] By 1919, Beard argued, disillusionment had set in as a result of the war and the social damages caused by unrestrained capitalist enterprise.

Capitalist enterprise was from the start the driving force in the opening of the middle and far west for settlement. The great banking and industrial corporations, which Jefferson had seen as being fundamentally antipathetic to his dreams of an agrarian democracy, swiftly followed the multitude of small-scale speculators who offered their services to the new settlers. Settlers and speculators alike faced considerable risks in their search for personal advancement. Banking, for example, was a perilous business undertaking for both the borrowers and the lenders. Some banks operated without charters and issued bills 'with only the word of the stockholders to protect the holders of the money'.[44] During the 1850s and 1860s the farmers also began to organize clubs and societies to protect their economic interests, to encourage new horticultural techniques and to provide credit on favourable terms for the organization of local fairs. Rates of interest on both loans and deposits tended to be high. Mortgage companies flourished, and in some areas foreclosures were common amongst the poor landholders.

Bartlett emphasizes the crucial role of private speculation and entrepreneurship in the development of the new urban centres of the west — a term becoming progressively more occidental as the frontier communities pushed out towards the Pacific. The great cities of the future such as Cincinnati and Chicago were initially the products of 'real estate bonanzas', and there were many others which despite intensive advertising and early settlement never became established or which disappeared entirely after a few initially promising years of growth. The subsequent location of railways and river steamship services was crucial. The relationship between urban growth and municipal improvement was frequently tenuous. There were mining towns which, having committed their ratepayers, albeit reluctantly, to municipal service improvements, found themselves left — after the unexpected exhaustion of minerals — with a fearful burden of public debt.

Developers used local newspapers to publicize the attractions of their new towns and especially to attract skilled workers and small businessmen such as blacksmiths, hoteliers and shopkeepers. Such publicity often included totally misleading illustrations of spacious tree-lined roads, churches and steamships moored along well laid out wharves, when the reality amounted to a few chipboard and sod-house dwellings. In other towns such as Leavenworth there were real if modest developments. Nonetheless emigrants were often deeply disillusioned on arrival by the primitive surroundings in which they had invested their savings and hopes. Occasionally churches and schools were given free sites by the municipality. As early as 1829 Tennessee passed a law giving any father of three or more children 200 acres of state land per child.[45] Similar policies were followed in parts of Nebraska and Kansas during the 1850s. There were frequent attempts, sometimes successful, by prospering townships to buy out whole rival townships or to attract settlers away from them.[46]

In the history of frontier expansion there are many examples of spontaneous local community organization for the purposes of mutual aid and protection. The cheap land was the magnet which drew the immigrant peoples in search of a better life. Land was synonymous with welfare. The allocation and sale of these lands was, however, often a confused and risk-laden undertaking, carried out in a thrusting entrepreneurial spirit and refereed with only partial effectiveness by the federal government. There were frequent disputes over claim boundaries, at a time when surveying techniques were imprecise. Along the expanding frontier there grew up many extra-legal organizations 'to protect the settler in his possession of the land and to act as an arbiter in the case of disputes'.[47] These 'claim clubs' were usually the product of local mass meetings, and their objective was to prevent the defrauding of settlers. Sometimes they were infiltrated by transient speculators intent upon fraud. Sometimes disputes over tenure divided the resident members. As

Everett Dick observes, 'Claim clubs varied greatly. On the one extreme, self interest ruled largely in most of the proceedings, while on the other the general interest and welfare of the settlements was the ruling principle.'[48] Within the new communities other themes of conflict emerged not only between white settlers and Indians but between the permanent settlers, the absentee claimants and squatters without legal rights. One of the purposes of the claim clubs was to push out the squatters wherever possible.[49] It would be interesting to add to our comparative research into the development of formal welfare policies in the United States and Britain further comparative studies of the voluntary activities of the British Friendly Societies and Collecting Clubs, their American counterparts in the new cities, and these frontier claim clubs.

Bartlett observes that 'The family was of especial importance in the new country, for it was the one social structure that provided stability. It antedated the coming of government, law and order, schools and churches. When children were orphaned due to disease, accident or Indian depredations, or left destitute by desertion, it was not at all unusual for a neighbouring family to take them in and raise them with their own.'[50] In some of the new states and territories the sex ratio was as high as six males to every woman. Some surprisingly enlightened attempts were made to attract more women of marriageable age to these districts. By the 1850s most of the states had passed legislation acknowledging the right of married women to hold property in their own names. In Wyoming in 1869 and Utah in 1870 women were granted not only such property rights but full suffrage, including an entitlement to vote, to serve on juries and to enjoy equal pay for equal work.[51]

There was a general lack of graciousness in the social life of the mid-nineteenth-century frontier towns. Dick reports that 'The wives and daughters of the respectable cultured class seldom walked on the streets and when they did, they wore veils or sun-bonnets to hide their faces from the men.' A minister of religion who slept overnight in Atcheson in 1865 complained that he was unable to rest 'on account of blasphemous language, groans of pain, and the ring of revolvers heard thro the night'.[52] There is no doubt that in the early years of town development, life on the frontier was often rough and rudimentary. Yet the amenities and styles of civilized living were desired and worked for by many of the citizens. The new townships wanted in the main to attract respectable and stable citizens, and those with large families were especially welcomed.

The subsequent arrival of more women and their growing influence in the new communities had an important effect on the quality of social life outside the family. Library and literary associations, sewing clubs, public readings and concerts, open air debates and organized church fêtes and galas became established features of the new townships. At the same time women were prime movers in the organization of Temperance Societies. It was the women jurors of Laramie, for example, who were the first to enforce licensing hours in a township already notorious for the number of its saloons. Associated with the Temperance movement were various lobbies and campaigns against gambling. These local interests came together and found common cause in the Anti-Saloon Leagues of the late nineteenth century. Travelling preachers, most of them non-conformist in affiliation, also provided sobering influences on frontier life, until permanent churches were built.

Domestic life on the frontier could be exceedingly hard, especially in winter. Basic items like wood and nails were expensive and scarce. Many cabins lacked doors and windows, their occupants making do with blankets or greaseproofed papers.[53] The traditional sod-houses were cut and shaped from prairie mud bricks. These constructions had certain advantages over the more highly esteemed wooden houses as they were cooler in summer and less cold in winter, but their roofs and walls were liable to collapse and also to infestation by vermin. The first habitation of a settler family might be no more than a dug-out in the side of a hill. Thereafter the pattern of progress would be measured out in constructional stages, from dug-out to the crudest sod-house, the addition of wooden doors and windows and eventually a complete log cabin. The ultimate index of success was a wooden frame-house. The initial living conditions of these families as settlers were frequently more primitive than those which they had left behind. As Dick observes, 'The sod-house dweller had to learn to migrate when it rained. If the rain came from the north . . . it was necessary to move everything to the southside; if from the south a move had to be made again. When the roof was saturated it dripped for three days after the sky was bright without.'[54] He also quotes one woman pioneer who recalled how 'In case of sickness, someone had to hold an umbrella over the patient in bed. One old settler remembers that they often had to dispense with kneeling at family worship because the floor was in puddles.'[55]

The characteristic social and economic living conditions of small-scale farmers in the old north-west between 1850 and 1860 are described in an essay by Carter, 'Rural Indiana in Transition'.[56] By mid-century the greater part of Indiana was already settled, but new communities were still being opened up in the northern part of the state. About a half of the population were still living in log cabins, and most of the others had brick or wooden frame-houses. One in two of the men were farmers who owned their land. There was a rudimentary rail system and a sufficient market for agricultural produce to provide modest farming incomes in good times. A typical farming household consisted of upwards of sixty-five acres and supported the farmer, his wife and four children as well as providing some employment for hired labourers. The most characteristic community undertakings centred upon the raising of barns and the husking of beans. Frontier weddings were the occasion of major celebrations. On the evening of a wedding there would be a 'charivari', with local townspeople gathering outside the young couple's home and making a great deal of noise with cowbells and saucepan lids until they were invited in for a party. The following day there would be another party for close friends and relatives.[57]

Carter observes that, although 'practically all individual effort was being rewarded with moderate success . . . confidence in the future rather than satisfaction with the present was the key-note insofar as material well-being was concerned'.[58] A farm labourer earned between eight and twenty dollars per month, but food was cheap, with eggs costing between four cents per dozen in summer and ten cents in winter and beef selling at three dollars per hundredweight.[59] Throughout the 1850s the price of food — and the price of land — rose steadily. Nonetheless the contrast in the standards of living of the 'rural poor' in these communities and those of the southern English agricultural counties of the time is a dramatic one.[60]

The greatest challenge facing the newcomers was 'getting a home' and surviving the first few years against the risks of 'adverse weather, crop failures, ill health' and the consequences of bad management. Levels of farming technology were generally low. Corn was planted, cut, stocked and husked by hand and cultivated by hoe, but Indiana was a progressive state, and during the 1850s new techniques were adopted. Wheat and cattle production per cultivated acre of land or head of cattle increased steadily. The state had one of the highest proportions of farmers in the Union. The transition from farming for a living to farming for profit was marked by the sponsoring of state fairs in Madison, Indianapolis and New Albany during the 1850s, with exhibitions and sales not only of farm produce but of an increasing range of modern agricultural machinery.

As the transition to a modern agricultural economy took place, the demand for hired and seasonal labour increased. Cox provides a useful summary view of this trend as it developed between 1865 and 1900,[61] and draws attention to a situation which became 'as much a social problem as were the conditions of employment in the early nineteenth century factories of England and America'.[62]

In southern states such as Louisiana the transition from slavery to freedom did not progress beyond the status of tenancy for many of the black people. Very few of them were destined to become owners, although it appears that there was a minority of black agricultural workers who held resident status and were thus able to bargain for better wages than those obtained by white seasonal or casual workers elsewhere. The demand for such labourers grew with the rapid development of fruit and vegetable production and other forms of market gardening.

The new immigrants were a vitally important source of labour. Cox describes how they were often recruited almost on arrival. Successive waves of 'Irish, Germans and Swedes took to the fields, then came the Italians and Poles. By the nineties, padrones were rounding up Italian families in Philadelphia for harvest work in New Jersey. Before the end of the decade, Polish people had replaced the Irish as the most important group of foreign born farm labour in Massachusetts.'[63] Many young immigrant boys were hired for work in tobacco fields. Cox also describes how the term 'help' was replaced by that of 'labour' during this period, and sees this change in title as indicative of the changing status of farm workers. Throughout the states of the eastern seaboard labour relations were becoming formalized. Cox quotes from a Report of the Maine Board of Agriculture that 'It is in the employment of many labourers and in the accumulated profits of those many labourers that he [the manufacturer] builds up his income. It is precisely so in farming.'[64] In this pursuit of profit wage rates tended to be kept as low as possible, and 'The farmer came to look upon the labourer not as a temporary member of his household but as an important item in the cost, and consequently in the profit, of his business enterprise.'[65]

By the 1870s many farmers were beginning to look for sources of labour even cheaper than those supplied by the European migration. As one Massachusetts farmer remarked, 'What is needed to improve the farming interest is more and cheaper labour. Let the Asiatic come. Ireland has almost run out, and those now here are getting much too Americanised to be very efficient help — the best working for themselves and buying farms and the others earning their wages as easily as they can.'[66] There are numerous references in the evidence submitted to a Congressional Committee of 1877 to the need for sources of labour which would be even cheaper to hire than the Chinese. Although the Senate passed anti-Chinese immigration legislation in 1882, the Chinese continued to make up the majority of transient labourers in the Californian vineyards and orchards. As the years passed, the most frugal and fortunate of these immigrants saved enough to set up as small-scale entrepreneurs and shopkeepers. For those who remained as labourers, wage rates and working conditions did not improve. They worked for as little as one dollar a day and slept in yards and barns. This new rural proletariat was in turn displaced during the depression of the 1890s by Japanese workers, who tended to be both better organized and more militant than the Chinese.

Conflicts arose between employers and workers not only over wages but as a result of the changing quality of labour relations. The fate of the much romanticized cowboy paradoxically exemplifies a growing trend towards a routinization of labour relations. Although he was traditionally considered to be the 'aristocrat of all wage-earners' the cowboy as a rule was simply a hired hand, working for eight months in the year at a monthly wage of twenty-five to thirty dollars. A strike of 325 cowboys in Texas during 1883 was apparently motivated 'not only by wage consciousness but also by resentment of the impersonal treatment and loss of status and of opportunity to become independent ranchers which accompanied the expansion of absentee corporate ownership'.[67] Union organization was also taking place during the 1890s amongst hired sheep hands.

The steady commercialization of farming was increasingly dependent upon a supply of migrant workers who could be hired and fired on a seasonal basis. There was 'a regular migratory movement of labour which characterized the entire western wheat country of the Great Plains until tractors and combine harvesters replaced them in the nineteen-twenties'.[68] Everett Dick suggests that this migratory pattern was established as early as the 1870s. Nonetheless it seems that from the 1890s onwards many of these workers, dissatisfied by their low wages and wretched living conditions, were moving to the new cities in search of better prospects. The indices of real wages for the period between 1866 and 1899 suggest a gradual falling behind of farm rates in comparison with those of non-farm workers. In addition to these relative deprivations the farm labour force found itself not only excluded from the traditional temporary inclusion in the farmer's household but also denied access to the gradually developing community-based services such as elementary schooling, which the citizens of the new townships were beginning to provide for their own children.

Amongst the many criticisms of the Turner thesis it has been suggested that the cities, rather than the rural frontier lands, provided until recent years the 'safety valve' for popular discontent.[69] Nonetheless the alliance between capitalists and workers which was to make possible the victory of the North in the Civil War found its most dramatic expression in the Homestead Act of 1862. The availability of free land contributed to giving both rich and poor a common commitment to the values of entrepreneurship and the economic market.[70] The Homestead Act provided that any head of a family who had reached the age of twenty-one could occupy up to 160 acres of the public domain, 'improve it for five years, and at the expiration of that time be given a legal patent to the land'.[71] The cost of such a transaction could be as little as ten dollars. There were several other ways in which land could be purchased cheaply — from the railroad companies, from land companies or through the provisions of the earlier Preemption Act of 1841. The risks of ruin, however, could be almost as great as the dangers of fraud. In many parts of the middle west the pioneer had to contend not only with climatic extremes, the dangers of drought and extreme loneliness, but with an acute shortage of timber and other basic materials. Nonetheless a multitude of immigrants moved into these open plains to pit their wits and energies against a frequently hostile environment. On the basis of the available evidence Hobsbawm warns us against exaggerating the number of actual beneficiaries under the Homestead Act — as distinct from the number of hopeful participants. He estimates the number of beneficiaries at less than 400,000 households.[72] Mencher, however, goes so far as to describe the

Homestead Act as 'the American counter-part to British concern about the poor laws'.[73]

In comparison with Britain the creation of new forms of community organization and consensus in the United States can be interpreted as following a more democratic course, unaffected by paternalistic concern or intervention by the central government. Houses, schools and churches had to be built, local defence organized and law and order enforced. The process of establishing these basic services and resolving local conflicts of interest helped to create structured communities out of scattered homesteads and to establish a tradition of participant democracy.[74] Inter-state migration initially endangered strong local ties of community, but with the passage of time it also created a new sense of national identity.[75] The social problems and challenges arising from immigration were, however, manifested more dramatically in the cities than in the frontier regions.

Self-help and mutual aid in an urban context

It was to study such problems that Thomas and Znaniecki prepared their classic study, *The Polish Peasant in Europe and America*.[76] Most of the Polish immigrants had originally lived in villages where family and local community ties sustained a network of social relationships based on 'common responsibility and prestige, reciprocal response, continuity of traditions, similarity of occupation, etc. — a complex and indivisible set of attitudes'.[77] These local communities, stable though they appeared to be, had nonetheless been subject to a sequence of radical political and economic changes. The emancipation of the Polish serfs had taken place in 1807. Since the freed peasants had not received any allotment of lands, many of them became labourers on the estates of their landlords, to whom they paid relatively high rents. After the Polish rising of 1861 the tsarist government in 1864 instituted a series of land reforms, under which small allotments of porperty were made to these labourers from the estates of the nobility. The main purpose of the reforms was to alienate the peasantry from the Polish aristocracy.

The transition of rural emigrants from peasant communities to an acceptance of new forms of social organization serves as a central theme in Handlin's study, *The Uprooted*.[78] In writing of the nineteenth-century Polish communities before the period of land enclosures, Handlin comments on their 'simple but profound division of labour based on sex, familial status and age',[79] with the 'family and land in the village . . . locked in an unyielding knot. And the heart of the bond was the marriage system.'[80] The 'knot', however, was made to unravel by the intrusions of economic change. The gradual consolidation of holdings by the larger landlords gradually separated and trans-formed the peasantry into two main groups — the smaller of these was composed of independent farmers renting large areas of land on long-term leases, with a majority reduced to short-term tenancies of smallholdings. The income from these tenan-cies had to be supplemented by day or seasonal labour. The traditional bases of land-holding, including the sharing of common fields, gradually gave way to more efficient forms of organization in response to the growing demand of the new towns for more food.

By the end of the century the characteristic forms of land tenure amongst the better-off peasants were family holdings, secured on twelve-year leases, and one-year leases, held by manorial servants. It was a way of life which afforded a measure of protection against dire want but offered little scope for personal advancement. In times of economic distress it was customary for help to be given by the local lord and for such help to be accepted without loss of social standing. On such occasions help would only be stigmatizing if the provider attempted to 'interfere with personal or family life, except in the case of those who depended on him personally and had no land'.[81] It seems that emancipation had encouraged the growth of the qualities of independence and regard for personal privacy.

Although wages were generally very low in Poland before 1914, there is some evidence to suggest that industry was deve-loping fast enough to absorb the surplus agrarian workers. Pros-pective emigrants often faced official hostility and the dis-approval of their local communities. In some country districts the managers of estates complained of a scarcity of labour, which may be attributable to the seasonal migration of peasants to Prussia as well as the migration to America.[82] Thomas and Znaniecki suggest that most of the Polish emigrants were poorly paid workers and small farmers. They were concerned to pre-serve or enhance their standards of living although they came 'in general . . . from the less stable and less organized elements of Polish society'.[83] Seasonal migration to Germany had often been 'the first step in preparing the individual, psychologically and economically for the idea of transocean emigration'.[84]

Thomas and Znaniecki lay considerable emphasis, however, on the fact that the prospect of emigration only quickened the disposition of certain individuals and their families to break with a traditional way of life which had long ceased to satisfy them.

The immigrants who survived and prospered were those who were quick to acquire the qualities of self-help and independence — qualities which were to inhibit the growth of public social services in the United States during the succeeding decades. It was in the new cities rather than the frontier regions that the failures rather than the successes of the immigrants first began to attract sustained public anxiety. They were amongst the earliest concerns of American social workers and of the few public social services which existed. In each wave of immigrants there were those who could not make the difficult transition from one way of life to another. Thomas and Znaniecki undertook their great survey between 1918 and 1920, with the particular object of examining a process of 'social disorganization' and setting out 'the materials for a rational social policy'.[85] They attempted to describe the ways in which personality and social structure were modified in the process of migration. Their theoretical interests were focused on the interactions of individual and social phenomena and the processes through which individual attitudes were modified by the objective cultural elements of social values. They were equally interested in the extent to which these objective facts of social organization were in turn influenced and redefined by individuals. This concern with the interrelationship between social structure and personality provided the conceptual framework for a study which still stands as a major, if neglected, contribution to the development of symbolic-interactionist theory.

The authors summarized their approach in stating that 'The cause of a social or individual phenomenon is never another social or individual phenomenon alone, but always a combination of a social and an individual phenomenon.'[86] The student of social change must analyse not only the action of individuals but also the social context in which it takes place, as well as the pre-existing attitudes on the basis of which this action was performed. In this way it may be possible to understand how and why new social attitudes develop — and in the case of Polish migration to the United States how a new cultural element of that society was created.[87] Thomas and Znaniecki's study thus draws upon both sociological and psychological perspectives in seeking to explain major processes of change at individual and institutional levels of activity. They emphasize the importance of studying change in its various situational contexts and consequently they are able to provide an analytical framework which can be applied to the study of both the formal and the informal aspects of social welfare, ranging from institutional levels to the most transient and spontaneous of individual welfare practices. Their approach has been criticized by Herbert Blumer on the grounds that the distinction between social 'values' and individual 'attitudes' is a vague and confusing one, which weakens the explanatory potential of their theory.[88] This criticism is, in my view, a valid one, but it can be applied to any social theory which is concerned with differentiating between the causes and the characteristics of social and individual behaviour. Very similar criticisms have been levelled more recently at the 'culture of poverty' thesis. They are useful cautions against attributing too much causal significance to either individual or social variables.

Although the Polish peasants were historically and culturally different from their Russian counterparts, Poland had been a part of the Russian Empire for over a century (apart from a brief Napoleonic interlude). The Polish system of land-holding and conditions of life were therefore subject directly and indirectly to the policies of the Russian government. Furthermore there were enough cultural similarities to justify our using Thomas's and Znaniecki's findings in a cross-national study of social welfare.

Of all the new American cities Chicago attracted the largest single concentration of Polish immigrants, who numbered about 360,000 at the time of the study. Approximately three million Poles had migrated to the United States before the First World War, and of these roughly 30 per cent are thought to have returned home.[89]

These Polish immigrants came to Chicago as strangers in a hostile environment, which lacked all of the traditional Polish forms of mutual aid based on the extended family and the local community. Successive groups of Polish immigrants settled as near as possible to the fellow nationals who had preceded them, and, as the number of immigrants increased in these localities, the original residents moved away. The highly localized nature of these settlements was strengthened by the establishment of Polish estate agencies, building societies, loan clubs and savings banks. The building of new churches and parish schools and the publication of Polish newspapers accelerated the process. Thomas and Znaniecki observed that, whenever these colonies reached a membership of between 100 and 300, the Polish immigrants invariably founded a 'society'. The major function of these 'societies' was the provision of mutual aid against the contingencies of sickness, death and unemployment. The alacrity with which the 'societies' were founded indicates how little time elapsed before the immigrants came to feel the lack of their traditional forms of mutual aid. The new forms of association were not, however, based on the traditional notion that entitlement to help rested solely on the idea of common membership in a community. In the early days there were a number of 'societies' which were intended to provide assistance on an *ad hoc* basis, but they were swiftly replaced by regularized insurance schemes, often small in scale but governed by economic rather than social principles.

During the three years when he was the Director of the Emigrants Protective Society, Znaniecki collected extensive material about the kinds of social problems and risks which beset the Polish immigrant communities. He found that 'Pauperism, sexual demoralization and the whole scale of delinquency [were] represented among American Poles in a much larger measure than among the population of Poland from which the immigrants [were] recruited.'[90] The incidence of mental illness was also disturbingly high. Although the immigrant population included a relatively high proportion of 'abnormal' persons, who were therefore at risk, Znaniecki found what he considered to be 'overwhelming evidence' that much of the 'social disintegration' had its origins in the 'novelty' and uncertainty of the social situation. The immigrant was often unable to 'define situations which surge up in the course of his life', and the resulting uncertainties destroyed 'whatever remnants of normal habit he had left and [drove] him finally into mental chaos'.[91] These changes had a particularly damaging effect on the morale of the womenfolk. In their village communities in Poland the women had derived social significance from the various horticultural tasks which were their traditional responsibility. They had kept livestock, tended vegetable gardens and made a significant contribution to their household economies. Isolated in their Chicago tenements, however, many of these women tended to become isolated and depressed and a prey to sloth and drunkenness.

The most notable changes occurred with regard to the care of the sick and the deviant. In the Polish villages physical and mental handicaps had been contained within the extended family, and 'however disabled physically an individual . . . there [was] some place for him in the family economy of peasant life, even if it [was] only the supervision of children in the absence of parents. His position [might have been] inferior but not abnormal in consequence of the mere fact that his work [was] not equivalent to the expense of his support.' Even the totally helpless had a clear and unequivocal claim to support, with little consequent risk of stigma. Under the pressures of the new urban life 'economic interests' became 'divorced from other interests and individualized', so that simple membership of the community was no longer a sufficient claim to mutual aid. Znaniecki and Thomas postulated a clear connection between economic dependency and 'economic demoralization', interpreting the growth of mutual aid insurance as a collective attempt to prevent wherever possible this transition from dependency to loss of self-respect.[92] The alternative to mutual insurance was poor relief and charity. The doctrines and procedures of these public organizations were, however, of such a kind that they were bound to conflict with the traditional attitudes and beliefs of the Polish immigrants. Their effect was to hasten rather than check the process of demoralization.

The Polish peasant brought to America a deeply familial notion of altruism. He feared and resented the intervention of charitable outsiders. Collectively this resentment was expressed in the view that 'Every Pole who accepts the help of American institutions is . . . considered not only disgraced as a pauper, but as disgracing the whole Polish colony.'[93] In Poland those who had resorted to public relief had suffered personal humiliation. In Chicago the applicant for relief also brought collective shame upon his group. For the uninsured, the sick or the disabled person the public hospital, with its connotations of alien charity, meant public disgrace as well as pauperization. Znaniecki describes instances of destitute and sick Poles committing suicide rather than seeking help from the county authorities, and he refers to 'an unmitigated aversion to the use of hospitals and to allowing the county or the city to bury the dead'.[94] In times of dire crisis, however, some of the immigrants were inevitably driven to overcome their revulsion from relief; furthermore they tended 'after the first step' to become 'very bold and exacting' in their future requests for help. From the point of view of Thomas and Znaniecki and from that of the Polish immigrant communities this subsequent willingness to use public relief was evidence of further demoralization, and the ultimate price paid by these applicants was total exclusion from 'respectable' society.

There were degrees and stages in this process of humiliation. Immigrants who accepted only material help were less to be despised than those who were subjected to personal investigation and advice on family matters. Znaniecki and Thomas were highly critical of the relief and social work agencies, which ignored or were ignorant of 'the specific social psychology of the immigrant', and they argued that there would have been less damage to morale if the agencies had 'simply pledged a definite amount of relief for a definite period in cases of real need, and abstained from all active interference'.[95] It seems evident that, in seeking to check moral disintegration among the immigrant communities, some social agencies were actually hastening the process. They were bringing about the incorporation of the 'failed' Polish immigrants into the wider American society, but at the lowest level of civic status and self-esteem.

The replacement of the traditional forms of mutual aid based on the values of the social market by the economic principles of insurance created further social divisions in the immigrant communities. The insurance schemes were at best a compromise between claims for aid based on common membership of a social group and a developing tendency to rely on evidence of self-help and success as the index of desert. In the traditional village communities only the incorrigible 'anti-socials' had been excluded, but the new immigrant communities were far less tolerant of the 'inefficient and misadapted' and far more disposed to judge new members in terms of their capacity for self-help. Thomas and Znaniecki suggest that 'The more coherent and self-conscious the community becomes, the less it is inclined to bother with the misadapted and the disabled. This is simply a manifestation of the tendency of the group to self-preservation, made possible by the facility of excluding the weak members from, or more exactly, of not including them in the community system.'[96] Urban living gave a greater freedom to the new immigrants, including the freedom to enhance the welfare of their own families and to deny responsibility for 'the innumerable cases of family decay, juvenile delinquency, alcoholism, vagabondage, crime'[97] which were appearing in their neighbourhoods.

These changes in the traditional forms of mutual aid at local levels were complemented by the growth of new forms of national consciousness. Although the local mutual aid 'societies' were characteristically American in their underlying values and practices, most of them were initially affiliated to larger associations which maintained strong emotional ties with Poland. The two largest associations were the Polish National Alliance and the Roman Catholic Union, both founded in the 1880s. Both associations provided training in local leadership through their mutual insurance schemes, but the Polish National Alliance was also committed to wider political objectives, including the preservation of links between the home and the immigrant communities through the provision of funds for the national liberation movement. This patriotic attachment to Poland became weaker with the passage of time. The Polish National Alliance became less concerned with political objectives and more preoccupied with preserving the solidarity of Poles as a distinctive ethnic group within the United States.[98] By the turn of the century the Polish National Alliance was also predominantly concerned with working for the 'prestige, security and solidarity of Polish-American Society',[99] and the American branch of Pilsudski's Committee of National Defence collapsed through lack of support, when the immigrants declared that they would no longer take instructions from 'abroad'.

Insurance became the central activity of the Polish National Alliance and the source of its considerable financial strength. By 1918 the membership had risen to just over 126,000, and the revenue was in excess of seven million dollars. The insurance scheme was based on a network of nearly 1,700 local groups, federated into twenty-six sections. Over half the membership was concentrated in Illinois, Pennsylvania, Michigan and Wisconsin. The funds were administered by seven commissions, each one concerned with a particular kind of provision, of which sickness and death benefits and the building of schools were the most important. The task of one of these commissions was 'to grant assistance to members who present certificates of complete destitution'.[100] These business activities were intended not so much to create a social bond as 'to stabilize and extend a social cohesion which otherwise would manifest itself only irregularly and within narrower limits'. As Znaniecki and Thomas point out, 'Mutual insurance is not a basis of association but of organization.'[101]

The Polish Roman Catholic Union was the second largest of the Polish immigrant associations. It was mainly concerned with the preservation of ethnic and cultural unity and was generally critical of the Polish National Alliance, whose leaders were suspected of both socialistic and masonic tendencies.[102] The Roman Catholic Union was in turn the subject of frequent attacks by the smaller Polish political associations, which put forward the argument that it should spend less of its resources on parish schools and give more support to political work. The leadership of the Union replied by pointing out that 'Every insurance of ours is literally a benefit . . . taking into account the unusually low assessments in the Union in proportion to the amount of insurance. We receive here raw, simple, often very dark people . . . you will not attract such poor fellows who come here for bread by lofty ideals and high aspirations.'[103] The Roman Catholic Union appears to have continued as a parish-based association, which was concerned as much with charity as with insurance.

The Polish National Alliance and the Roman Catholic Union were substantially correct in their assessment of the needs and aspirations of their members. The primarily political associations attracted only a very small minority of supporters. The Alliance of Polish Socialists had a membership of only 2,000, and it was one of the largest political groups. Although many of the immigrant families suffered periods of intense hardship, and although a minority of them were broken by these experiences, discontent was never sufficiently widespread to give rise to systematic political protest. As increasing numbers of the immigrants grew more prosperous and began to invest in property, they became more closely integrated into a newly emergent Polish-American culture as well as the wider American way of life, while the dissident 'nationalist' and 'socialist' groups gradually lost the little influence which they had once exerted.

As these new communities evolved, they developed distinctive forms of participant democracy and leadership. Traditional forms of mutual aid gave way to schemes of mutual insurance which were increasingly based on the individualistic values of self-help and independence. Elements of the old culture remained, but the welfare ideals of the new immigrants were both more ambitious and more exclusive. These individualistic qualities found a natural affinity and inspiration in the dominant values of the economic market rather than those of the social market. The idea of welfare and its practical modes of expression underwent a dramatic transformation within the space of half a century.

These processes of change in one large immigrant community helped in turn to reinforce the popular basis of belief in the virtues of the free market which later inhibited the development of publicly financed social services in America. Any analytic framework which defined social welfare largely in terms of statutory intervention and administrative processes would largely pass over these fundamental changes in welfare practice and living standards as topics of marginal importance. In the same way the historian of welfare is tempted to leave blank the periods of human endeavour and achievement in which neither the political intelligentsia nor the benevolent public administrator played a major role.

It may be that in other immigrant cultures the patterns of social change were different, and that the idea of welfare was expressed in other forms. The settler minorities most likely to succeed are probably those who adopt most readily the dominant values of their new country, whatever those values happen to be. We need to know far more about the part played by these complex patterns of cultural interaction in the formation and transformation of welfare ideals, before we can presume to judge whether one set of ideals is morally superior to any other. This kind of knowledge will also help us to study the aims and functions of formal welfare bureaucracies and agencies within their total societal contexts. There is nonetheless much that we still need to learn about the welfare practices of ordinary people in the areas of social life which are unregulated by formal policies and expert opinions. We can add a new dimension to our knowledge if we give more attention to the times when the range of such formal regulation was far more limited than it is today.

In this chapter I have concentrated on certain informal aspects of social welfare practice which have been neglected in the past rather than on the development of formal social policies in the United States — which has been the subject of extensive study elsewhere. Community is a term which lends itself more readily to description than definition. The forms of mutual aid based on community organization vary dramatically between different societies and within any given society over time. A comparison of the Russian mir and typical forms of community development on the American frontier illustrates how striking these differences can be. Of even greater interest, perhaps, are the differences which can emerge under conditions of change, when an alien culture like that of the Polish *émigrés* from tsarist Russia is translated into a new societal context. In studying such changes it becomes necessary to use terms like individualism and collectivism with great caution. The American experience reminds us that collectivism is not necessarily synonymous with extensive intervention by the state — or incompatible with individualism. In Thomas's and Znaniecki's study of urban life we can observe a trend towards the emergence of new forms of collective enterprise and aid based on the ethics of the economic rather than the social market.

A similar trend can be observed in the farmers' co-operative movements such as the Grangers, the Southern Alliance and the National Farmers' Alliance which grew up in the populist midwestern states of the 1870s.[104] These movements encouraged the co-operative pooling of capital resources and began campaigns for objectives such as railway nationalization and monetary reform. Turner emphasizes two features of this reconciliation between individualism and collectivism — the desire to make a reality of the 'ideal of democracy' and the willingness of the pioneers to sacrifice 'the ease of the immediate future for the welfare of their children'.[105] But the forms of collective intervention were fundamentally different from those which occurred in Britain, and the key differences lay in the fact that welfare provision remained a strictly personal concern. The role of the government was to ensure that the individual entrepreneur had a fairer chance in the competitive struggle for survival.

These co-operative movements found their urban counterpart in the reformist programmes of the Progressive Party during the 1880s and 1890s. Despite the introduction of local schemes of social insurance and factory legislation in cities such as Madison, Cincinnati and Cleveland 'progressivist' ideas influenced federal policy for only a brief period during the presidency of Theodore Roosevelt, who won a massive presidential victory in 1904, with an electoral programme of imperialism and social reform. It was in part Roosevelt's inability to carry through these social reforms that caused him to adopt a more radical position and to stand unsuccessfully as presidential candidate for the Progressives in 1912.[106] His successor, Woodrow Wilson, carried on the progressive tradition of American politics in a more moderate form. The main beneficiaries were the railway workers and seamen, whose conditions of work were improved, as well as the independent farmers, who secured government aid for land improvement and road construction. The economic market was more carefully regulated, but it remained largely uncomplemented by social service provision.

The almost total inadequacy of public social services was revealed during the depression of the 1930s. Nonetheless even during the peak years of unemployment 'An interesting feature of popular discontent was a tendency towards self help in contrast to the emphasis on assistance'.[107] Protest organizations like the Bonus Army, the Townsendites and the Old Age Pensions Movement campaigned for limited objectives based largely on principles of self-help. Franklin Roosevelt's New Deal was a programme to save capitalism, not to destroy it. The Social Security Act of 1935, while compromising between the claims of the economic and social markets, emphasized 'contractual' rather than 'social' rights.[108]

Piven and Cloward argue that the primary function of the American public relief system was and continues to be to preserve the efficiency and continuity of the economic market, either by alleviating conflict or by forcing men to work 'on any terms' when employment is available.[109] The thesis is an interesting one, but it neglects what seems to be the most interesting and obvious points of all. Despite the eagerness with which social scientists diagnose and publicize the gross injustices and inadequacies of American society, no other country has had to protect itself so thoroughly against such a legion of prospective new members.

Despite the persistence of racial and ethnic discrimination and residual poverty in America, the relative lack of collective welfare provision in that country was for a remarkably long period as conducive to consensus as has been its increasing availability in Britain. The American Supreme Court was for many decades an impediment to social reform,[110] but the major obstacle has been the sheer success of capitalism in America. Neither socialism nor the social gospel movement made any substantial impact on this general attachment to economic market values.[111] The socially deprived in both the United States and Britain have been gradually reduced through economic progress or social reform to a residual minority. Sociologists may question the evidence regarding the process of embourgeoisement. The fact is that, if the deprived and the despised were not a residual minority in most Western democracies, it would not be necessary for social scientists and other pressure groups to urge their claims with such vigour. In America the social theories of Spencer and Sumner have proved at least as reflective of popular opinion as either the reformist tradition in American sociology, which originated in the Chicago school, or its more recent radical manifestations.

Conclusion

Carrier and Kendall warn us against seeking to identify 'critical' periods in the historical development of social policies.[112] Nonetheless it is very difficult to undertake comparative studies without noticing some periods which seem to be more important than others, and there seems to be no reason whatever why they should not be mentioned in a speculative way.

In the case of Britain it can be hypothesized that the Great Depression of the 1870s hastened a retreat from individualism to collectivism that was already under way within the social market. Britain was slow to adopt protectionist economic policies, but this was because Britain had always had a uniquely powerful tradition of free trade. Furthermore for the greater part of the nineteenth century free trade was the best policy by which Britain could further its own economic interests.

Russia had to face the challenge of industrialization in the twentieth century with the political attitudes and administrative resources of an eighteenth-century despotism. Its best ministers tried to adopt policies which were essentially mercantilist but which could not succeed without the unequivocal support of a ruling class and the adoption of foreign policies which avoided rather than welcomed the prospect of war. After the revolution the goal of industrialization was pursued with extreme ruthlessness and out of exclusively national interests. Events did not allow Russia a period of adjustment or adaptation. Under the tyranny of tsarism all the criteria of economic, social and political desert in the allocation of welfare goods and services were employed in such inconsistent and inefficient ways that the regime finally lost every credible basis of loyalty and support. The revolution of 1917 expressed widespread longing and demand for economic and social justice, but the aims of the revolution were subsequently pursued by priority being given to the criterion of political loyalty and desert. The constituency of the privileged was kept small, partly because there were so few goods and welfare services to distribute, and partly because public opinion was effectively cowed by the totalitarian political system. Stalin in his domestic and foreign policies adopted a singularly brutal version of mercantilist doctrines as the means of creating socialism — down to the eventual recovery of the last kilometre of the former Russian Empire.

The United States also suffered from the great recession of the 1870s, though not to the same extent as Britain. Until the close of the nineteenth century it possessed the economic asset of seemingly free land. The popularity of the doctrines of individualism and competition was sustained by real prospects of opportunity and personal advancement. The gradual adoption of protectionist trade policies was not accompanied or followed by any significant growth of collectivist social policies at home. In the United States it was the Great Depression of the inter-war years which shattered confidence in the unregulated free market. In addition to the ruin of countless urban enterprises the agricultural communities also suffered greatly. Unemployment rose from just over 1½ million in 1929 to nearly 13 million in 1933, and during the same period 'One out of every eight farmers was forced to give up his property.'[113]

The New Deal had little if anything to do with socialism, and it was at best a cautious experiment in collectivist social welfare. Nonetheless it marked a beginning and created a precedent from which retreat was to prove difficult. The subsequent resistance to collectivist proposals for policies such as a free health service has been a sustained and at times a successful one. Under the Truman administration between 1946 and 1952 the post-war Fair Deal programme enjoyed some successes in the provision of low-rent housing and the improvement of schemes for old-age and survivor's insurance. These developments are associated with the aftermath of the Second World War and the Korean War as much as the period of Johnson's 'Great Society' programme and the war on poverty is linked with the intervention in Vietnam. The over-all effectiveness of these gradual but massive extensions of the involvement of government in social welfare has been the subject of intense debate. Taken together, however, they constitute a significant shift in governmental policy — and presumably also in public opinion — through the weight which they added to collectivist intervention.

The belated adoption of collectivist policies in the United States has been paralleled by dramatic internal movements in population. Perhaps the drift of over 20 million black and white Americans from rural to urban areas between 1940 and

1970 has had the most significant implications for social policy. The rural basis of welfare individualism has vanished. The ghetto problems of the cities have become the new focus of collectivist welfare priorities. They are problems, however, which require solution through economic opportunity as well as better social services. The inhabitants of these inner city areas are now far more likely to be indigenous black citizens than recently arrived white immigrants of the kind studied by Thomas and Znaniecki.

Both Britain and the United States experienced at different stages in their development a crisis of confidence in the capacity of their economies to provide without governmental regulation for the welfare of their citizenry. In Britain the collectivist reaction began in the 1870s, gathered momentum in the years prior to and during the First World War, and reached a second peak during and after the Second World War. In the USA the crisis came later, during the inter-war depression, but the advance of collectivist sentiments and policies was again coincident with two international conflicts, namely, the Second World War and the war in Vietnam.

The ideological resistance to these changes in welfare philosophy and policy has been sustained and powerful, because its supporters could appeal to the dramatic success of capitalism as a creator of wealth and welfare in both countries. If in Britain past successes and promises for the future were epitomized in the ideals of international free trade, in America they originally found expression in the ideals of the Covenant and the frontier, and of entrepreneurial opportunity. Both were sets of ideals which stressed the morality of self-help and yet linked this morality with a sense of belonging to a much wider community.

In Russia the collectivist tradition of mutual aid was shaped by the needs of a subsistence agrarian economy and a centralized despotism which was both inefficient and corrupt. Industrialization began the destruction of this old order; defeat in war and the subsequent revolution completed it. The collectivist doctrines of Bolshevism were as much at variance with the old system of mutual aid based upon the mir as with the values of capitalism and the interests of the new entrepreneurial class. The crisis in confidence was so fundamental that one political order was replaced by another. Thereafter new criteria of political loyalty took precedence over both economic and social considerations in the allocation of welfare. The objective of the new revolutionaries was not simply to industrialize but to industrialize in a particular way and towards a specific political end.

References

[1] John C. Miller, *The Federalist Era, 1789-1801*, Harper Torchbooks, 1963, pp. 71-3; and R. Hofstadter, *The American Political Tradition*, New York, 1948, pp. 176-7.

[2] See also David W. Noble, *Historians Against History: The Frontier Thesis and the National Covenant in American History*, University of Minnesota Press, Minneapolis, 1965.

[3] Richard Rose, 'A Model Democracy?', in Richard Rose (ed.), *Lessons from America*, Macmillan, 1974, p. 133.

[4] Rose, op. cit., p. 135.

[5] Sidney Fine, *Laissez-Faire and the General Welfare State: A Study of Conflict in American Thought, 1865-1901*, University of Michigan Press, Ann Arbor, Geoffrey Cumberlege, Oxford University Press, London, 1956, p. 126.

[6] ibid., p. 140.

[7] Rose, op. cit., pp. 140-1.

[8] ibid., p. 140.

[9] ibid., p. 146.

[10] ibid., p. 148.

[11] loc. cit.

[12] ibid., p. 159.

[13] Samuel Mencher, *Poor Law to Poverty Program*, University of Pittsburgh Press, Pittsburgh, 1967, p. 237. See also Oscar Handlin, *The Uprooted*, Watts & Company, London, 1953, pp. 217-19.

[14] Frank Thistlethwaite, *The Great Experiment*, Cambridge University Press, London, 1955, pp. 156 et seq.

[15] Charles A. Beard and Mary R. Beard, *A Basic History of the United States*, New Home Library, Blakiston Company, Philadelphia, 1944, pp. 117 and 209-13; and Richard Hofstadter, William Miller and Daniel Aaron, *The American Republic, Vol. I, to 1865*, Prentice-Hall, New Jersey, 1959, pp. 390-3.

[16] Blanche D. Coll, 'Public Assistance in the United States: Colonial Times to 1860', in E. W. Martin (ed.), *Comparative Development in Social Welfare*, Allen & Unwin, London, 1972, p. 130.

[17] Mencher, op. cit., pp. 131 et seq. and 148-51.

[18] Coll, op. cit., p. 130.

[19] Marcus Lee Hansen, *The Atlantic Migration, 1607-1860*, Harper Torchbooks, New York, 1961, pp. 255-61.

[20] Terry Coleman, *Passage to America*, Hutchinson, London, 1972, pp. 224-7.

[21] ibid., p. 230.

[22] ibid., p. 233.

[23] Marcus Lee Hansen, op. cit., p. 273.

[24] ibid., pp. 273-4.

[25] ibid., p. 274.

[26] ibid., p. 165.

[27] F. J. Turner, *The Frontier in American History*, Holt, Rinehart &

Winston, New York, 1962, p. 275.

[28] ibid., pp. 30-1.

[29] ibid., p. 30.

[30] ibid., pp. 60-1.

[31] Mody C. Boatright, 'The Myth of Frontier Individualism', in Richard Hofstadter and Seymour Martin Lipset (eds), *Turner and the Sociology of the Frontier*, Harper Torchbooks, New York, 1968, pp. 45-8.

[32] Richard A. Bartlett, *The New Country: A Social History of the American Frontier, 1776-1890*, Oxford University Press, New York, 1974, p. 32.

[33] Turner, op. cit., pp. 259 and 263.

[34] ibid., p. 202.

[35] ibid., pp. 219-20.

[36] ibid., p. 277.

[37] ibid., pp. 277 and 305.

[38] ibid., pp. 348-9.

[39] ibid., p. 358. See also 'Max Weber on Bureaucratization in 1909', in J. P. Mayer, *Max Weber and German Politics: A Study in Political Sociology*, Faber & Faber, 1954, 'it is still more horrible to think that the world could be filled one day with those little cogs, little men clinging to little jobs and striving towards bigger ones — a state of affairs which is to be seen once more . . . playing an ever-increasing part in the spirit of our present administrative system', p. 127.

[40] Noble, op. cit., p. 51; and Turner, op. cit., pp. 357-8.

[41] Turner, op. cit., p. 286.

[42] Charles and Mary Beard, *A Basic History of the United States*, p. 380; see also Noble, op. cit., p. 56.

[43] Noble, op. cit., p. 68.

[44] Everett Dick, *The Sod-House Frontier, 1854-1890*, Appleton-Century, New York and London, 1943, p. 89.

[45] Bartlett, op. cit., p. 361.

[46] Dick, op. cit., pp. 42-3.

[47] ibid., p. 21.

[48] ibid., p. 28.

[49] Bartlett, op. cit., p. 59.

[50] ibid., p. 363.

[51] ibid., pp. 357-8.

[52] Dick, op. cit., p. 68.

[53] ibid., p. 77.

[54] ibid., p. 114.

[55] ibid., pp. 115-16.

[56] Henry L. Carter, 'Rural Indiana in Transition, 1850-1860', *Agricultural History*, 20, 1946, pp. 107-21.

[57] Dick, op. cit., p. 73.

[58] Carter, op. cit., p. 108.

[59] ibid., p. 115.

[60] See John Burnett, *Plenty and Want: A Social History of Diet in England from 1815 to the Present Day*, Penguin, Harmondsworth, 1968; and G. E. Mingay, 'The Transformation of Agriculture', in Institute of Economic Affairs, *The Long Debate on Poverty*, p. 56.

[61] Lauranda F. Cox, 'The American Agricultural Wage Earner, 1865-1900', *Agricultural History*, 22, 1948, pp. 95-114.

[62] ibid., p. 95.

[63] ibid., p. 99.

[64] loc. cit.

[65] ibid., p. 100.

[66] loc. cit.

[67] Quoted ibid., p. 104.

[68] ibid., p. 106.

[69] See Hofstadter and Lipset (eds), op. cit.; and Noble, op. cit., especially in the former, Everett S. Lee, 'The Turner Thesis Re-examined', pp. 66-7; Fred A. Shannon, 'A Post-Mortem on the Labor-Safety-Valve Theory', pp. 172 et seq; and Hofstadter's Introduction, p. 7. Shannon suggests that the 'frontier thesis' may be most usefully treated as 'a special case of a more general theory of migration', p. 66.

[70] Charles and Mary Beard, *The Rise of American Civilization*, Vol. I, Jonathan Cape, London, 1927, pp. 648-9; and Moore, op. cit., p. 130.

[71] Bartlett, op. cit., p. 113.

[72] Eric Hobsbawm, *The Age of Capital 1848-1875*, Abacus, Sphere, London, 1977, p. 167.

[73] Mencher, op. cit., p. 238.

[74] S. Elkins and Eric McKitrick, 'A Meaning for Turner's Frontier: Democracy in the Old North West', in Hofstadter and Lipset (eds), op. cit., p. 127; and Boatright, op. cit., p. 48.

[75] Turner, op. cit., p. 30.

[76] W. I. Thomas and Florian Znaniecki, *The Polish Peasant in Europe and America*, Vol. I, Dover Publications, New York, 1958, p. 350.

[77] ibid., p. 1,688.

[78] Handlin, op. cit.

[79] ibid., p. 9.

[80] ibid., p. 12.

[81] Thomas and Znaniecki, op. cit., p. 1,698.

[82] ibid., p. 98.

[83] ibid., pp. 94 and 1,500.

[84] ibid., p. 98.

[85] ibid., p. 350.

[86] ibid., p. 44.

[87] ibid., p. 1,469.

[88] Herbert Blumer, *An Appraisal of Thomas and Znaniecki's The Polish Peasant in Europe and America*, Social Science Research Council, New York, 1939. See also Larson, op. cit., pp. 101-8, for a useful summary of this theoretical approach.

[89] Thomas and Znaniecki, op. cit., p. 1,511.

[90] ibid., p. 76.

[91] ibid., p. 1,690.

[92] ibid., p. 1,688.

[93] ibid., p. 19.

[94] ibid., p. 1,697.

[95] ibid., pp. 1,698-701.

[96] ibid., p. 34.

[97] ibid., p. 1,586.

[98] ibid., p. 84.

[99] ibid., p. 1,602.

[100] ibid., p. 1,634.

[101] ibid., p. 1,577.

[102] ibid., p. 1,602.

[103] ibid., p. 1,640.

[104] Frank Thistlethwaite, op. cit., pp. 259-62.

[105] Turner, op. cit., pp. 348-9.

[106] There are useful summaries of the rise and decline of the Progressive Party in Thistlethwaite, op. cit., pp. 268-72; and Fine, op. cit.

[107] Rimlinger, op. cit., p. 201.

[108] ibid., pp. 204-5 and 230.

[109] Frances Fox Piven and Richard A. Cloward, *Regulating the Poor: The Functions of Public Welfare*, Tavistock Publications, London, 1972, pp. xiii and 33.

[110] Fine, op. cit., pp. 126 et seq. and 140 et seq.

[111] Charles Howard Hopkins, *The Rise of the Social Gospel in American Protestantism 1865-1915*, Yale University Press, New Haven, 1961.

[112] John Carrier and Ian Kendall, 'Social Policy and Social Change: Explanations of the Development of Social Policy', *Journal of Social Policy*, 2, 3, 1973, pp. 209-24; and 'The Development of Welfare States: The Production of Plausible Accounts', *Journal of Social Policy*, 6, 3, 1977, pp. 271-90.

[113] Donald R. McCoy, *Coming of Age: The United States During the 1920s and 1930s*, Penguin, Harmondsworth, 1973, p. 178.

10 Settlement, Migration and the Search for Welfare

The values of the economic market assert the right and the obligation of the individual to seek his own welfare where it can best be maximized. The values of the social market place greater emphasis on the right of the individual to receive at least a guaranteed subsistence in the community of his own choice. In their extreme forms the one philosophy stresses the obligation of the individual to seek work wherever it can be found, and the other emphasizes the obligation of society to bring work to the worker.

Britain and the United States were the first great nations to become industrialized. Government intervention when it occurred, was designed to give greater scope to the free play of market forces. The governments of both countries resorted to coercive poor laws in order to create a mobile industrial labour force. This chapter explores the process by which the terms of the rights to work and welfare were modified and extended. In Britain throughout the seventeenth and eighteenth centuries the movement of labour within the economic market was regulated by a variety of mercantilist laws. There were restrictions upon both internal migration and emigration. The social markets of relief were highly localized, and under the Acts of Settlement the individual had a right to relief in a particular parish.

During the nineteenth century these mercantilist restrictions upon labour mobility were gradually removed. Industrialization created a national labour market. The administration and provision of relief, however, remained a local matter, under the jurisdiction of local authorities. It also became British policy to encourage emigration, preferably of paupers and other persons who could not find employment at home. Successive American governments for their part encouraged immigration but increasingly gave preference to those who appeared to be potentially the most economically productive. (The flow of emigrants was contingent upon the export of British capital, without which economic expansion in the United States could not have been sustained.)[1] Today the local provision of relief has become primarily the responsiblity of the central government. The boundary demarcations regarding rights to welfare and obligations to assist, which once were drawn between local communities within nations, now occur mainly between nations. At the same time the international movement of labour has been significantly restricted. Nations only admit immigrants whose skills are in short supply, and even these exceptional cases are frequently denied entitlement to welfare rights in the social market.

The English Settlement Acts continued to operate throughout the period during which *laissez-faire* was a dominant influence in economic life, and so they provide an illuminating counterpoint to the process by which freedom in the mobility of labour was gradually extended. This freedom was related to the value placed by the economic market on the labour of the individual. The price of individual failure in the economic market was a loss of civic freedoms in a much wider sense.

The terms on which goods and services were exchanged between nations were radically modified in Britain by the transition from mercantilist protection to free trade. The terms on which labour was allowed to move also changed, but in a far more inconsistent and complex manner. Goods unsold are a loss to their owner, but labour unhired implies a cost to someone other than the labourer, and this responsibility had traditionally been charged to the ratepayer and discharged through the poor law. The decision as to which particular group of ratepayers was chargeable was made by reference to the Acts of Settlement.

The general effect of the English laws of settlement throughout the seventeenth and eighteenth centuries was to inhibit the free movement of labour within the country. Their major purpose was 'to enable the justices, on complaint of the churchwardens or overseers, to remove any newcomers from a parish, though not applying for relief, if they think or profess to think that he is likely to become chargeable'.[2] We need look for no better example of an exclusive and highly conditional definition of obligation and entitlement which is based on residence in a local community. Although the repressive aspect of these laws has always been emphasized, the idea of settlement also expressed a person's legal right to benefit from poor relief, subject to his having resided in a given locality for a prescribed period of time. For many of the poorest migrant labourers, however, the process of relief began with an act of rejection and dissociation and ended with their return to communities of which they were only legally members and in which they would not be made welcome.

Adam Smith was in no doubt concerning the deleterious effects of the settlement laws upon the creation of wealth. In Book I of *The Wealth of Nations* he observes that 'Whatever obstructs the free circulation of labour from one employment to another obstructs that of stock likewise.'[3] While the corporation laws impeded the movement of skilled workers and entrepreneurs, the settlement laws had the same effect on labourers. Smith's attack on these laws, however, went beyond a concern for greater economic efficiency, since in his view 'To remove a man who has committed no misdemeanour from the parish where he chooses to reside is an evident violation of natural liberty and justice.' In his opinion there was 'scarce a poor man in England of forty years of age . . . who has not in some part of his life felt himself most cruelly oppressed by this ill-contrived law of settlements'.[4]

Thomas Hardy gives an interesting example of the way in which the settlement laws could be manipulated by farmers to their own advantage in the period to which Smith refers. The old maltster in *Far from the Madding Crowd* describes how, at the turn of the eighteenth century, he worked eleven years for one farmer, who 'wouldn't hire me for more than eleven months at a time, to keep me from being chargeable to the parish if so be I was disabled'.[5]

The authors of the 1834 Poor Law Report concluded that the settlement laws were often operated in a corrupt and fraudulent manner. Their proposals for change, however, were modest and amounted to little more than a recommendation that the grossest anomalies be removed. They were not prepared to recommend 'settlement by residence'. They agreed that this was 'the most natural and the most obvious' solution, and that its adoption 'would often prevent inconvenience to particular parishes, from the return in age or infirmity of those who have left there in youth and vigour, and inconvenience to the paupers themselves, from being removed from friends and residences to which they have become attached, to places in which they have become strangers'.[6] Nonetheless these advantages were outweighed by several 'powerful' objections.

The authors of the Report condemned modes of obtaining settlement which encouraged 'perjury and fraud' and which imposed arbitrary limits on the employer's choice of his labourers and the labourers' rights to sell their labour to best advantage. Any unconditional granting of a right to settlement simply by residence would give the labourer a right to poor relief which he would lose should he subsequently move to another parish in search of new or better employment. The authors compared the unsettled labourers, who 'At present . . . are confessedly superior, both in morals and in industry, to those who are settled in the parishes in which they reside.' 'Make that residence give a settlement', they went on to argue, 'and they will fall back into the general mass.'[7]

These views were reflected in the provisions of the Act of 1834. The Act made provision for the enlargement of areas of residence by allowing the guardians of the new unions to treat their union as if it were one parish for the purposes of settlement, subject to the approval of the Poor Law Commissioners. The Act also abolished the rights of persons to acquire settlement by hiring, by service or by serving an office or an apprenticeship in sea service. This provision left only the conditions of birth, apprenticeship (other than in sea service), renting, ownership of an estate or payment of rates. Legitimate children took the settlement of their fathers, but, if the fathers had no settlement, they took that of their mothers. Until such details had been resolved, legitimate children, like bastards, took settlement from their birthplaces. One parish could only charge another if a pauper was eligible for removal.

Throughout the mid-nineteenth century, the conditions of irremovability were made increasingly stringent. After 1846 a person could not be removed from a parish in which he had resided for five years. This term was reduced to three years in 1861 and then to one year in 1862. The 1861 Statute also defined residence in terms of the union and not a parish of that union, leaving guardians no choice in the matter. Any period of time which a pauper had spent in a workhouse, a hospital or a prison was deducted from the stipulated time.

The primary purpose of the 1834 Poor Law Amendment Act was to reduce the cost of poor relief by forcing the destitute to seek their own salvation in the free economic market. The new poor law was the instrument by which *laissez-faire* could be made to work, as one of the most important prerequisites of an efficient market economy was the free movement of labour. Paradoxically the actual system of poor relief was based on highly localized unions, while anything less than a truly national system of poor relief was certain to militate against the creation of a truly national labour market. Thus it came about that, within the very institution which had been designed to create a mobile labour force, the older mercantilist traditions, embodied in the settlement laws, survived with remarkable tenacity throughout the hey-day of nineteenth-century *laissez-faire*.

The laws of settlement did change nonetheless, albeit in a slow and piecemeal way. By the 1860s the scope of obligation under the poor law had been extended from parish to union. If one of the traditions of community care can be said to have had its origins in the laws of settlement it was certainly tenacious in its survival and grudgingly narrow in its compass.

One cannot but note the striking paradox which had resulted from the combined effects of change in economic policy through the liberalization of trade and change in social policy through the reform of the poor law. The labourer was now encouraged to move wheresoever the market required it in order to secure employment and preserve his independence. If that economic independency was lost, however, he stood in danger of compulsory return to pauperdom in the union of his origin. As the authors of the 1834 Report explained, 'No man can be removed until he himself, by applying for relief, gives jurisdiction to the magistrates.'[8] They recognized the misery and hardship that could be caused by compulsory removal but rested their case on the grounds that 'A person who applies to be maintained out of the produce of the industry or frugality of others must accept that relief on the terms which the public good requires.' The small minority whose destitution was not caused by their 'own indolence, or improvidence, or misconduct' could be saved from removal by charitable agencies.[9]

These sentiments expressed a very narrow view of social obligation, but there is little doubt that they reflected the attitudes of many guardians and ratepayers. Yet these definitions of obligation were consistent with a period in which travel was still difficult and in which many local communities were geographically isolated. To the ratepayers of Okehampton or Coldstream the pauper delivered from London or Birmingham must have seemed as alien as the immigrant from Uganda or Pakistan seems to our metropolitan ratepayers today.

Emigration offered the pauper an alternative to removal, provided that he could raise the passage money and was reasonably fit. Migrationist policies gained favour in response to the rising incidence of pauperism in the countries of Western Europe which were becoming industrialized. In Britain the authors of the 1834 Poor Law Report were 'of opinion that emigration, which has been one of the most innocent palliatives of the evils of the present system, could be advantageously made available to facilitate the application of the remedies which we have already suggested'.[10] They went on to quote with approval 'numerous instances' in which local parishes were already sponsoring the emigration of paupers. By the middle of the nineteenth century there was an increasing number of European states which were attempting to solve the problem of a rising demand for poor relief by encouraging emigration.

Those who made the Atlantic crossing were to discover prosperity or destitution on the same terms as those prevailing in Britain. The workhouses which had been built by the communities of the eastern seaboard were regulated by laws deriving directly from the Elizabethan poor law. The movements of the travelling poor were similarly controlled and sanctioned under enactments modelled on the English settlement laws. The deterrent philosophy of the New Poor Law was rapidly adopted by the eastern seaboard states after 1834, as the tide of immigrants increased in volume. Workhouses and almshouses were built in greater numbers and access to relief was generally curtailed.

Coll emphasizes the important role played by these institutions in coping with the increasing number of immigrants arriving throughout the 1840s and 1850s at the various eastern seaboard ports. Well over 3 million immigrants disembarked during this period, and many of them had to seek immediate relief from the destitution authorities.[11] An extensive literature exists on the perils of the Atlantic crossing, and the costs of coping with so many destitute immigrants clearly evoked much hostility and resentment in cities such as Boston and New York. Coll observes that 'No detailed study of public assistance in the middle west and western states has been made', but she goes on to suggest that 'Their poor laws followed and sometimes copied verbatim the wording used by the older settlements in the east.'[12]

The Atlantic migration to America was the most dramatic expression of the search for welfare in modern times. The United States was built on the hopes of the 33 million immigrants who came to its shores between 1821 and 1924.[13] In addition a further 22 million people emigrated to South America, Canada, South Africa, Australia and New Zealand. The great majority of all these migrants, well over 80 per cent, settled in North and South America.[14] Cipolla estimates that the 'average annual overseas emigration from Europe amounted to *circa* 377,000 individuals per year in the period 1846-1900, somewhat around 911,000 in 1891-1920 and about 366,000 in 1921-1929'.[15]

A relatively high proportion of these emigrants subsequently returned home again. Carr-Saunders observes that 'While few figures can be given . . . 30% of those who entered the United States between 1821 and 1924, and 47% of those who entered the Argentine between 1821 and 1924 are believed to have returned home again.'[16] Whether they returned home because of success or failure, we cannot be sure. Charlotte Erickson remarks on the very inadequate statistical records of migration from Europe. The available data do not distinguish between nationalities, between settlers and transients before 1853, between cabin and steerage passengers before 1863 or between those who stayed and those who returned home before 1895.[17]

There were other important migrations of population within Europe during the nineteenth century. Moller suggests that the migrations included a relatively high proportion of skilled workers such as Lancashire cotton operatives, Cornish miners and Welsh iron workers, and German, Italian and French tradespeople, who carried their skills across the continent of Europe as far as Russia in search of the best working conditions and wages.[18] It was workers of this kind whom the inhabitants of the new frontier townships of North America were particularly eager to attract.

The connections between patterns of migration and demographic and economic changes are very difficult to interpret. Habakkuk advances the view that one consequence of the growth of population during the eighteenth century was that it stimulated agricultural innovation and increases in food supplies, which in turn weakened the traditional restraints on early marriage and child-bearing.[19] He suggests that 'There was a fall in mortality in the last two or three decades of the eighteenth century',[20] which was less likely to have been caused by improvements in the food supply than by improvements in medical knowledge and care, notably the spread of the practice of innoculation against smallpox.[21] The trend towards an increase in family size may be accounted for by a fall in the age at marriage, particularly in areas where the 'proportion of women in *industrial* employment' was rising[22] and in areas where owner-cultivation was giving way to tenant-farming and wage labour. Habakkuk suggests that 'Marriages depend upon housing, and the provision of cottages for labourers instead of accommodation within the farmhouse is likely to have led to a fall in the age at marriage.' In the past 'living-in' was a positive restraint on marriage, as had been in the past the expectation of land inheritance. Conversely the 'proletarianization' of agricultural labour might have encouraged 'recklessness and early marriage'.[23] Habakkuk concludes that there were a number of factors which could have accounted for changes in the patterns of marriage. It is possible that 'People were marrying earlier . . . because conditions had changed so that exercise of the same degree of prudence dictated earlier marriage. On this reading of events, economic development offered positive opportunities for earlier marriage, as abundant land did in early nineteenth century America.' It is also arguable that these changes were 'partly due to social disorganization. People married early . . . because they were so depressed that they had nothing to hope for.'[24]

The authors of the 1834 Poor Law Report emphasized the fact that the dramatic increase in population had been 'nearly as rapid' in the agricultural as in the industrial counties.[25] Under these conditions the generous provision of poor relief encouraged fecundity and wasted funds which would have been better spent in the creation of new industries. As the poor law investigators observed, 'The income which maintains an able-bodied pauper in idleness would, if not so expended, be applied directly or indirectly to the employment of labour.'[26]

As for the effects of economic change on the patterns of migration, Hansen suggests with regard to the Atlantic traffic between Europe and North America that 'The periods of greatest volume correspond with the eras of liveliest industrial activity in the United States. With a regularity which, however, does not exhibit perfect co-ordination, the westward movement (to the Pacific) was strongest at times of economic depression.'[27] Thomas concludes that there was 'an inverse relation between home investment and the level of income in Britain, on the one hand, and emigration and capital exports on the other; a positive relationship between immigration, investment and income in the United States, and correspondingly disharmony between the rates of economic growth on the eastern and the western sides of the Atlantic.'[28]

There is some evidence that prior to the 1870s increases in the level of American business activity tended to follow increases in immigration, which suggests that 'push' factors from Europe were perhaps more important than 'pull' factors from America.[29] This interpretation gives some support to Habakkuk's thesis that increases in the supply of labour served under certain circumstances as a stimulus to business activity and economic innovation.

In writing about migration from Britain in the late nineteenth century, Erickson suggests that 'Except in the case of the disaster of the Irish famine, emigration was more a means of escaping from relative rural poverty in regions touched by economic growth and structural change than a flight from pure Malthusian crisis.'[30] Erickson stresses the extent to which English emigration was 'entirely an individualistic movement, drawing off persons from all occupations and regions at times when opportunities abroad looked promising'.[31] She goes on to illustrate the links between the changes in migratory patterns and those in economic opportunity by reference to the building and mining trades. Her analysis of passenger lists during the 1880s shows that 18 per cent of the migrants were workers in the building trade and 8 per cent were miners. The 1880s were a time of recession in the British building industry and a boom period in that of the United States. During the following decade the recession in the American building industry coincided with a boom in Australia and South Africa, where new mineral discoveries were being exploited. The migratory patterns of English and Scots building workers and miners closely followed these trends.[32]

On the basis of the available evidence Hansen concludes that the majority of the emigrants was composed of 'peasants and artisans . . . swept by a longing for personal improvement'.[33] America, as the 'common man's Utopia', was contrasted with a Europe, 'doomed to destruction',[34] in which 'The land hungry German understood only with difficulty a society in which the sum he now paid for an annual rental would purchase complete title of a farm twice as large as his present holding.'[35] It was not only the attraction of land- and property-ownership which drew the migrant to the New World. The United States had the attraction of a country in which the worker could work for his own welfare, free from the interference of tax and tithe collectors, recruiting officers and policemen. It was a land in which government agencies did not interfere without good reason in the private lives of citizens.[36] The United States was also a place in which early marriage was possible and large families were an asset and a cause for congratulation rather than a liability and a cause for social disapproval. As one settler wrote home to his friends, 'Mr. Malthus would not be understood here.'[37]

Migration rates were greatly affected, as they are today, by the policies of the governments which stood respectively to gain or to lose population. These policies were in turn influenced by both mercantilist and *laissez-faire* economic doctrines. Throughout the seventeenth and eighteenth centuries it was the mercantilist doctrine of population control which had the dominant influence on migration; until the beginning of the nineteenth century most European governments tried to discourage or actually to forbid emigration. It was not until the 1840s that the 'shovelling out' of paupers by certain European countries became a widely noted and resented practice in the New World. Thereafter the seaboard towns of the United States began to apply increasingly severe sanctions to indigent immigrants, although it was not until the early 1880s that the federal government began to impose systemic limitations on the inflow from Europe and Asia. By this time the other major recipient nations such as Canada and Australia were also beginning to impose stricter controls on immigration. In Britain the old Acts of Settlement had lost much of their authority, only to become internationalized as the notion of conditional altruisim extended from the boundaries of parishes to the frontiers of nation states.

It is possible that the strength of popular commitment to *laissez-faire* in the United States can be explained at least in part by the existence of free land. Not until the end of the nineteenth century were the frontiers completed and the supply of free land exhausted. The myth of free competition and the eternal frontier in one sense outlasted the reality, acting as an ideological barrier to collectivist social reform. But in another sense there had always been premonitions regarding the finite nature of the nation's resources. The early settlers, for example, never considered that there was enough land to share with the 2 million Indians. And as early as the 1830s the maritime states had begun to impose controls on immigration.[38]

Throughout the nineteenth century there was increasing popular pressure to have the flow of immigration checked. Congress passed its first major acts in 1882. Some of these restrictions were based on principles of individual selection. They singled out those in greatest social need — or those likely to become a charge on public funds — paupers, lunatics, criminals and prostitutes.[39] The Chinese Exclusion Act of the same year singled out the first of the social groups to become the subject of discrimination on ethnic grounds.

There were a number of reasons for this policy of restriction. The trades unions feared that cheap labour would reduce wage levels. But it was the arrival of so many destitute immigrants which alarmed local authorities and ratepayers. Immigration control was a response to the European governments which from mid-century onwards adopted the policy of 'shovelling out' their paupers.[40] During the 1850s and 1860s certain groups of immigrants became increasingly defined as a threat to the American way of life, as American nativism became a more influential force in local political life.[41] In academic circles writers like John Fiske and Herbert Adams identified themselves with these anxieties and gave them a more articulate expression. This growth of patriotic sentiment helped to create widespread fears of politically subversive immigrants from Germany and Eastern Europe.[42] Further restrictions were imposed in the twentieth century, including literacy tests and a quota system.

A similar trend towards restriction occurred in Canada, Australia, New Zealand and South Africa.[43] The criteria of exclusion were almost identical. The process was, as Richmond suggests, 'a logical concomitant of any nation state's claim to autonomy and some control over its economic and social policies.[44]

In a similar manner the ideal of *laissez-faire* was gradually restricted to national frontiers. As the terms of trade became less favourable to America during the nineteenth century an influential section of the public began to campaign for tariff protection. The dilemma throughout the period was that of reconciling the farmers' interest in low tariffs and the need of 'infant industries' for protection.[45]

After the Civil War America became increasingly protectionist. The anti-trust Sherman Act of 1890 was complemented by the McKinley Act of the same year, which imposed high levels of tariff. This act was followed by economic recession and a high incidence of bitter labour disputes. The initial response to these social troubles was a vigorous imperialist foreign policy initiated by McKinley and carried on by Theodore Roosevelt during his term of office.

Despite its formal commitment to the values of individualism and free enterprise there has been a gradual if uneven extension of collectivist social services in America. The persistence of ethnic discrimination and disadvantage has done as much violence to economic criteria of justice as it has to the claims of social need and political justice. The continuing strength of local and state governments within a federal system has also helped to create sharp disparities in welfare policy and provision which make generalizations difficult and usually misleading.

What we cannot reliably assess is the range and depth of popular commitment to the values of the economic market amongst the underprivileged in the United States. In a society in which the consensus of popular opinion favours the enhancement of welfare in the economic market and equates citizenship with economic independence, social welfare becomes intrinsically stigmatizing to its recipients. In this kind of society it may be a genuinely equal right to compete in the economic market rather than an equal right to share in the social market which is most conducive to social consensus.

Patterns of migration provide a poor guide to the expression of welfare preferences in both tsarist and Soviet Russia. The traditional restraints on labour mobility obstructed but did not entirely prevent either emigration or the internal movement of labour. Approximately 1 million Russians emigrated to the United States between 1873 and 1902, the majority leaving after 1890.[46] Most of these emigrants were Jews. As the pace of land reform increased, the movement of population to Siberia also grew in volume after 1900. Between 1900 and 1914 approximately 3.5 million Russians migrated east of the Urals — almost as many as those who had done so throughout the preceding century.[47] We should, however, note that despite the political, legal and social disadvantages suffered by them, the indigenous populations of Siberia and central Asia were not subjected to extreme treatment such as mass deportation or genocide. Russians settled in these localities but were rarely allowed to usurp the land and means of livelihood belonging to the native peoples.[48]

Immediately after the Bolshevik revolution there was a sizeable exodus of political emigrants. By the early 1930s the regime had imposed stringent and effective controls on emigration. (The most widely publicized welfare state of all time has never been seriously troubled by immigration.) Internal movements of the Russian population have been largely determined by political decisions rather than voluntary choice in the search for welfare. If the ultimate expression of negative discrimination under democratic welfare states is the ghetto, under

Stalin's form of totalitarianism it became the labour camp. In more recent times coercion and terror as means of enforcing labour mobility have been largely replaced by economic incentives and additional welfare inducements such as housing and preferential social security benefits. With regard to negative sanctions it is significant that the punishment for parasites, vagrants and beggars remains the traditional one of enforced exile — for periods of up to five years. And the Soviet government today continues to astonish the world with the harshness of its general controls on emigration and in particular its discriminatory treatment of prospective Jewish emigrants.

In conclusion a truly comparative approach to the study of migration policies and their relationship to social welfare compels us to review some of the typical questions and answers which are traditionally presented in this area of study. Considerable attention has been given to the supposed selfishness of Western parliamentary democracies in their imposition of increasingly rigorous immigration controls. Such criticisms are frequently only a part of more wide-ranging indictments of mixed capitalist economies and prescriptions for their radical transformation into socialist societies.

Far less attention is given by social policy analysts to the even stricter controls imposed on prospective emigrants from the USSR and other Eastern European socialist societies — or to the fact that none of these societies is as yet troubled by a clamorous waiting-list of immigrants.

After sixty years of the recurring crises and contradictions of capitalism and the progressive rise of socialism the situation has not changed. The most savage mercantilist type of law controlling the international movement of labour today is to be found not in capitalist but in communist countries. The most dramatic example of this in recent times has been the building of the Berlin Wall. Despite a massive expansion of social services in the German Democratic Republic the flight from this totalitarian form of a welfare state had reached a figure of 2¼ million refugees by 1961, when the Wall was built. So long as the choice existed for the German-speaking people between a welfare state organized on totalitarian principles and one based on a compromise between social and economic criteria, there was no doubt whatever about the way in which ordinary people defined their own best interests, and they expressed their preference in the time-honoured practice of migration. But for the factor of a common patriotic attachment — as well as a keen interest in the acquisition of much-needed skilled workers — it might have been the West Germans who built a wall, using the time-honoured expedient of immigration control.

One possible interpretation of this state of affairs — which might at least fit into a Marxist frame of reference — is that prospective migrants to the West have been possessed in epidemic proportions by a collective false consciousness. Throughout history many emigrants have suffered loss and disappointment, and it is still true today that the search for a new world of welfare under capitalism can begin in hope and end in disillusionment. Nevertheless this may still be a better fate than life in a society in which it is a social disgrace to become disillusioned and a crime to make plans for a more congenial life in a different country.

References

[1] See Leland Hamilton Jenks, *The Migration of British Capital to 1875*, Jonathan Cape, London, 1938; J. B. Brebner, *North Atlantic Triangle*, Yale University Press, New Haven, Ryerson Press, Toronto, Geoffrey Cumberlege, Oxford University Press, London, 1946, pp. 109-10 and 120; Brinley Thomas, *Migration and Economic Growth: A Study of Great Britain and the Atlantic Economy*, Cambridge University Press, Cambridge, 1954, pp. 30-4.

[2] S. G. and E. O. A. Checkland, *The Poor Law Report of 1834*, Penguin, Harmondsworth, 1973, p. 243.

[3] Adam Smith, op. cit., p. 123.

[4] ibid., p. 128.

[5] Hardy, op. cit., p. 99.

[6] S. G. and E. O. A. Checkland, op. cit., p. 474.

[7] ibid., p. 475.

[8] ibid., p. 472.

[9] ibid., p. 475.

[10] ibid., p. 487.

[11] Coll, op. cit., p. 135.

[12] ibid., p. 140-1.

[13] Herbert Moller, *Population Movements in Modern European History*, Macmillan Company, New York, Collier-Macmillan, London, 1964, pp. 73 et seq. See also Frank Thistlethwaite, *Migration from Europe Overseas in the Nineteenth and Twentieth Centuries*, reprinted from XIe Congrès International des Sciences Historiques, Stockholm, 1960, Rapports, V, Historie Contemporaine, Almquist & Wiksell, Göteborg-Stockholm-Uppsala, 1960, pp. 32-60.

[14] Thistlethwaite, *Migration from Europe Overseas*, pp. 74-7; C. M. Cipolla, *Economic History of World Population*, Penguin, 1964, p. 102.

[15] Cipolla, op. cit., p. 102.

[16] Carr-Saunders, op. cit., p. 49.

[17] C. J. Erickson, 'Who were the English and Scots Emigrants to the United States in the Late Nineteenth Century?', in D. V. Glass and Roger

Revelle (eds), *Population and Social Change*, Edward Arnold, London, 1972, p. 350.
[18] Moller, op. cit., p. 81.
[19] H. J. Habakkuk, *Population Growth and Economic Development Since 1750*, Leicester University Press, 1971, pp. 33 and 37.
[20] ibid., p. 29.
[21] ibid., pp. 34-5.
[22] ibid., p. 39.
[23] ibid., pp. 42-3.
[24] ibid., p. 45.
[25] S. G. and E. O. A. Checkland, op. cit., p. 484.
[26] ibid., p. 486.
[27] Marcus Lee Hansen, op. cit., p. 16.
[28] See Brinley Thomas, op. cit.
[29] See also Moller, op. cit., pp. 86-7.
[30] Erickson, op. cit., p. 347.
[31] ibid., p. 353.
[32] ibid., pp. 364-5.
[33] Marcus Lee Hansen, op. cit., p. 162.
[34] ibid., p. 164.
[35] ibid., p. 157.
[36] ibid., p. 159.
[37] ibid., p. 164.
[38] C. and M. Beard, *A Basic History of the United States*, p. 418; Terry Coleman, op. cit., p. 232; and Marcus Lee Hansen, op. cit., pp. 256-60.
[39] F. James-Davis, *Social Problems, Enduring Major Issues and Social Change*, Free Press, New York, 1970, pp. 296-8.
[40] As late as 1959 four-fifths of the states were found to impose residence qualifications for poor relief in the hope of discouraging domestic and foreign immigrants (Mencher, op. cit., p. 385).
[41] The intense xenophobia of the Know Nothing Party was one of its more dramatic if transient manifestations. A number of towns and states began to deport undesirable immigrants. See Terry Coleman, op. cit., Ch. 14.
[42] Marcus Lee Hansen, op. cit., p. 272; and Thistlethwaite, *The Great Experiment*, p. 210.
[43] See Carr-Saunders, op. cit., pp. 211-16.
[44] A. Richmond, 'Sociology of Migration in Industrial and Post-Industrial Societies', in J. A. Jackson (ed.), *Migration*, Cambridge University Press, London, 1969, p. 240.
[45] The 1850s were the hey-day of the Democrat free-traders, and although Lincoln won the presidency in 1860 on a protectionist programme he secured only a minority of the votes. The other two features of his electoral programme were free homesteads and opposition to slavery. This programme represented two of the three main centres of capital growth in the republic — the industrial north-east and the free-farm areas of the west (Moore, op. cit., p. 115). The slave-based cotton industry of the south, representing the third area, was anti-protectionist but also opposed to the extension of independent farming into the west. Slavery was an obstacle not only to democracy but to the operation of a free economic market based on equal opportunity and competition (ibid., pp. 150-3).
[46] See also Jerome Davis, *The Russian Immigrant*, Macmillan, New York, 1922, p. 10.
[47] Carr-Saunders, op. cit., p. 56; and Stephenson, op. cit., pp. 94-6.

[48] Seton-Watson refers to protest movements and revolutionary activities amongst various national minority groups in Siberia during the years 1905-6, *The Decline of Imperial Russia*, pp. 241-2.

11 A Comparative Typology of Social Welfare

In this chapter I shall be drawing together the main themes of my enquiry into a classificatory framework and looking forward to some of the issues which I shall explore in the future. One of the problems associated with the comparative study of social welfare stems from the lack of a classificatory framework which would help us to distinguish the key institutional and normative features of different kinds of welfare system from the mass of descriptive data which research is making available for study. The classificatory framework outlined in this chapter should be treated as a set of working hypotheses about the development of social welfare systems and the reasons for their apparent similarities and dissimilarities.

Nearly all the societies which currently lay claim to the title 'welfare state' are either highly industrialized or in the process of becoming so. The way in which social policies have developed in different societies has been profoundly influenced not only by the process of industrialization but by the kinds of political context within which such changes occurred. A valid distinction can be drawn between the societies in which industrialization took place without the extensive intervention of the government and those in which it was imposed on the population by a small ruling élite. A second distinction can usefully be made between the societies in which the gradual extension of the franchise made it necessary for governments to create the broadest possible basis for social consensus and those in which governments ruled by force and needed only to generate sufficient public loyalty and support to enable them to continue doing so.

Sharp distinctions of this kind are of analytical value if they are treated as extreme types, located at the ends of their respective continua. Most societies come within the middle ranges, and their positions are subject to change over time. Nor does it follow that the position of a society on one of these scales necessarily determines its place on the other. Democratically accountable governments may sometimes attempt to lead public opinion and set aside popular expressions of short-term preference in the pursuit of what they define as long-term national interests. Nonetheless some account will always be taken of the variety of beliefs concerning social justice and welfare priorities out of which a measure of consensus has to be created — even in totalitarian societies. An effective classificatory framework must also enable us to specify the relative importance of the criteria employed by the government in the allocation of welfare resources.

There would seem to be three major criteria by which material welfare goods and services are allocated in social life. In the economic market the criterion is one of utility, or price; in the social market the criterion is one of need. There is, however, a third criterion — that of political desert — which also operates in all societies.[1] Within the economic market there is discrimination between like cases of need in terms of price. Those with an equal ability to pay can enjoy equality of provision. Within the social market the allocation of welfare provision is governed by the principle that like cases of need should be treated in a like manner. Political criteria may take the form of ideological, religious or ethnic discrimination. Within groups whose members share the same publicly recognized need, such as the need for housing or health care, some individuals will receive more or less provision without regard either to the similarity of their needs or to their ability to pay — because they have succeeded or failed in meeting one or more of the criteria of political desert.

The operation of these systems of exchange, with their different criteria of entitlement, is of central importance in the study of social policy. In each society the conflict between these criteria is posed and resolved in a different way, according to the extent and type of governmental intervention in the process of economic change and according to the quality of the relationship between rulers and the ruled. Since a concern for welfare is not the prerogative of governments, some account must also be taken of the role of public opinion and community sentiment.

Comparative studies of social policy are, of necessity, often focused at such an abstract level that they fail to take account of the growth in interactions of mutual aid and welfare sentiments at the level of everyday life. Our comparative analysis should try to rediscover something of the experience of the ordinary people who laid the foundations of mutual aid and local participant forms of democracy in both long-established and new communities, taking account of the social processes by which ordinary people made their own welfare, before the term 'welfare state' was invented, and continue to do so in the present.

At the same time it has to be recognized that the values of local community impose their own limits upon the scope of welfare altruism. Industrialization weakens the moral framework of traditional forms of mutual aid which are rooted in local loyalties and the bonds of kinship. It is all too easy to become sentimental about these attachments after their demise, to forget that, while the new values of the economic market distinguish between 'givers' and 'receivers' on the basis of a dispassionate utilitarianism, the older values of local community often discriminated with equal harshness between members and strangers.[2]

Any programme of social development and reform carries with it connotations of sacrifice made by one generation on behalf of another. Within the context of nuclear and extended families, altruism finds its most natural and total expression in the deference which one generation shows to the needs of the next. Shared experiences and common endeavours over long periods of time can inspire similar but less unconditional forms of altruism between members of small local communities. At a national level these altruistic qualities remain an authentic part of human consciousness. But the idea of welfare at this level is always the product of varying degrees of compromise between numerous sectional interests, including those of family, locality and class affiliations. The nature of these compromises is expressed in the ordering of welfare priorities and in the nature of the criteria employed in this ordering. Consensus in such matters is always of a provisional kind.

We must also take account of societies in which industrialization was originally imposed by governments ruling by force rather than popular consent and where it frequently happens that the government defines industrialization not as an end in itself but as a means to creating or confirming a new kind of political order. Ideological considerations will determine the extent to which a competitive market economy is allowed to operate, but, in the absence of democratic political institutions, the scope for government intervention is wide and the disposition to intervene is generally strong. In practice all the major societies which experienced periods of forced industrialization of this kind did so with the aid of high tariffs and policies designed to regulate emigration and internal labour mobility. This was true at various stages in the industrial development of Germany, Russia and Japan.

In societies where industrialization is imposed, and where there is a high degree of centralized economic planning, social policies are often used as a means of securing and reinforcing the loyalty of one group at the expense of another. The privileged minorities will be just sufficiently large to ensure the survival of the regime and the efficient pursuit of its various political objectives.

Since the giving and the withholding of welfare goods and services are such effective instruments of labour discipline, collectivist social welfare policies become component features of economic life at a very early stage in processes of forced industrialization. As the process of industrialization succeeds in generating greater wealth, social services may be used to enhance the welfare of a larger proportion of citizens, and in this way the social basis of a genuine consensus can be greatly extended. As this process occurs, the economic criterion of utility will become increasingly important in the allocation of welfare goods and services. Nonetheless the criterion of political loyalty will still operate to exclude hostile groups and individuals. In this respect the key distinction between democratic and non-democratic societies is that in a democracy, once a contingency such as illness or old age has been taken into consideration in the allocation of welfare resources, for economic and/or social reasons, political criteria *are not subsequently used to discriminate between like cases of need.*

The political variable also determines to a great extent the relationship between national and international welfare provision. Governments will frequently advance the welfare interests of one section of their population at the expense of another. They will also, under certain circumstances, insist on the subordination of all immediate and personal welfare preferences to the pursuit of what is defined as a national interest or a long-term political or economic objective. What governments will not do — irrespective of their political type — is to jeopardize what are popularly defined as national welfare interests in order to enhance the welfare of any other society. Some marginal account is taken by most governments of the claims of international welfare, but in these cases it can be argued that any such concessions are made despite rather than because of the popular will. Account must also be taken of the extent to which the majority of citizens will set aside their domestic disagreements regarding internal issues of social justice and combine to invoke the sovereign power of the state to protect and enhance their collective welfare interests, if need be, at the expense of other nations.

There is indeed evidence to suggest that at an international level today the dominant trends in the development of welfare services, the revision of tariff preferences and the regulation of migration are still operating in favour of richer nations and at the expense of poorer ones.[3] Titmuss suggests that the notion of a welfare society expresses a more altruistic spirit than that of a welfare state, insofar as a welfare society is more clearly committed to the ideals of an international community.[4] In welfare terms, I suggest, such a community has yet to find its founding member.

We would appear, therefore, to be faced with the situation that, at a time when most advanced industrial societies can lay some claim to being 'welfare states', the ideals of international welfare are still very far from realization. This truism has inspired more moral indignation than systematic analysis. I have already implied that there is a close connection between the search for internal political consensus and the enhancement of welfare. But the point of central importance is that rulers and the ruled are never in such close agreement as they are at a time when decisions are taken which affect the balance of welfare advantages between their own nation and the outside world.

The comparative study of social welfare draws attention to the exclusive as well as the inclusive features of social policy. The criteria of eligibility for social services provide both an index of community membership and an indication of which people are defined as internal or external strangers or deviants and are therefore denied such membership. One of the tasks of comparative study is to describe and analyse the forms of external discrimination, thus complementing the exhaustive work which has already been carried out on discrimination within nations. Patterns of migration provide one of several possible indices for measuring the scope and limits of social altruism.

Compared with other industrial societies, Britain has been slow to impose controls on immigration as a means of preserving standards of living. The imperial tradition and a lingering sense of commonwealth unity and obligation may have helped to delay this process. Nonetheless as early as 1870 an Extradition Act was passed, qualifying the rights of refugees to claim political asylum. The Aliens Acts of 1905, 1914 and 1919 regulated the entry of east European refugees.[5] Although there were no further major extensions of control until 1953, the recent upsurge of legislation reflects a variety of long-standing and widely shared anxieties — the fear of 'cheap labour', the 'abuse' of welfare services and the subversion by aliens of our British way of life. In practice the operation of these acts has been highly selective and attentive to the manpower needs of the national economy, especially those of our social services. The most significant feature of these legislative trends during recent years is that government immigration policies have been based on the assumption that they enjoy a wide measure of public support. It is currently most unlikely that either of the two major political parties would risk a return to more liberal policies, or that any other party would achieve electoral success by promising to do so.

The history of modern British social services began in a period of imperialist expansion. The socially adverse consequences of industrialization were mitigated in a piecemeal way which did not prevent the achievement of a reasonably popular balance between the claims of the economic and social markets. For a brief period after the Second World War the British, in their insular manner, assumed that the welfare state was a phenomenon unique to the British way of life. And in the dying days of Empire relatively little attention was given to the question of which members of the Commonwealth were uniquely British. In recent years a heightened consciousness of our diminished national territory and vanished imperial destiny has brought the question to a more central position in the debate about welfare priorities and immigration control. The process of adjustment has also left us psychologically ill-prepared for re-entry into any community wider than our own.

One of the future tasks of social analysis will be to explore more thoroughly the scope and limits of altruism as it is manifested generationally over the dimension of time, and also as it is revealed throughout the various levels of social organization — familially, locally, nationally and internationally — at any one time.

One of the dominant assumptions in the study of social administration has been that men and women are by nature communally orientated and altruistically motivated, and that the process of democratization makes manifest these natural and public virtues. From this assumption it becomes possible to argue that the welfare state is a staging post along a path which leads upwards from one form of collective enterprise to the next. In this sense liberal reformers cling to their trust in the inevitability of community with the same fervour as that with which radical Marxists believe in the inevitability of class war.

In this chapter I have suggested an alternative hypothesis, which questions this 'optimistic' collectivist view of social policy development at both national and international levels. In Britain and America, where democratic choice has existed, it can be argued that economic rather than social criteria have accorded most closely with popular notions of welfare and justice. Collectivist welfare policies were adopted as a last resort in Britain, when confidence in the free play of economic market forces was undermined, although the eventual compromise between individualism and collectivism was a more equable one than that which occurred in the United States. In both cases the balance struck made for consensus rather than conflict. The nature of these compromises suggests that while the enhancement of welfare has been a primary concern of both governments, collectivist social policies have never had more than a residual function in either society. Even in Britain the compromise leaves the claims of social need subordinate to those of the economic market. In tsarist Russia the attempt to create a property-owning autocracy came too late, and the Bolsheviks never submitted their revolutionary programme to a popular vote. Despite the rejection of the profit motive Soviet social policies have continued to display highly utilitarian criteria of evaluation.

If, as Dicey has suggested, 'A collectivist never holds a stronger position than when he advocates the enforcement of the best ascertained laws of health',[6] the individualist, for his part, is never so universally popular as when he advocates in the name of welfare the extension of the private ownership of property and its protection in law. Perhaps the most neglected index of popular welfare preference has been the private ownership of land, either as a means of livelihood or as a location for property. If kinship remains the natural focus of altruism, the commonest expression of this familial search for security is the acquisition of property and its transmission from one generation to the next. It is a search which can only be checked or denied by force.

There are also good reasons for giving to patriotism as much attention as we have given to socialism in welfare studies. It is arguable that there has never been a natural affinity between the values and aims which inspired the growth of welfare states and the ideals of international welfare. The balance of evidence supports a contrary view — that these two manifestations of human altruism are in many respects mutually antipathetic.

Before the emergence of the modern welfare state emigration was a traditional means by which men tried to provide for their own welfare on their own terms. Migration serves as a catalyst in the creation of community and national sentiments which, in turn, redefine the limits of social altruism. But these migratory processes and the growth of new community and patriotic feelings interact, making the enhancement of social welfare a predominantly national concern.

To countless Europeans America offered throughout the eighteenth and nineteenth centuries a prospect of relative welfare, freedom and justice, although it was not a welfare state in social market terms. Many were driven out of their homelands by the harshness and persecution of others. There were few immigrants who hesitated, once they were established in new lands, to persecute, displace or destroy indigenous communities. The treatment of American Indians and slaves, African Bushmen, Hottentots and Bantus, Australasian aborigines, Tasmanians and Maoris serves as a counterpoint to the history of social welfare. In post-revolutionary Russia and in Nazi Germany the same human propensity to discriminate was expressed in political, racial and religious terms.

As new nations discovered a sense of national identity and achieved a measure of prosperity, they sought to preserve them by regulating migration and erecting tariffs. Their criteria of selection encouraged the immigration of those with scarce economic skills and discouraged the entry of those who were in the greatest social need; as the supply of free land decreased, the controls became more stringent. The new nations built mainly from immigrant stock have long ceased to accept the 'bad risks' and 'failures' of the older nations, and, as emigration rates have declined and the standard of living has improved in the older nations, similar policies have been adopted with regard to underdeveloped countries.

If war is the natural extension of diplomacy carried on by 'other means',[7] discriminatory migration and tariff policies are the other means by which modern welfare states continue to enhance the well-being of their subjects. Trends in migration control would appear to be a significant index of the way in which both governments and popular opinion have come to share a common definition of the proper scope and limits of welfare altruism. Tariff protection has always been a more contentious issue, but both protectionists and free traders have based their arguments, in popular debate, upon nationalist rather than internationalist premises. The modern systems of welfare provision which have developed in both the new and the older nations have become objects of financial anxiety as well as a source of comfort to their members, resources to cherish rather than share. Viewed in comparative perspective, the internationalist ideals of social welfare seem almost to become ambivalent corrections scribbled in the margins of history.

References

[1] T. H. Marshall uses very similar criteria in his essay, 'Value Problems of Welfare-Capitalism', *Journal of Social Policy*, 1, 1, 1972, pp. 15-32. I lay greater emphasis on the significance of political variables, including in this category a wider range of discriminatory criteria.

[2] See Pinker, *Social Theory and Social Policy*, pp. 165-75, for a more detailed analysis of this distinction.

[3] On general trends in trade policies and capital movements see Gunnar Myrdal, *The Challenge of World Poverty*, Penguin, Harmondsworth, 1971, pp. 280 et seq. See especially Titmuss, *Commitment to Welfare*, Ch. XI, for a general review; and Oscar Gish, *Doctor Migration and World Health*, G. Bell & Sons, London, 1971, for a more detailed study of trends in medical care services. There is a useful article by Tom Soper, 'Western Attitudes to Aid', in *Lloyds Bank Review*, 94, 1969. The case for a more generous provision of foreign aid is developed in the work of Myrdal and the work of Jack L. Roach and Janet K. Roach, who provide an introduction to the work of other authorities in *Poverty: Selected Readings*, Penguin, Harmondsworth, 1972. An alternative view is presented by P. G. Bauer in *Dissent on Development: Studies and Debates in Development Economics*, Weidenfeld & Nicolson, London, 1972, and summarized in 'The Case Against Foreign Aid', *The Listener*, 21 September, 1972.

[4] Titmuss, *Commitment to Welfare*, p. 127.

[5] See Cedric Thornberry, *The Stranger at the Gate: A Study of the Law on Aliens and Commonwealth Citizens*, Fabian Research Series 243, 1964; David Stephens, *Immigration and Race Relations*, Fabian Research Series 291, 1970; and John A. Garrard, *The English and Immigration: A Comparative Study of the Jewish Influx 1880-1910*, Institute of Race Relations, Oxford University Press, London, 1971.

[6] Dicey, op. cit., p. lxxiv.

[7] Carl von Clausewitz, *On War*, Vol. III, Kegan Paul, Trench, Trubner & Company, London, 1940, 'war is nothing but a continuation of political intercourse, with a mixture of other means', p. 121.

12 Three Models of Social Welfare

Normative choices in social welfare

Keynes and Beveridge both believed that the reform of capitalism offered the best prospect for enhancing welfare and that collectivist social policies could make a vitally important contribution to that reform. At the time there were those who opposed this thesis and argued in defence of the *status quo*. There were others who saw the replacement of capitalism by socialism as the only way of creating a more just and humanitarian society. There was a rift in socialist opinion between those who thought that social policies could serve as an important instrument in effecting this transition and those who maintained that radical political changes would have to precede social policy reforms.

By 1945 all three major political parties were committed in varying degrees to manifestos embodying Keynesian and Beveridgean prescriptions for change, but the election of that year put the Labour Party into office, and thereafter collectivism and socialism seemed for a time to be synonymous. Within the discipline of social policy and administration this tendency to associate collectivism with socialism has become stronger and now represents, in normative terms, the conventional wisdom of the subject. Of the various major writers on British social policies only Marshall, and possibly Donnison, seem to have accepted with a measure of equanimity the values of the mixed capitalist economy, which have survived largely intact in our society throughout the post-war years.

In the last part of this chapter I shall discuss the issues of political choice which are implicit in these various interpretations of the ends of social policy, and their relationship with the collectivism of Keynes and Beveridge, as well as the traditions of Marxist and classical economic theory which were their historical antecedents. My purpose will be to question the terms on which we have grown accustomed to making these choices.

Titmuss frequently reminded us of the need to make these

choices and of the implications of the dilemmas of choice at every level of social policy debate. In my view, however, he oversimplified the general issue by treating it as a choice between no more than *two* alternatives — the values of the economic market and those of the social market. He thus defined the problem in such a way as either to exclude the middle way of the mixed economy from serious consideration or to place it firmly within the context of the economic market alternative. In so doing he effectively severed the discipline from its most vigorous normative roots, which in turn had been nourished by the most productive welfare tradition of all.

By defining the problem in this way Titmuss was inviting those who were attracted neither by capitalism nor by socialism to choose what would be for them the lesser of two evils, when there was no reason why they should choose either. It should also be noted that Titmuss equated the values of the social market with socialism and that he did not include Marxism in this side of his dichotomy. Consequently both the tradition of collectivism which had contributed so much to the creation of welfare systems under capitalism and the tradition of Marxism which had provided the most forceful and sustained critique of welfare-capitalism were effectively left out of the debate as possible choices. Titmuss left out Marxism because he thought that it was a morally repugnant doctrine. Repugnant or otherwise, it remains an important political option in the world today.

Any theory of social policy must be firmly grounded in the institutional and psychological realities of its time. Analytical models based upon oversimplified distinctions between egoism and altruism fail to take into account the ambivalent nature of perceived interest and of felt obligation stemming from a variety of institutional loyalties which may be based upon family, community, nation or class. Three major normative assumptions may be said to underlie the various theories which seek to explain and evaluate the relationship between social order, social change and social welfare. These can be broadly described as classical economic theory, Marxism and its socialist derivatives, and the traditions of mercantile collectivism.

Classical economic theory is based upon the premise that there is no basic incompatibility between the competing interests and loyalties which characterize a free society. Marxist theory asserts not only that these interests and loyalties are incompatible but that only through the intensification of such conflict and the heightening of class conflict in particular is change possible and real freedom attainable. The ultimate objective of change is the abolition of the forms of property and the division of labour out of which sectional interests and inequalities arise.

China, Russia, all the nations of the east European bloc, and many of those in the Third World are committed to the eventual creation of societies based on the teachings of Marx. In addition to socializing the means of production they have already built up complex systems of collectivist social services. It is not so easy to identify a comparable group of societies which are actively committed to a significant enlargement of the scope of the free market and private enterprise.

Wilensky describes how in all the richer nations of today collectivist sentiment and economic individualism coexist, so that 'pro-welfare-state doctrines are perhaps as widely popular as the ideology of success'.[1] Friedman bitterly laments the growth of total government spending in the USA from about 10 per cent of national income in the years before 1929 to about 40 per cent today.[2] In the United Kingdom the level has gone still higher, and the same trend in levels of government spending has been observed in the other major Western nations. This general trend towards collectivism has in the main only tenuous connections with socialism and in some cases none at all. While Marxists argue that these massive collectivist interventions in industry and welfare are designed merely to preserve capitalism, many liberal economists complain that they are certain to destroy it.

It can be argued that collectivism on this scale does not have to be consistent with either capitalism or socialism and that its influence has already been sufficiently pervasive to create a new social system which will subsequently develop without regard for either of these doctrines. What this new version of collectivism lacks is a coherent body of theory, a set of explicit normative assumptions, and an articulate and committed political movement which will continuously assert and remind us of its distinctive properties. These properties do, however, enjoy a historical pedigree antedating both capitalism and socialism, as they represent a modern revival of the much modified mercantilist doctrines challenged by the rise of classical political economy, although the continuing and distinctive influence of mercantilist doctrines can be traced not so much through protective social policies as through protectionist economic policies.

Given that it is collectivist, this revived neo-mercantilist tradition stands in ideological opposition to the individualistic values of classical political economy. Insofar as it is not socialist in the terms of Marxist theory and may indeed appear in societies which are anti-socialist, it stands equally in opposition to Marxist collectivism. This is not to advance another version of the 'convergence thesis'. The possibility still exists that some, if not all, of the present socialist societies will move towards a state of communism which accords with Marxist theory. The history of capitalist societies so far suggests a general trend towards governmental regulation of the free market, but we cannot rule out the possibility of a reversal of that trend.

Contemporary Marxists reject the assertion that the extent of governmental intervention can go so far in a capitalist society that that society will cease to be capitalist to any significant degree.[3] Their argument is that, so long as the means of production remain even nominally in private ownership and so long as the forces of production are organized and rewarded on the basis of economic market values, the society will remain essentially capitalist. A welfare capitalist society is still a society in which the members of a ruling class — the owners of the means of production — further their own interests at the expense of the workers through the agencies of the state. At the same time, as I have noted, contemporary liberal economists would attribute most of the deficiencies which they observe in such a society to its gradual abandonment of capitalist virtues. Thus we are left with two interpretations, one of which asserts that however much state intervention occurs in a capitalist society, it remains capitalist in every important respect. The other interpretation measures the mixed economy against an ideal of perfect competition and finds it substantially wanting in every important respect.

My own position is based on the view that both classical economic theory and its ideal state of capitalism and Marxist theory and its ideal state of communism offer attractive prescriptions for the maximization of human welfare which, when they are put into practice, also become instruments of oppression and diswelfare. The same criticism can be levelled at the third model of welfare — a form of mercantile collectivism in which the state comes to serve so many coalitions of interest that for all practical purposes it ceases to be the instrument of any single ruling class. Nonetheless I recognize that circumstances can arise in which it will become such an instrument, and the nature of such outcomes is more difficult to predict than it would be in the case of overtly free-market or socialistically controlled societies. The reason for such a high degree of uncertainty is obvious — mixed economies occupy the middle ground with regard to the balance between freedom and control and the choice between the totalitarian styles of either the left or the right wings of political theory and practice.

We commit a fundamental error, however, if we judge all the alternative and possible forms of social organization by reference to the two paradigms of capitalism and communism, since this makes us voluntary prisoners of two historical modes of thought, both of which embody highly deterministic theories of social development. Capitalism does not necessarily collapse or suffer irreparable damage if the free play of market forces is modified. Neither does it inevitably give way to socialism when the time and circumstances are ripe. It is perfectly reasonable to argue that capitalism will develop in ways which we are not able to anticipate or predict; it has done so in the past.

Furthermore the factor of nationality and national culture is regularly underestimated by theorists of social change. It would be rash to predict the eventual outcome of the impact of Western ideas on the new nations of the Third World. The indigenous culture of a nation is a catalyst which transmutes alien philosophies like capitalism and socialism in ways which we simply do not understand at present. How many metamorphoses will these societies have to undergo before we can cease to use such terms to categorize them? If we admit that there is a high potential for cultural autonomy and innovative response among the countries of the Third World, why should we not allow as much of the industrialized nations of the West? We have reached a stage in social thought at which we allow Marxists — as we once allowed classical political economists and the founding fathers of the Christian church before them — to define in advance our universe of discourse, to set out the very questions of import which we are required to answer before we can ask our own questions, and to lay down for all times and all places what are in fact intelligent analyses of earlier times and places as paradigms, against which the past, the present and the future must be judged and found worthy or wanting. No doubt at the time of the Reformation it was sensible to judge Protestantism largely by reference to the canons of Roman Catholicism, or in the early stages of the Industrial Revolution to judge new modes of capitalist enterprise by reference to an unreformed and backward-looking mercantilism. But there came a time when Protestantism and capitalism had to be understood not only by reference to their antecedents but in terms of what they had become in their own right. Equally we cannot rule out the possibility that in their historical development societies rediscover and take on modified forms of much earlier traditions of thought and organization. The recent revival of the notion of community, for example, owes much to the earliest traditions of thought about social organization. Similarly the precepts of mercantilism survived with remarkable tenacity even in the hey-day of *laissez-faire* Victorian England.

This third approach therefore rejects the possibility of either a natural harmonization of welfare interests through the free play of economic market forces or the inevitability of a conflict, with the eventual reconciliation of these interests being effected by the replacement of capitalism by socialism. It is possible to argue that the welfare ideals of this tradition can best be realized in a society that is neither capitalist nor socialist in any ideal sense.

Social administration has tended to develop a set of concepts and theories of the middle ground which are collectivist in value orientation and critical of capitalism, but lacking in any explicit political theory which might convincingly explain either how what is deemed to be a defective economic system can be changed or what alternative social order might take its place. In this sense the subject mirrors the contradictions and ambivalences of the societies in which it has grown to maturity as a discipline and in which collectivist social policies have been used to modify the free play of market forces. The perceptive student might conclude that these reformist theories of the middle ground suffer from the analytical weaknesses which arise from normative uncertainty — and from a failure to make logical connections between political means and ends. In contrast the theories both of classical political economy and of Marx may be said to suffer from the weaknesses that arise from over-certainty regarding the connection between these means and ends.

It was never likely that social policy and administration would provide a significant theoretical and normative vindication of the values and aims of the free market. Its doing so now would amount to a singularly impressive demonstration of professional altruism. Nonetheless an important individualist approach to the study of social welfare has persisted, largely outside the mainstream of normative thought within the discipline itself, like the sociological critiques from the welfare state which drew their inspirational theory from Marx.

What follows now is an attempt to relate more clearly the potential and actual contributions of thinking in social policy and administration to my concern with the collectivist renaissance in recent British history and its affinities with the institutional framework of obligation, entitlement and exchange. In my historical approach I have focused on a subject which has been largely neglected in social policy studies — the relationships between free trade, protection and reform — partly because the poor law has received very extensive attention, and partly because the subject has allowed me to concentrate on certain developments in economic policy and thought which prepared the ground for the positive assertion of collectivist philosophies from the 1870s onwards.

The welfare theories of the individualist tradition can be traced from Smith and Ricardo, through Spencer, Sumner and Dicey, to Hayek, Powell and Friedman. It is harder to find agreement about what constitutes the Marxist tradition in the West, if we limit ourselves to those who gave special attention to social policy. George's and Wilding's choice of Laski, Strachey and Miliband as its exemplars in the British context is open to question, but it is hard to find better alternatives.[4] Between these polar extremes of classical economic individualism and Marxist collectivism George and Wilding also recognize another collectivist tradition, but their interpretation of this tradition differs from my own.

They do their best to identify its main elements by distinguishing between the 'reluctant collectivists' represented by Keynes, Beveridge and Galbraith and the 'Fabian socialists' represented by Tawney, Crosland and Titmuss. In seeking to explain their classification George and Wilding distinguish between those who 'saw the extension of public ownership not as an end in itself but as vitally necessary to the general achievement of socialist objectives' and those who believed that 'public ownership is to be used pragmatically and selectively for the achievement of specific objectives'.[5] The traditions of 'Fabian socialism' and Marxist collectivism are further differentiated from that of reluctant collectivism by their rejection of acquisitive individualism as a commendable human motive, and their rejection of capitalism on the grounds that the free market system inevitably leads to an undemocratic distribution of power, an unjust and unequal distribution of wealth and an inefficient use of resources. Furthermore 'The free market system has not abolished, will not, and cannot abolish poverty, let alone inequality.'[6]

In my view it is misleading to attribute a quality of reluctance to the collectivism of Keynes and Beveridge on the grounds that they were not enthusiastic nationalizers. Keynes and Beveridge were enthusiastic collectivists with regard to social policy because they were both anti-socialist. Similarly the way in which George and Wilding define acquisitive individualism does not do sufficient justice to Keynes's and Beveridge's views about economic morality. Keynes and Beveridge believed that the profit motive and competitive self-interest, like most other human sentiments, swiftly become unlovable when taken to excess. In their different ways, however, they also believed that, unless the spirit of entrepreneurship was allowed to flourish in a free society, there would never be a general increase in prosperity sufficient to abolish poverty.

George's and Wilding's choice of Laski, Strachey and Miliband as examples also restricts their scope for exploring a further distinction of vital importance within the Marxist tradition. They note that Laski, Strachey and Miliband opposed 'the use of violence to achieve their ends'[7] and believed that a peaceful transition to socialism was possible. These convictions set them apart from the central tradition of Marxist thought exemplified particularly in the writings of Marx, Engels and Lenin, who accepted violence as a regrettable but necessary means to the political end of achieving socialism and eventually a communist society. So far history offers no example of a party which is committed to these ends achieving and retaining power by non-violent parliamentary means.

This difference among Marxists over the choice of means seems to me to be of greater political importance than any declared identity of ends. The weight of historical evidence suggests that revolutionary Marxists are correct in their choice of means, even if they choose violence only as a last resort. George and Wilding would have brought out this fundamental distinction more clearly if they had given the Webbs a central role in their analysis. The Webbs had far greater illustrative significance in the development of collectivist thought than Laski, Strachey or Miliband because, more than any other authority, they helped to give intellectual coherence to the

Fabian doctrine of gradual collectivist reform. Having done so, they renounced Fabianism, when in their last years they were converted to Soviet communism and accepted the necessity of violence at least in countries other than their own.

When the choice of means is between violence and non-violence, this carries such profound implications for the ends of political action that it seems to me to represent a distinction of fundamental importance within the tradition of Marxist collectivism. The advance of collectivism under conditions of parliamentary democracy owes much to coalitions of interest among a variety of ideological groupings. But collectivism has ideological affinities with non-socialist as well as socialist political movements. Collectivism may involve no more than commitment to a significant degree of state intervention in the maintenance and enhancement of welfare. It can have ideological connections with either the Left or the Right. The errors lie in equating collectivism only with socialism and in assuming that collectivism without socialism always implies a 'reluctant' commitment to state intervention. Although socialism is inevitably associated with collectivist welfare policies, the converse does not follow. In the history of Western Europe, North America and industrializing nations in other continents we can observe many versions of collectivism, ranging from communist societies, through various types of mixed economy and corporate state, to outright fascism.

Keynes and Beveridge provided the intellectual and philosophical framework within which our post-war collectivist social policies developed. They set out the theoretical and normative case for Britain to follow a middle way between the free market and the command economy. In large part post-war developments in British economic and social policy have followed the direction of their prescriptions until very recently. In 'Social Policy and Social Justice' I discussed some of the reasons why the post-Beveridge era of social security is coming to an end, with particular reference to Beveridge's 'fundamentally inegalitarian view of family life' and his insistence on the necessary association between citizenship and the insurance principle. At the same time I regretted the decline of the 'spirit of community' and the erosion of the 'common moral framework' at a national level which were characteristics of British society so deeply valued by Beveridge and Keynes.[8]

It is, however, a central part of my thesis that the collectivist tradition represented by these qualities still has an important role within the discipline of social policy and administration. Mine is an approach which sees no fundamental incompatibility between the enhancement of social welfare and the values of the mixed economy and a pluralist social order. Indeed the subject and the richness of its potential contribution to the policy sciences would be diminished if this tradition were not to prosper in the future.

At the present time the tradition is intellectually closest to the pluralist theories elaborated by political scientists like Braybrooke, Lindblom and Dahl, with their emphasis on disjointed incrementalism as a technique of social reform, on the role of the state as one among several creations of power and influence in society, on the virtues of diversity and the delegation of authority and the reconciliation of conflicts within a broadly consensual political framework.

Donnison recognizes the contribution of pluralist theory to our understanding of the role of interest groups in the ordering of social priorities and to the actual workings of the political process. He identifies it with a particular view of the good society which abjures Utopian planning and is administered on a basis of piecemeal engineering directed towards gradual improvement. He also criticizes the lack of a historical dimension in pluralist analysis and its indifference to the ideological aspects of social life. In this sense pluralism lacks the synoptic vision of Keynes and Beveridge, although it may still help to elucidate the types of change and the problems of decision-taking which are most likely to occur in a mixed economy.

Our understanding of the functioning and the distinctive nature of the mixed economy, which is neither capitalist nor socialist, owes much to pluralist theories. It is true that these theories lack historical perspective[9] and that, as Halebsky has recently argued, they tend to underestimate the extent to which the least powerful interest groups are neglected in democratic processes and in the resistance of the private industrial sector to collective interests.[10] In a lengthy preface to the new edition of *Politics, Economics and Welfare* Dahl and Lindblom respond to such criticisms of their approach to pluralist theory. They admit that in neither the USA nor Britain have the problems of poverty and racial inequality yielded significantly to piecemeal reform, and that in pluralist societies powerful minority groups can delay for long periods changes which are in the common interest.[11] They also recognize that collectivist policies of social reform have little hope of success while income inequalities buttress political inequalities.[12]

At the same time Lindblom and Dahl argue that, despite these valid criticisms by social scientists in the West, social pluralism is winning more support from authorities in Eastern Europe and in the communist parties of Western Europe. If pluralist societies tolerate too much organized autonomy, socialist societies suffer in other ways from too little.[13] The temptation in the West is to adopt more highly centralized systems of political control, but, they add, those who move towards that goal are likely to meet equally disillusioned Marxists travelling cautiously in the opposite direction. Thus Lindblom and Dahl remain committed to incremental rates of change and limited structural reforms.[14] In the Soviet Union and China they identify the concentration of power in the state as a major obstacle to change. In the USA they admit that the free market is a cause of social inequalities, but they also claim that it is a major source of innovation. In recognizing the need to revise their original formulation of pluralist theory Lindblom and Dahl restate the case for a middle way between the Utopian paradigms of the free market and the command economy of the highly centralized state. In their analysis they come very close to a mercantile collectivist position which lays greater emphasis on social unity than social conflict, and on change within existing social structures rather than change through the overthrow of those structures.

I have emphasized the need for social administrators to give more attention to the theoretical and philosophical issues involved in an understanding of the relationship between social policy and social change and the relationship between social policy and different conceptions of the good society. Nonetheless one of the enduring strengths of the discipline has been the involvement of so many of its practitioners in specific problems of policy and administration and developments in particular service fields. Again it is this concern which accounts for the growing importance of political science theories in recent social policy analysis. I have already referred to Hall's, Land's, Parker's and Webb's study, *Change, Choice and Conflict in Social Policy*,[15] which makes extensive use of such theories. The basic framework of analysis is taken from Easton's systems analysis model, but the authors go on explore the use of class theories and pluralism in their analysis of political processes. They formulate their hypothesis in such a way as to take account of both these approaches: 'that the making of day-today policy on social issues in Britain does operate within a distinctly pluralist *process*, but that the *limits* of policy-making are set by élites which for many purposes are indistinguishable from what Miliband calls a ruling class'. This emphasis on limitations refers to the authors' characterization of 'the policy process as *bounded pluralism*', although they add that the class model does not necessarily explain 'the nature of the boundaries within which the process operates'.[16]

I have referred again to this study because its authors show that it is useful to apply more than one theoretical approach to the same social policy problem. In exploring the links between policy changes and change at a broader societal level they clearly find class theory more useful than systems and pluralist theories. They also illustrate the extent to which normative theories can be employed with impartiality, especially within a discipline which is able to draw on a number of such theories. Furthermore the variety and range of the case studies in *Change, Choice and Conflict* remind us that a large part of social policy is conducted at a level of enquiry at which conflicts over basic values need not arise, although, as Kogan suggests, it is not always easy to distinguish between the issues of policy principle and those of administrative process.[17]

Although social policy and administration is frequently criticized for being too widely derivative in its borrowings from the other social sciences, I think there is a case to be made that it has not been sufficiently eclectic. The pluralist theories which I have discussed owe more to political science than they do to sociology, but their actual and potential contribution to social policy studies tends to be underrated by sociologists of welfare. The same could be said of the contribution of history, philosophy and economics. Sociologists of welfare often talk as if sociology ought to have a special relationship with social policy and administration, and several consequences follow from this assumption. First, it licenses sociologists to berate from time to time their dull, pragmatic relations for being a-theoretical. Secondly, it allows them to assume that their discipline has a near-monopoly of theories which are relevant to social policy studies. Thirdly, it encourages sociologists to believe that the majority of social administrators are — or ought to become — sociologists. In fact the majority of social administrators are not sociologists either by training or choice, and a small but increasing minority could point out that they entered on their careers as social administrators and not sociologists. This is not to deny that sociology has something of value to offer to social administration — as one among several contributory disciplines.

Such eclecticism can be defended on two grounds. First, it preserves the discipline from catching any of the ideological infections which may be afflicting the related social sciences, and sociology in this respect has a singularly bad health record. Secondly, eclecticism can provide a more comprehensive basis for the development of theories and concepts which are indigenous to social policy and administration as a subject. Given the variety of disciplinary interests which already coexist under the name of social policy and administration, it is neither likely nor desirable that any one of them will make a dramatic theoretical contribution which will swiftly and unanimously be understood and adopted within the subject. Social administrators are jointly engaged in a difficult interdisciplinary exercise. Learning from the range of relevant disciplines is a slow and piecemeal process. Nonetheless, so long as a balanced universe of discourse is maintained, there is likely to be a gradual development of theory indigenous to the subject, some of which will no doubt have its origins in sociology. We can already observe in the works of Titmuss, Donnison and Marshall (who is a sociologist) contributions which are social policy and administration in an eponymous sense.

I believe that there are other potential contributions from sociology which have not yet been exploited in social policy studies. Among these I would pick out the work of Elton Mayo and his school which has been drawn to our attention by John Smith in his recent reappraisal and commentary.[18] The problems which Mayo studied in industrial life, namely, those stemming from the need to develop the skills and status of citizenship in the work situation, are the same as those which Marshall emphasizes in the context of social policy and political life. Similarly, as Smith observes, Mayo's interest in the practical possibilities of delegation and decentralization in decision-taking has obvious relevance to current debates about the same issues in social administration.

At the same time there are clear signs of a developing and productive relationship between social policy and administration and legal studies which will deepen our understanding of the links between public opinion and law and between changes in law and changes in social policy. The contribution of O. R. McGregor from his earlier study of divorce to his recent work on the Finer Committee reminds us that in studying the legal aspects of social welfare we may often acquire a clearer understanding of the inconsistencies which characterize our divided treatment of citizens on the one hand as members of families and on the other hand as workers. McGregor observes, for example, that 'The inescapable conclusion from many recent studies of women's experience in trying to reconcile the claims of marriage, motherhood and work is the existence of a firmly rooted double standard of occupational morality. As a society, we pay lip-service to equality for women whilst practising discrimination.'[19] Similarly the pioneering work of Kathleen Bell and her colleagues on national insurance tribunals has brought out other inconsistencies and anomalies in our treatment of citizens, once they become welfare appellants, in what is a relatively new but increasingly important context of adjudication.[20]

A discipline which is well grounded and also involved in issues both of a general theoretical and normative nature and of a more immediate and practical kind is not likely to be overwhelmed by ideologies which prescribe total and chiliastic solutions for our social ills. It will abjure the extremes of moral sentiment, recognizing that any ideal Kingdom of the Saints, religious or secular, would be a discomfiting place to live in. As a genuinely humane discipline social policy and administration would work towards the making of a welfare society in which the terms of exchange and the understandings of obligation and entitlement were decently conditional, neither vulgarly egoistical nor impossibly altruistic.

Each of the major traditions of thought to which I have referred expresses the conviction that it alone offers the best prescription for the enhancement of social welfare and the creation of a better society. What I have tried to do is to rehabilitate one of these traditions within the discipline of social administration because I think that it has fallen into neglect, if not disrepute, and that this has happened in large part because the terms of the debate have been progressively narrowed. In my view the range of normative choice within a discipline ought to be set out as generously as possible. With a variety of theoretical resources at their disposal, the practitioners of the discipline should find scope for co-operation and compromise as well as conflict.

Risk, retrenchment and reform

I have tried to demonstrate that three major theoretical traditions have contributed to our understanding of the role of social policy in enhancing the welfare of industrial societies. Both classical economic theory and Marxist theory have their intellectual origins in the Industrial Revolution and the rise of capitalism. Classical economic theory was the intellectual vindication of these momentous events. In outlining an alternative to capitalism Marx became its most formidable and influential critic, and his social theory inspired a range of revolutionary and reformist socialist prescriptions for the transformation of capitalism. The origination of mercantilist doctrine coincided with the rise of the modern nation state which preceded the Industrial Revolution and the rise to influence of the other two doctrines. Throughout the nineteenth century mercantilist doctrine continued to exercise a greater influence on the course of economic policies in continental Europe than was the case in either Britain or the USA. More recently, as I have suggested, Keynes rehabilitated significant elements of mercantilist economic theory, albeit in greatly modified forms. These and other aspects of the doctrine have played a large part in the growth of collectivist social policies and the development of theories of the welfare state. This revival has been sufficiently radical and sufficiently extensive to bring about significant changes in the structure and values of most of the advanced capitalist societies of the West. It has provided the normative and instrumental rationale for the emergence of the modern welfare state, as we know it.

Nonetheless, despite the record of its real achievement, the third way — the pluralist commitment to the mixed economy — with its emphasis on social protection and mitigating reforms, evokes among social administrators at best a defensive apology rather than a positive commitment. By contrast neither the classical economic nor the Marxist paradigm of welfare has so far been adopted in its ideal form, nor has either one proved to be particularly effective in a modified form. This situation is all the more difficult to account for if social policy and administration is taken to be a subject characteristic of the forms of applied social science which are specifically required and nurtured by the mixed economies of mercantilist collectivism.

This state of affairs can be partly explained by the way in which the subject has developed over the past twenty years. This period has seen the adoption of a dominant normative consensus, which regards the values of the competitive economic market with such hostility that it cannot sustain coherent theories of social consensus or change which are at all sympathetic to those values. Any theory about the enhancement of social welfare must be addressed to issues of consensus and change, and it must be normative, in the sense that it will single out certain policy objectives and outcomes of change as being morally preferable to others.

One of the main problems in British social policy and administration is that too many of its practitioners feel that the social services as agencies of both consensus and change have to function in a society whose basic values are antipathetic to its own social policies. This fallacious model is preserved by the practice of treating the economic and social markets as if they were separate institutional entities. Consequently it is impossible to analyse in any consistent way the various functional and dysfunctional relationships which hold between the processes of production and distribution. Whatever else can be said of classical economic theory and Marxist theory, they do not fall into this error, both displaying a normative consistency between the means and the ends which they prescribe for the enhancement of human welfare, and it is this consistency which accounts for their conceptual unity and explanatory appeal.

In discussing the character of social policy and administration Titmuss denied that it was merely 'a messy conglomeration of the technical *ad hoc*', and he argued that 'Its primary areas of unifying interest are centred in those social institutions that foster integration and discourage alienation.'[21] Within the terms of his personal value commitment, however, it is difficult to see how social policies could serve these ends, even in a mixed economy. From what we know of Titmuss's beliefs about the alienating qualities of the economic market, integration of this kind could only be achieved within a socialist society, one moreover in which the majority of the citizens were committed socialists. In default of this ideological transformation a Titmussian social administrator would find himself in conflict with the dominant values of the mixed economy and with the ends of the social services as defined by those values — unless those services bore a remarkably high degree of normative autonomy.

The way out of this problem has been to treat the values of the social market as if they possessed a self-evident moral superiority to those of the economic market. In discussing concepts like 'market', 'need' and 'justice' itself we have reached a point at which we use the term 'social' as if it were synonymous with 'sacred'. Even the norm of reciprocity, which is essential to the creation of wealth, stands lower in the moral hierarchy of welfare studies than the norm of unilateral gift-giving.

In his critique of 'welfare sociologists' Gouldner indicts them for having colluded in some systematic way with the 'powers-that-be' in helping to preserve the mixed economy of welfare capitalism, or, as he describes it, the 'welfare-warfare' state.[22] It would perhaps have been more accurate to accuse some 'welfare sociologists' of pretending that social policies could be used as instruments for the peaceful transformation of capitalism into socialism and others of lacking any clear commitment to either capitalism or socialism. In both cases the outcome has been the same — the assumption of a holier-than-thou attitude towards the values and imperatives of the economic market.

Since the Second World War British social policy analysts have tended to adopt a largely critical attitude towards industry and industrial values. It is symptomatic of this generally negative cast of mind that throughout the major works of Titmuss economic forces are described in the main as exploitative forces, or as the cause of social costs for which society must offer compensation through social policies. The cause of national efficiency and the association of social policy with patriotic sentiment which Beveridge brought as an Edwardian legacy to his Report have ceased to be dominant themes in social policy studies. Yet within this tradition social policy and administration had a vitally important intellectual and practical role to perform.

With the demise of this tradition, we are left with a residue of ill-assorted philosophies of welfare which point at one and the same time towards gestures of international altruism on behalf of strangers and towards the revival of local community loyalties on behalf of our next-door neighbours. Such moral imperatives appear to be somewhat irrelevant at a time when Britain is seeking its future as an economic pauper in the very continent on whose behalf it lost an empire, little more than twenty years after the inception within its national boundaries of a new multi-racial society based upon the peoples of that lost empire. These immigrants were brought into the country to meet short-term labour needs, and they now constitute a growing proportion of the economically and socially disadvantaged. If their social and economic circumstances are not improved, these immigrants are likely to become a danger to political stability. Yet our policies for social and economic renewal at home continue to be financially impoverished, while we maintain — in a state of post-imperial euphoria — a programme of international aid.

A concern with the immediacies of human suffering is a natural and commendable quality. Indeed it can be argued that one of the most admirable features of social administration is the reluctance of its practitioners to treat even minority groups as means to the realization of more glorious societal ends, whether they be perfect competition or perfect communism. But social administrators must have a broader concern in social welfare than the needs of poverty-stricken minorities, because these needs can only be met if the relatively privileged are willing to make some sacrifices on their behalf. Since the privileged are no more altruistic than the poor, there is no reason to assume that they will be content to make sacrifices in an unconditional and continuing sense. They will require some consideration of their own needs and some regard for their own conception of justice, which will probably have more in common with the values of the economic market than those of the social market.

A satisfactory compromise between these competing claims is most likely to be achieved in a society with some overriding sense of collective purpose and pride in its common productive endeavours. A collective purpose of this order requires accommodation rather than conflict between the claims of the social market and those of the economic market, yet the present relationship is so clearly based on an assumption of conflict that the very notion of a 'welfare right' is taken by many social administrators to be vested exclusively in the values and practices of the social market. Nonetheless every 'welfare right' implies a claim on someone else's productive obligation, and the increase in the number of academic courses in 'welfare rights' for students of social policy and social work indicates a perilous insulation of these subjects from economic realities and popular notions of justice. This one-sided idea of a welfare right fits naturally into a discipline which conceptualizes social services as a defence against an essentially predatory economic system. Carried to extremes in a society fighting for economic survival, such a philosophy of welfare will end by converting social services into predators on the economic system, thereby prejudicing still further our chances of social survival.

Until recently most of our deprived minorities have been poor, because they have been unemployable or only marginally employable. These minorities include the old, the physically and mentally ill or handicapped and children in care. They will continue to be a central and proper concern of the social services. Today we face new challenges in the form of a dramatic increase in the incidence of unemployment among the able-bodied and the growth of a large minority of coloured citizens who suffer from a variety of disadvantages, including poor educational and employment prospects.

In response to these relatively new challenges many social policy analysts will undoubtedly take a more comprehensive view of the relationships between the economic and social markets and the processes of production and distribution. Any such reappraisal is likely to lead to a deepening of ideological differences within the discipline. There will be those who interpret our present economic crisis as further evidence of the impending collapse of welfare capitalism, with some prescribing socialism as the remedy and others recommending a return to a more competitive free market.

A third school of thought will argue that the mixed economy of welfare capitalism is capable of overcoming the present crisis, just as it has survived similar episodes in the past. Indeed it will be claimed that our present state of affairs has much in common with the crisis which occasioned the collectivist renaissance of the 1940s, that is, a serious loss of productive efficiency and the return of mass unemployment. Today, however, there are no collectivists of the intellectual stature and influence of Keynes or Beveridge who share their conviction that the mixed economy of welfare capitalism is worth saving.

Social policy and administration retains its instrumental links with the mixed economy of welfare capitalism, but the positive commitment to this kind of society embodied in the contributions of Keynes and Beveridge is no longer a major influence. Yet even the middle way of cautious and prudential reform requires a measure of committed support, if it is to succeed. There is, of course, less scope for Utopian speculation in attempts to repair an existing social system which is malfunctioning than there is in attempts to replace it with a totally new system. A normative commitment of this order, if it is to recover its place in the debate about welfare, must take its stand on an explicitly anti-Utopian basis. It entails an acceptance of the imperfections of human nature and hence of all possible human societies and it offers no more than a highly conditional optimism about our future. It will have to balance the necessity of economic risk-taking against the need to reduce social and political risks to a minimum.

Classical political economy and Marxism are both doctrines which offer us dramatic welfare possibilities, but, in inviting us to play for the highest stakes, they also require us to take the greatest risks. Moreover all prescriptions for radical change lay it open to the political barbarians of our time to assume the governance of our lives. In the last analysis the idea of welfare must embody non-material as well as material components, among which the notion of freedom and the right to a measure of self-determination have to be included.

The continuing influence and popularity of the classical economic and Marxist paradigms of welfare can be partly explained by the fact that their respective protagonists are still able to claim that they have not yet been in a position to prove their theories workable. Another explanation lies in the fact that both paradigms explicitly postulate an ideal future state in which there will be an inevitable reconciliation between individual and collective welfare interests. Nonetheless in their different ways both theories do presume to determine the conditions of our freedom: in the one case we are free to fulfil ourselves only within the terms of economic market imperatives; in the other we are free only to ride on the locomotive of history.

The third possibility offers an equally conditional view of freedom, but it seeks the most equitable accommodation between the various liberties and constraints which determine the conditions of life in any type of society. We return here to the structural problem described by Marshall to which he says that there is 'no purely structural solution', namely, the problem of reconciling 'a man's value in the market (capitalist value), his value as a citizen (democratic value), and his value for himself (welfare value)'.[23] Indeed there is no solution to this problem, and the third tradition does not presume to offer one; it does, however, provide through the procedures of representative government and the influence of mitigating social reforms some protection against the danger that any one of these moral imperatives might achieve sufficient predominance to threaten the relative authority of the others.

This approach to the problem of distributive justice rests on the assumption that the idea of welfare is sustained by a number of moral imperatives and that a relative preponderance of any one of these will rapidly produce a situation of diminishing returns. It is part of a philosophy of welfare which, far from heralding the 'end of ideologies', recognizes their prevalence but itself offers policies of incremental and prudential change as a sensible way of keeping a tight ship and avoiding storms on an increasingly hazardous political sea. The purpose of the voyage is not to discover new continents but to keep the ship afloat and steer clear of the various eldorados along the shore, where the life is rumoured to be less arduous than the life on board — rumours belied only by the warnings of fugitives from those alien shores, clamouring to be taken along. Of course the voyage is worthwhile only if the crew come to love their ship and discover the joys of good seamanship; without that common bond they might as well scuttle and be damned.

Though social policy and administration retains its instrumental affinities with the tradition of mercantile collectivism, it has lost that sense of national destiny and common purpose which inspired Keynes and Beveridge. Indeed our love for Britain seems to be conditional on its becoming a society that is radically different from what it is and what it has been. Yet, if a popular loss of confidence in a nation's economic future customarily precedes a revival or an intensification of mercantilist sentiment, it would be reasonable to look for signs of such change at the present time. The signs are undoubtedly there, but in disheartening forms. On the far Left we are exhorted to retreat into the mentality and practices of a socialist siege economy, protected by high import quotas and rudely divorced from the European Economic Community. On the far Right we are offered a different version of the siege economy, explicitly xenophobic and viciously discriminatory not only towards the outside world but towards a minority of our own citizens. It would be a sad thing if the sentiment of patriotism were to become by default the prerogative of two sets of extremists, either of which would speedily transform the basic culture and traditions of British society.

In the end we have to choose between competing philosophies of welfare. In this chapter I have emphasized one of these philosophies partly because I believe that it has more than enough contemporary relevance to merit recovery from its present state of neglect, and partly because the range of choice ought to be as wide and as open as possible. Although the cautiously prudential mood of this philosophy has much in common with the political and economic uncertainties of the present time, it will not have an instant and obvious appeal for idealists. Its objectives, like its expectations, are modest.

In contrast classical economic theory and Marxist theory can be seen as the inspiration of assertive and expansionist political doctrines. They are assertive in their confidence regarding a better future for humanity in terms of both individual and collective welfare. They are expansionist in their respective claims to international relevance. As macro-theories they can be fully tested only in an international context. In this respect both theories generate a mood of intellectual imperialism and optimistic expectation, and both equally imply commitment to a high degree of economic and political risk.

The tradition of mercantile collectivism can best be described as a reactive set of political doctrines. It possesses neither the theoretical coherence nor the consistency of classical political economy or Marxism. Given the various political ends to which mercantilist forms of collectivism may be directed, it is impossible to speak of it as a singular tradition. We can put forward the hypothesis that the doctrines of mercantile collectivism are most likely to gain ascendancy at times when political confidence in the present and the future has been badly shaken. These are doctrines which react to events, in contrast to doctrines which, forearmed with systematic theories, presume both to anticipate and to make the future. Mercantile collectivism is expansionist only in the sense that its doctrines gain in popularity insofar as they follow the adversities of political and economic life from one nation to another. As reactive doctrines the forms of mercantile collectivism might well be adopted by nations whose confidence either in the free market or in socialism has been undermined by sudden disaster or gradual decline. Alternatively a nation in the early stages of industrialization might simply move from one form of pre-capitalist mercantilism to another, which is more suited to the exigencies of industrial life, as happened in the case of Hohenzollern Germany.

Mercantile collectivism gives rise to national rather than international doctrines. Doctrines of this sort are the intellectual heirs of fear rather than hope, of uncertainty about the present rather than confidence in the future, and of a disposition to avoid rather than to take risks and to accept collective responsibility for risks which cannot be avoided.

The literature of social administration abounds with examples of this prudential philosophy, but it is most concisely and elegantly expressed by Titmuss, when he rejects the 'argument for allowing the social costs or diswelfares of the economic system to lie where they fall', on the grounds that in modern societies it is 'increasingly difficult to identify the causal agent or agencies' of those 'diswelfares'. He concludes that 'Non-discriminating universalist services are in part the consequence of unidentifiable causality.'[24] This view of individual responsibility and the right to collective safeguards against risk can be compared with the views of Captain Shotover in *Heartbreak House*, when he caustically explains to his son-in-law, Hector, 'I did not let the fear of death govern my life; and my reward was, I had my life. You are going to let the fear of poverty govern your life: and your reward will be that you will eat, but you will not live.'[25] A more authentic expression of the philosophy of the free market was of course made by Chief Inspector Davy, when he advised the Royal Commission on the Poor Laws in 1906 that 'The unemployed man must stand by his accidents' and 'suffer for the good of the body politic'.[26]

This disposition to sacrifice the welfare of single individuals in the interests of broader principles and long-term objectives has its parallel in Lenin's views on the costs and risks involved in the building of socialism. He writes that during the transition from capitalism to communism political suppression by 'the state' will still be necessary. Nonetheless he goes on to say, 'The suppression of the minority of exploiters by the majority of the wage slaves *of yesterday* is comparatively so easy, simple and natural a task that it will entail far less bloodshed than the suppression of the risings of slaves, serfs or wage labourers, and it will cost mankind far less.'[27]

Perhaps we should stop judging the mixed economies of the West simply on the basis of their divergence from the ideals embodied in the theories of classical political economy or Marxism. Neither of these systems of thought is a body of revealed truth in a sense which gives it a right to define all other systems as heresies or deviations. In most other countries of the West the history of social and economic development has tended to follow or to revert to policies which have their origins in the mercantilist doctrines of the seventeenth and eighteenth centuries. Social policies now assume an important role in that development, because governments now possess the wealth, the will and the administrative expertise to regulate economic life in ways which were not open to them in the past. Social policy and administration is at best an irrelevance and at worst a threat to the political and economic ideals of both classical economic theory and Marxist theory. Some of its practitioners at least should bear witness to their affinities with the third tradition, which alone allows that they may have something useful to say about social welfare and justice.

It is tempting for those of us who live amongst the recurring crises and contradictions of Western parliamentary democracy to equate the middle way of the mixed economy with a seemingly endless *via dolorosa*. Yet the comparative history of social policies does not appear to offer any less arduous form of pilgrims' progress to a better world. Each path has its own Slough of Despond, its Doubting Castles and its Vanity Fairs, and we have yet to see the Celestial City at any of their journeys' ends.

References

[1] Harold L. Wilensky, *The Welfare State and Equality: Structural and Ideological Roots of Public Expenditures*, University of California Press, Berkeley, 1975, p. 37.

[2] Friedman, op. cit., p. 10.

[3] See for example R. Miliband, *The State in Capitalist Society*, Weidenfeld & Nicolson, London, 1969, p. 49; and R. Blackburn (ed.), *Ideology in Social Science*, Fontana, London, 1972.

[4] Vic George and Paul Wilding, *Ideology and Social Welfare*, Routledge & Kegan Paul, London, 1976, p. 85 et seq.

[5] ibid., p. 70.

[6] ibid., pp. 70-1.

[7] ibid., p. 93.

[8] Pinker, 'Social Policy and Social Justice., *Journal of Social Policy*, 1974, pp. 14 and 18.

[9] A classic exposition of a pluralist approach to public policy is Robert Dahl's and Charles Lindblom's *Politics, Economics and Welfare*, University of Chicago Press, 1976. This edition includes a new preface by the authors.

[10] Sandor Halebsky, *Mass Society and Political Conflict*, Cambridge University Press, 1976, Ch. 6 et seq.

[11] Dahl and Lindblom, op. cit., pp. xxi and xxii.

[12] ibid., pp. xxxi-xxxii.

[13] ibid., pp. xxxiii and xxxiv.

[14] ibid., p. xlii.

[15] Hall *et al.*, op. cit.

[16] ibid., pp. 150-1.

[17] Maurice Kogan, 'Social Policy and Public Organizational Values', *Journal of Social Policy*, 3, 2, 1974, pp. 97-111.

[18] Elton Mayo, *The Social Problems of an Industrial Civilization*, with a new Foreword by J. H. Smith, Routledge & Kegan Paul, London, 1975.

[19] O. R. McGregor, 'Equality, Sexual Values and Permissive Legislation', *Journal of Social Policy*, 1, 1, 1972, p. 58. See also McGregor *et al.*, op. cit.; and Finer Report.

[20] See Kathleen Bell, Peter Collison, Stephen Turner and Susan Webber, 'National Insurance Local Tribunals: A Research Study', Parts I and II respectively in *Journal of Social Policy*, 3, 4, 1974, pp. 289-311, and 4, 1, 1975, pp. 1-24.

[21] Titmuss, *Commitment to Welfare*, p. 22.

[22] Alvin W. Gouldner, *The Coming Crisis of Western Sociology*, Heinemann Educational Books, London, 1971, pp. 342 et seq.

[23] T. H. Marshall, op. cit., p. 30.

[24] Titmuss, *Commitment to Welfare*, p. 133-4.

[25] *The Complete Plays of Bernard Shaw*, Odhams Press, London, *Heartbreak House*, p. 790.

[26] *Report of the Royal Commission on the Poor Law, 1905-9*, Vol. I, Cd 4625, para. 3,290 et seq.

[27] Lenin, op. cit., p. 144.

Bibliography

Ashworth, William, *An Economic History of England 1870-1939*, London, 1960.

Bartlett, Richard A., *The New Country: A Social History of the American Frontier, 1776-1890*, New York, 1974.

Bauer, Peter, 'A Myth of Our Time', *Encounter*, 1974.

—— *Dissent on Development: Studies and Debates in Development Economics*, London, 1972.

—— 'The Case Against Foreign Aid', *The Listener*, 1972.

Bayley, Michael, *Mental Handicap and Community Care*, London, 1973.

Beard, Charles A. and Beard, Mary R., *A Basic History of the United States*, Philadelphia, 1944.

—— *The Rise of American Civilization*, Vol. 1, London, 1927.

Beerman, R., 'A Discussion on the Draft Law Against Parasites, Tramps and Beggars', *Soviet Studies*, 1958.

—— 'Laws Against Parasites, Tramps and Beggars', *Soviet Studies*, 1958.

—— 'The Parasite Laws', *Soviet Studies*, 1961.

Bell, C. R., *Middle Class Families: Social and Geographical Mobility*, London, 1968.

Bell, Kathleen, *Disequilibrium in Welfare*, U. of Newcastle upon Tyne, 1973.

Bell, Kathleen, Collison, Peter, Turner, Stephen and Webber, Susan, 'National Insurance Local Tribunals: A Research Study', Parts I & II, *Journal of Social Policy*, 1974-5.

Bendix, Reinhard and Lipset, Seymour Martin (eds), *Class, Status and Power: Social Stratification in Comparative Perspective*, 2nd ed., Routledge and Kegan Paul, 1967.

Berger, Peter, *Pyramids of Sacrifice: Political Ethics and Social Change*, New York, 1974.

Berlin, Isaiah, Preface to Venturi, Franco, *Roots of Revolution*, London, 1964.

Bernhardi, General Friedrich von, *Germany and the Next War*, Edward Arnold, 1914.

Beveridge, William, *Voluntary Action: A Report on Methods of Advance*, London, 1948.

—— *Full Employment in a Free Society: A Report*, London, 1944.

Beveridge Report: *Social Insurance and Allied Services*, Cmd 6404, H.M.S.O., 1942, 1958.

Black, Cyril E. (ed.), *The Transformation of Russian Society*, C.U.P. and Harvard U.P., 1960.

Blackburn R. (ed.), *Ideology in Social Science*, London, 1972.

Blake, Robert, *The Conservative Party from Peel to Churchill*, Eyre and Spottiswoode, 1970.

Blatchford, Robert, *My Eighty Years*, London, 1931.

Blau, Peter M., *Exchange and Power in Social Life*, New York, 1964.

Blumer, Herbert, *An Appraisal of Thomas and Znaniecki's The Polish Peasant in Europe and America*, New York, 1939.

Boatright, Mody C., 'The Myth of Frontier Individualism', in Hofstadter, Richard and Lipset, Seymour Martin (eds), *Turner and the Sociology of the Frontier*, Harper Torchbooks, 1968.

Bodelsen, C. A., *Studies in Mid-Victorian Imperialism*, London and Berlin, 1924.

Brebner, J. B., *North Atlantic Triangle*, Yale U.P. and O.U.P., 1946.

Bunyan, James and Fisher, H. H., *The Bolshevik Revolution, 1917-18: Documents and Materials*, Stanford U.P., 1965.

Burnett, John, *A History of the Cost of Living*, Penguin, 1969.

—— *Plenty and Want: A Social History of Diet in England from 1815 to the Present Day*, Penguin, 1968.

Burrow, J. W., *Evolution and Society: A Study in Victory Social Theory*, C.U.P., 1970.

Bury, J. P. (ed.), *The New Cambridge Modern History*, Vol. X, *The Zenith of European Power, 1830-1870*, C.U.P., 1967.

Byrnes, Robert F., *Pobedonostev, His Life and Thought*, London, 1969.

Carr, E. H., *The Bolshevik Revolution 1917-23*, London, 1969.

Carrier, John and Kendall, Ian, 'Social Policy and Social Change: Explanations of the Development of Social Policy', *Journal of Social Policy*, 1973.

—— 'The Development of Welfare States: The Production of Plausible Accounts', *Journal of Social Policy*, 1973.

Carr-Saunders, A., *World Population, Past Growth and Present Trends*, Frank Cass, 1964.

Carter, Henry L., 'Rural Indiana in Transition, 1850-1860', *Agricultural History*, 1946.

Central Council for Education and Training in Social Work, *Social Work Curriculum Study: The Teaching of Community Work*, London, 1974.

Checkland, S.G. and E.O.A., *The Poor Law Report of 1834*, Penguin, 1973.

Cipolla, C. M., *Economic History of World Population*, Penguin, 1964.

Clark, Colin, 'What's Wrong with Economics?', *Encounter*, 1958.

Clausewitz, Carl von, *On War*, Vol. III, London, 1940.

Coats, A. W., 'The Classical Economists, Industrialisation and Poverty', in Institute of Economic Affairs, *The Long Debate on Poverty*, London, 1972.

Coleman, D. C. (ed.), *Revisions in Mercantilism*, Methuen, 1969.

Coleman, Terry, *Passage to America*, London, 1972.

Coll, Blanche D., 'Public Assistance in the United States: Colonial Times to 1860', in Martin, E. W., (ed.), *Comparative Development in Social Welfare*, London, 1972.

Conquest, Robert, *Agricultural Workers in the USSR*, London, 1968.

Conze, Werner, 'The German Empire', in Hinsley, F. H. (ed.), *The New Cambridge Modern History*, Vol. XI, *Material Progress and World-Wide Problems, 1870-1898*, C.U.P., 1970.

Cox, Lauranda F., 'The American Agricultural Wage Earner 1865-1900', *Agricultural History*, 1948.

Cross, Colin, *The Fall of the British Empire, 1918-1968*, London, 1970.

Cunningham, William, article on Free Trade in *Encyclopaedia Britannica*, 11th ed., Cambridge, 1910-11.

Dahl, Robert and Lindblom, Charles, *Politics, Economics and Welfare*, U. of Chicago Press, 1976.

Dahrendorf, Ralf, *Society and Democracy in Germany*, Weidenfeld and

Nicolson, 1968.

Dalton, George, 'Economic Theory and Primitive Society', in LeClair, E. E. Jr., and Schneider, H. K., *Economic Anthropology: Readings in Theory and Analysis*, New York, 1968.

— *Economic Systems and Society*, Penguin, 1974.

Dalton, Hugh, *High Tide and After: Memoirs 1945-1960*, London, 1962.

Davis, Jerome, *The Russian Immigrant*, New York, 1922.

Dicey, A. V., *Law and Public Opinion in England During the Nineteenth Century*, London, 1962.

Dick, Everett, *The Sod-House Frontier, 1854-1890*, New York and London, 1943.

Dickens, Charles, *Bleak House*, Penguin, 1978.

Dilke, Charles Wentworth, *Greater Britain: A Record of Travel in the English-Speaking Countries During 1866 and 1867*, Vols. I & II, Macmillan, 1868.

Dillard, Dudley, *The Economics of John Maynard Keynes*, London, 1963.

Durkheim, Emile, *The Division of Labour in Society*, London, 1964.

— *Moral Education*, Free Press of Glencoe, 1961.

Eekelar, J., *Family Security and Family Breakdown*, Penguin, 1971.

Ekeh, P., *Social Exchange Theory*, London, 1975.

Eliot, George, *Felix Holt the Radical*, Panther.

Eliot, T. S., *Little Gidding*, Faber & Faber, 1942.

Elkins, S. and McKitrick, Eric, 'A Meaning for Turner's Frontier: Democracy in the Old North West', in Hofstadter and Lipset (eds), *Turner and the Sociology of the Frontier*, New York, 1968.

Encounter, 'Going into Europe', Symposia II and IV, in *Encounter*, 1963.

Erickson, C. J., 'Who Were the English and Scots Emigrants to the United States in the Late Nineteenth Century?', in Glass, D. V. and Revelle, Roger (eds), *Population and Social Change*, London, 1972.

Feinberg, Joel (ed.), *Moral Concepts*, London, 1969.

Ferro, Marco, article in Pipes, R. (ed.), *Revolutionary Russia*, Harvard U.P. and O.U.P., 1968.

Fieldhouse, D. K., *The Colonial Empires: A Comparative Study from the Nineteenth Century*, London, 1865.

Fine, Sidney, *Laissez-Faire and the General Welfare State: A Study of Conflict in American Thought, 1865-1901*, Ann Arbor and London, 1956.

Finer Report: *Report of the Committee on One-Parent Families*, Vols I, Cmnd 5629, and II, Cmnd 5629-1, H.M.S.O., 1974.

Firth, R. (ed.), *Two Studies in Kinship in London*, London, 1957.

Fletcher, Ronald, *The Family and Marriage*, Penguin, 1962.

Florinsky, M. T., *The End of the Russian Empire*, New York, 1971.

Frank, Joseph, 'The World of Raskolnikov', *Encounter*, 1966.

Friedman, Milton, 'The Line We Dare Not Cross', *Encounter*, 1976.

Fuchs, Carl Johannes, *The Trade Policy of Great Britain and Her Colonies Since 1860*, Macmillan, 1905.

Garrard, John A., *The English and Immigration: A Comparative Study of the Jewish Influx 1880-1910*, London, 1971.

Geertz, Clifford, *The Interpretation of Cultures*, New York, 1973.

George, Vic and Wilding, Paul, *Ideology and Social Welfare*, London, 1976.

Gilbert, Bentley B., *British Social Policy 1914-1939*, London, 1970.

Ginsberg, Morris, *On the Diversity of Morals*, London, 1962.

Gish, Oscar, *Doctor Migration and World Health*, London, 1971.

Glass, D. V. and Revelle, Roger (eds), *Population and Social Change*, London, 1972.

Glynn, Sean and Oxborrow, John, *Interwar Britain: A Social and Economic History*, London, 1976.

Gouldner, Alvin W., 'The Norm of Reciprocity', *American Sociological Review*, 1960.

—— *The Coming Crisis of Western Sociology*, London, 1971.

Habakkuk, H. J., *Population Growth and Economic Development Since 1750*, Leicester U.P., 1971.

Halebsky, Sandor, *Mass Society and Political Conflict*, C.U.P., 1976.

Hall, Phoebe, Land, Hilary, Parker, Roy and Webb, Adrian, *Change, Choice and Conflict in Social Policy*, Heinemann Educational Books, 1975.

Handlin, Oscar, *The Uprooted*, London, 1953.

Hansen, Alvin H., *A Guide to Keynes*, New York, 1953.

Hansen, Marcus Lee, *The Atlantic Migration, 1607-1860*, New York, 1961.

Hardy, Thomas, *Far From the Madding Crowd*, London, 1974.

Harris, Jose, *William Beveridge: A Portrait*, Oxford, 1977.

Heath, A., *Rational Choice and Social Exchange*, C.U.P., 1976.

Heckscher, E., *Mercantilism*, London, 1955.

Hicks, John, *A Theory of Economic History*, Oxford, 1969.

Hill, Christopher, *Lenin and the Russian Revolution*, Penguin, 1971.

Hillery, Richard, 'Definitions of Community: Areas of Agreement', in *Rural Sociology*, 1955.

Hinsley, F. H., Introduction to Hinsley, F. H. (ed.), *The New Cambridge Modern History*, Vol. XI *Material Progress and World-Wide Problems 1870-1898*, C.U.P., 1970.

Hobsbawm, E. J., *Industry and Empire: An Economic History of Britain Since 1750*, London, 1968.

—— *The Age of Capital 1848-1875*, London, 1977.

Hofstadter, R., *The American Political Tradition*, New York, 1948.

—— Introduction to Hofstadter, R. and Lipset, S. M. (eds), *Turner and the Sociology of the Frontier*, New York, 1968.

Hofstadter, Richard and Lipset, Seymour Martin (eds), *Turner and the Sociology of the Frontier*, New York, 1968.

Hofstadter, Richard, Miller, William and Aaron, Daniel, *The American Republic*, Vol I, to 1865, Englewood Cliffs, N. J., 1959.

Homans, George C., *Social Behaviour: Its Elementary Forms*, London, 1973.

Hopkins, Charles Howard, *The Rise of the Social Gospel in American Protestantism 1865-1915*, New Haven, Conn., 1961.

Huxley, T. H., 'The Struggle for Existence: A Programme', *Nineteenth Century*, 1888.

Institute of Economic Affairs, *The Long Debate on Poverty*, London, 1972.

Jackson, J. A. (ed.), *Migration*, London, 1969.

James, M. R., *Social Problems and Policy During the Puritan Revolution 1640-1660*, George Routledge and Sons, 1930.

James-Davis, F., *Social Problems, Enduring Major Issues and Social Change*, New York, 1970.

Jenks, Leland Hamilton, *The Migration of British Capital to 1875*, London, 1938.

Joll, James, *Europe Since 1870: An International History*, Penguin, 1976.

Joubert, Carl, *Russia as It Really Is*, London, 1905.

Kamenka, Eugene, *Nationalism: The Nature and Evolution of an Idea*,

London, 1976.

Kennan, G. F., article in Pipes, R. (ed.), *Revolutionary Russia*, Harvard U.P., and O.U.P., 1968.

Keynes, John Maynard, *The General Theory of Employment, Interest and Money*, London, 1960.

—— *Laissez-Faire and Communism*, New York, 1926.

Kidd, Benjamin, *Social Evolution*, London, 1894.

—— *The Science of Power*, London, 1919.

Knapp, J., 'Economics or Political Economy', *Lloyds Bank Review*, 1973.

Kogan, Maurice, 'Social Policy and Public Organizational Values', *Journal of Social Policy*, 1974.

Kropotkin, Peter, *Mutual Aid: A Factor of Evolution*, ed. and with an Introduction by Avrich, Paul, London, 1972.

Larson, Calvin J., *Major Themes in Sociological Theory*, New York, 1973.

Leach, Edmund, *Lévi-Strauss*, London, 1970.

—— 'Claude Lévi-Strauss — Anthropologist and Philosopher', *New Left Review*, 1965.

LeClair, Edward E., Jr., and Schneider, Harold K., *Economic Anthropology: Readings in Theory and Analysis*, New York, 1968.

Lee, Everett S., 'The Turner Thesis Re-examined', in Hofstadter and Lipset (eds), *Turner and the Sociology of the Frontier*, New York, 1968.

Lenin, V. I., *The State and Revolution*, Moscow, 1951.

Levin, Alfred, *The Second Duma: A Study of the Social-Democratic Party and the Russian Constitutional Experiment*, Hamden, Conn., 1966.

Lévi-Strauss, Claude, *The Elementary Structures of Kinship*, Eyre and Spottiswoode, 1969.

—— *World on the Wane*, London, 1961.

—— *Race and History*, UNESCO, 1952.

—— *The Savage Mind*, Weidenfeld and Nicolson, 1966.

—— *Structural Anthropology*, Allen Lane, 1968. (See also Leach, E., and Geertz, C.)

Lichtheim, George, *Imperialism*, Allen Lane, 1971.

Litwak, Eugene, 'Extended Kin Relations in an Industrial Society', in Shanas, Ethel and Streib, Gordon F., *Social Structure and the Family: Generational Relations*, Englewood Cliffs, N.J., 1965.

Lloyd, T. O., *Empire to Welfare State: English History 1906-1967*, O.U.P., 1970.

McBriar, A. M., *Fabian Socialism and English Politics, 1884-1918*, C.U.P., 1962.

McCoy, Donald R., *Coming of Age: The United States During the 1920s and 1930s*, Penguin, 1973.

MacDonagh, Oliver, *A Pattern of Government Growth 1800-1860*, London, 1961.

McGregor, O. R., 'Equality, Sexual Values and Permissive Legislation', *Journal of Social Policy*, 1972.

McGregor, O. R., Blom-Cooper, L., and Gibson, C., *Separated Spouses*, London, 1971.

Madison, Bernice, 'The Organization of Welfare Services', in Black, Cyril E. (ed.), *The Transformation of Russian Society*, Harvard U.P. and C.U.P., 1960.

Marquand, David, *Ramsay Macdonald*, London, 1977.

Marris, P., *Widows and their Families*, London, 1958.

Marshall, Alfred, *Principles of Economics*, London, 1907.

Marshall, T. H., 'Value Problems of Welfare Capitalism', *Journal of Social Policy*, 1972.

Martin, E. W. (ed.), *Comparative Development in Social Welfare*, London, 1972.

Marx, Karl, *Grundrisse*, Penguin, 1977.

—— *Capital*, Vols I & II, London, 1946.

Marx, Karl and Engels, Frederick, *The German Ideology*, Part I, London, 1970.

—— *Manifesto of the Communist Party*, Moscow, 1959.

Matza, David, 'The Disreputable Poor', in Bendix, Reinhard and Lipset, Seymour Martin (eds), *Class, Status and Power: Social Stratification in Comparative Perspective*, 2nd ed., London, 1967.

Mayer, J. P., *Max Weber and German Politics: A Study in Political Sociology*, Faber and Faber, 1954, containing article (no author given) 'Max Weber on Bureaucratization in 1909'.

Mayo, Elton, *The Social Problems of an Industrial Civilization*, London, 1975. With a new Foreword by J. H. Smith.

Medlicott, W. N., *Contemporary England, 1914-1964*, Longman, 1967.

Mencher, Samuel, *Poor Law to Poverty Program*, Pittsburgh, 1967.

Miliband, R., *The State in Capitalist Society*, London, 1969.

Miller, John C., *The Federalist Era, 1789-1801*, New York, 1963.

Miller, M., *The Economic Development of Russia, 1905-14*, 1926.

Milligan, Sandra, 'The Petrograd Bolsheviks and Social Insurance, 1914-1917', *Soviet Studies*, 1969.

Mills, E., *Living with Mental Illness*, London, 1962.

Mingay, G. E., 'The Transformation of Agriculture', in Institute of Economic Affairs, *The Long Debate on Poverty*, London, 1972.

Moller, Herbert, *Population Movements in Modern European History*, New York and London, 1964.

Monod, Jacques, *Chance and Necessity*, Glasgow, 1974.

Moore, Barrington, Jr., *Social Origins of Dictatorship and Democracy*, Penguin, 1967.

Morgan, D. H. J., *Social Theory and the Family*, London, 1975.

Morris, Pauline, *Prisoners and their Families*, London, 1965.

Myrdal, Gunnar, *The Challenge of World Poverty*, Penguin, 1971.

Nisbet, Robert A., *The Sociological Tradition*, Heinemann Educational Books, 1970.

—— *The Quest for Community*, O.U.P., 1970.

Noble, David W., *Historians Against History: The Frontier Thesis and the National Covenant in American History*, Minneapolis, 1965.

Nove, A., *An Economic History of the U.S.S.R.*, (quoting Gerschenkrov), Allen Lane, 1969.

Orwell, George, 'Notes on Nationalism', in *Decline of the English Murder and Other Essays*, Penguin, 1975.

Pares, Bernard, *Russia*, Penguin, 1975.

Pearson, Karl, *National Life from the Standpoint of Science*, London, 1905.

—— *The Ethic of Free Thought*, London, 1888.

—— *Socialism and Natural Science*.

Pinker, Robert, 'Social Policy and Social Justice', *Journal of Social Policy*, 1974.

—— *Social Theory and Social Policy*, Heinemann Educational Books, 1971.

—— Preface to Reisman, David, *Richard Titmuss: Welfare and Society*, Heinemann Educational Books, 1977.

Pipes, Richard, *Russia Under the Old Regime*, Weidenfeld and Nicolson, 1974.

—— 'The Origins of Bolshevism', in Pipes, R. (ed.), *Revolutionary Russia*, Harvard U.P. and O.U.P., 1968.

Piven, Frances Fox and Cloward, Richard A., *Regulating the Poor: The Functions of Public Welfare*, London, 1972.

Plamenatz, John, 'Two Types of Nationalism', in Eugene Kamenka, *Nationalism: The Nature and Evolution of an Idea*, London, 1976.

Plant, Raymond, *Community and Ideology: An Essay in Applied Social Philosophy*, London, 1974.

Platt, J., *Social Research in Bethnal Green: An Evaluation of the Work of the Institute of Community Studies*, London, 1971.

Poggi, Gianfranco, *Images of Society*, Stanford U.P., 1972.

Polanyi, Karl, *The Great Transformation: The Political and Economic Origins of Our Time*, Boston, 1968.

Poor Law Report: *Report of the Royal Commission on the Poor Law, 1905-9*, Vol. I, Cd 4625, H.M.S.O.

Popper, K. R., *The Open Society and its Enemies*, Vol. I, London, 1957.

Pruger, Robert, 'Social Policy: Unilateral Transfer or Reciprocal Exchange', *Journal of Social Policy*, 1973.

Rawls, J., *A Theory of Justice*, London, 1972.

Reisman, David, *Richard Titmuss: Welfare and Society*, Heinemann Educational Books, 1977.

Ricardo, David, *The Principles of Political Economy*, Everyman edition, Dent Dutton, 1929.

Richmond, A., 'Sociology of Migration in Industrial and Post-Industrial Societies', in Jackson, J. A. (ed.), *Migration*, London, 1969.

Rimlinger, G. V., *Welfare Policy and Industrialization in Europe, America and Russia*, New York, 1971.

Roach, Jack L. and Roach, Janet K., *Poverty: Selected Readings*, Penguin, 1972.

Robbins, L. (ed.), *The Common Sense of Political Economy*, London, 1933.

Roberts, Robert, *The Classic Slum: Salford Life in the First Quarter of the Century*, Manchester U.P., 1971.

Robinson, Joan, *Economic Philosophy*, Penguin, 1964.

Roll, Eric, *A History of Economic Thought*, Faber & Faber, 1973.

Rose, Richard, 'A Model Democracy?', in Rose, Richard (ed.), *Lessons from America*, Macmillan, 1974.

Rosser, C. and Harris, J., *The Family and Social Change: A Study of Family and Kinship in a South Wales Town*, London, 1966.

Schumpeter, Joseph A., *History of Economic Analysis*, London, 1963.

—— *Capitalism, Socialism and Democracy*, London, 1961.

Schwarz, Solomon M., *The Russian Revolution of 1905*, Chicago and London, 1969.

Semmell, B., *Imperialism and Social Reform*, London, 1960.

Seton-Watson, H., *The Decline of Imperial Russia, 1855-1914*, London, 1960.

—— article (untitled) in Pipes, R. (ed.), *Revolutionary Russia*, Harvard U.P. and O.U.P., 1968.

Shanas, Ethel and Streib, Gordon F., *Social Structure and the Family: Generational Relations*, Englewood Cliffs, N.J., 1965.

Shannon, Fred A., 'A Post-Mortem on the Labor-Safety-Valve Theory', in Hofstadter and Lipset (eds), *Turner and the Sociology of the Frontier*, New York, 1968.

Shaw, Bernard, *Heartbreak House*, Penguin, 1970.

Smith, Adam, *The Wealth of Nations*, Vols. I and II, Dent Dutton, 1937.

Soper, Tom, 'Western Attitudes to Aid', *Lloyds Bank Review*, London, 1969.

Stacey, Margaret, *Tradition and Change: A Study of Banbury*, London, 1960.

—— 'The Myth of Community Studies', *British Journal of Sociology*, 1969.

Stavrou, Theofanis George, *Russia Under the Last Tsar*, Minneapolis, 1969.

Stephens, David, *Immigration and Race Relations*, London, 1970.

Stephenson, Graham, *History of Russia 1812-1945*, London, 1969.

Szamuely, Tibor, *The Russian Tradition*, London, 1974.

Taylor, A. J. P., *English History 1914-1945*, Penguin, 1975.

Thistlethwaite, Frank, *The Great Experiment*, London, 1955.

—— *Migration from Europe Overseas in the Nineteenth and Twentieth Centuries*, Göteborg — Stockholm — Uppsala, 1960.

Thomas, Brinley, *Migration and Economic Growth: A Study of Great Britain and the Atlantic Economy*, C.U.P., 1954.

Thomas, W. I. and Znaniecki, Florian, *The Polish Peasant in Europe and America*, Vol. I, New York, 1958.

Thompson, Lawrence, *Robert Blatchford: Portrait of an Englishman*, Gollancz, 1951.

Thomson, David, 'The United Kingdom and its World-Wide Interests', in Bury, J. P. (ed.), *The New Cambridge Modern History*, Vol. X, *The Zenith of European Power 1830-1870*, C.U.P., 1967.

Thornberry, Cedric, *The Stranger at the Gate: A Study of the Law on Aliens and Commonwealth Citizens*, London, 1964.

Thornton, A. P., *The Imperial Ideal and its Enemies*, London, 1963.

Titmuss, Richard M., *The Gift Relationship: From Human Blood to Social Policy*, Allen and Unwin, 1970.

—— *Commitment to Welfare*, Allen and Unwin, 1968.

Tocqueville, Alexis de, *Democracy in America*, New York, 1966.

Tönnies, Ferdinand, *Custom: An Essay on Social Codes*, Free Press of Glencoe, Ill., 1961.

Topliss, Eda, *Provision for the Disabled*, Blackwell and Martin Robertson, 1975.

Townsend, P., *The Family Life of Old People*, London, 1957.

Troyat, Henri, *Daily Life in Russia under the Last Tsar*, London, 1961.

Turner, F. J., *The Frontier in American History*, New York, 1962.

Urmson, J. O., 'Saints and Heroes', in Feinberg, Joel (ed.), *Moral Concepts*, London, 1969.

Venturi, Franco, *Roots of Revolution*, London, 1964.

Viner, Jacob, 'Power versus Plenty as Objectives of Foreign Policy in the Seventeenth and Eighteenth Centuries', in Coleman, D. C. (ed.), *Revisions in Mercantilism*, Methuen, 1969.

Wallace, Donald MacKenzie, *Russia*, London, 1912.

Walsh, Warren Bartlett, *Russia and the Soviet Union*, Ann Arbor and London, 1958.

Webb, Sidney and Beatrice, *Soviet Communism: A New Civilization*, 3rd ed., London, 1944.

Wicksteed, P., article in Robbins, L. (ed.), *The Common Sense of Political Economy*, London, 1933.

Wilensky, Harold L., *The Welfare State and Equality: Structural and Ideological Roots of Public Expenditures*, Berkeley, 1975.

Williams, Bernard, *Morality*, Penguin, 1973.

Willmott, P., *The Evolution of a Community*, London, 1963.
Wilson, Charles, 'The Other Face of Mercantilism', in Coleman, D. C. (ed.), *Revisions in Mercantilism*, Methuen, 1969.
—— *England's Apprenticeship 1603-1763*, Longman, 1965.
Wilson, Thomas, 'Sympathy and Self Interest', unpublished paper given at the Adam Smith Bicentenary Conference, 1976.
Wiltshire, D., *The Social and Political Thought of Herbert Spencer*, O.U.P., 1978.
Wolff, Kurt H., *The Sociology of Georg Simmel*, London, 1964.
Young, Michael and Willmott, Peter, *Family and Class in a London Suburb*, London, 1960.
—— *Family and Kinship in East London*, Routledge, 1957.

Subject Index

Name Index